N. Michael Murphy is a clinical professor in both the Department of Psychiatry and the Department of Family Practice at Albany Medical College in Albany, New York. He also founded a hospice in Albany, concentrating on his ideas on living and dying soulfully. Murphy runs workshops, and gives lectures in the United States, Belgium, Holland and Ireland. He lives near Albany, New York.

The Wisdom of Dying

Practices for Living

N. Michael Murphy M.D.

ELEMENT

SHAFTESBURY, DORSET • BOSTON, MASSACHUSETTS • MELBOURNE, VICTORIA

© Element Books Limited 1999
Text © N. Michael Murphy 1999

First published in the UK in 1999 by
Element Books Limited
Shaftesbury, Dorset SP7 8BP

Published in Australia in 1999 by
Element Books and distributed
by Penguin Australia Limited
487 Maroondah Highway, Ringwood,
Victoria 3134

Cover design by Slatter-Anderson
Text design by Behram Kapadia
Typeset by Bournemouth Colour Press, Parkstone
Printed and bound in the USA by Edwards Bros

British Library Cataloguing in Publication
data available

ISBN 1 86204 538 0

Thanks are given to Calder Publications, London, and Grove Press, New York
for permission to quote from *Exit the King* by Eugene Ionesco.

Contents

❦

CONTENTS

Dedication and Thanksgiving

Awriter needs an apprenticeship as a witness if he or she is to become an effective storyteller, and I would never have become a good witness if I had not come close to those who are dying. So my becoming a conscious witness is thanks to all those whose stories I was privileged to witness during my life among the living yet close to dying in St. Peter's Hospice in Albany, New York. My loving thanks to all those teacher-storytellers who graced the hospice as patients and family members, a few of whose stories I have recounted in these pages.

In my apprenticeship as witness, I was lucky to have as guides a most extraordinary gathering of human beings (who were also fellow apprentice-witnesses and staff), and I would like to name them all since each contributed a part of who I became. But that would be like naming all the parts of the body, each of which goes to make up the whole, so I will simply acknowledge with the deepest gratitude Sr. Jean Roche who was a key figure for me and for so many others. Jean modeled creativity, color, love, laughter, tears, and a form of religious being that connected and celebrated rather than strangled and controlled. Jean manifested our soul and spirit, and I want to thank her and the others with whom I spent that vital time in my life; I want to thank them all for their loving kindness, patience, and willingness to explore the darkness.

My ability to tell a coherent story is largely due to the forbearance and wisdom of Susan Davidson, a marvelous executive editor who took my breath away along with reams of garbled thoughts and endless streams of twisted grammar. Thanks also to Thomas Moore who has been a friend and source of soulful inspiration, and to all at Element Books, particularly Grace Cheetham, for their willingness to publish, and for their enthusiasm and polish during the process of launching.

Since I only became a conscious witness when I became close to those who are dying, I missed out on much of the magic of my children's growing up, and for that I am so sorry—for them and for me. But the joy is that they are awake and are not waiting to be close to death to be involved in soulful living. It has been a delight to wake up and experience the warmth and wisdom of my oldest daughter, Paula, who taught me the beginnings of humility and much else when we worked together in the hospice. It has been an amazing privilege to have co-facilitated many workshops with her and to have moved beyond the usual family friction to a relationship in which feminine and masculine are in creative harmony. Suzanne, Stephen, John, and Sandra are also jewels and balances in my life, key enablers of my storytelling, and I am in awe of them and all they have touched. My wife, Kathy, has been a fount of support, patience, and humor during the parturition of this work, and to her goes my love and thanks.

I visualize this book as being composed of images of all of us made more vivid and redolent of soul and spirit by the proximity of death, but these stories require the witnessing reader to make them come alive. So I wish to acknowledge all the different facets—storyteller, witness, and guide—that make up our oneness, and lovingly dedicate this book to all of us.

Note: To avoid clumsy constructions, the pronouns "he" and "she" are used in alternate chapters, and should be taken to indicate both genders.

Preface

It has been almost ten years since I first became acquainted with Mike Murphy's work with the dying at St. Peter's Hospice in Albany, New York. I was living nearby in the Berkshires of Massachusetts and participated in some of Mike's in-service training programs. On many occasions I met with his staff and talked about the relevance of mythology to the deep work of dealing with patients and families at the time of dying. Mike and I traveled sometimes to give workshops for nurses and doctors. I especially enjoyed talking with medical teams about their dream life, and I was amazed listening to Mike speak to them in the strongest terms challenging them to humanize their profession.

Mike is an articulate man of forceful conviction and sweet compassion. His impatience with systems that screen out the human dimension in the care of persons is palpable, but it is not sour or dark. His brilliant enthusiasm and vision never disappear behind the clouds of stark reality, and he never gives in to cynicism, although the opportunities to surrender to the thick-headedness of institutions must come to him daily. His optimistic realism comes through in the following pages as he describes his tough work, dealing on one side with an establishment that prides itself on its numbness to plain human need, and on the other with endless variations on lives stuck in senseless anger and misunderstanding, especially in families where imminent death brings to light the narrative patterns that have suppressed the soul over years and lifetimes.

The Celtic sensibility in Mike Murphy appreciates the role of stories, storytelling, and drama in the working through of emotional blockage and existential anxiety. Over the years I have encouraged Mike to tell his stories. I've heard them for many years and have been incredibly moved and instructed by them, and I'm convinced that stories pass more easily than do ideas and theories through the gates of our defenses and our habits of thought. This book contains good stories, stories that will encourage the reader to think fresh thoughts about medicine, death, and especially the motifs that keep families and other relationships from the free expression of their simple humanity.

Because it lacks dogma and an agenda, this book could serve as an excellent source of instruction for hospice workers, families facing a challenging death, or any person at all wishing to cut through the irrelevancies of psychological theory and method to find insight into those aspects of ordinary life that account for meaning and emotional engagement. Dying is a distilling process for the person at the edge of life and for families, friends, and even those providing professional care. It forces us to look at what is essential, at what has been covered over by the distractions to real living we cultivate daily in a society that denies life as much as it pretends that death is an aberration. Mike has a knack for tracking subtle avoidances and then shaking them out into the light of recognition.

We are all called upon to be hospice workers as we confront the reality of our own mortality, our illnesses, and the fragility of our lives, and when we are faced with the dying of parents and other family members or friends. In all its forms death is the great educator, teaching us how to live life as it is presented rather than in its illusory forms. A visitation from death is an opening to the soul, a way of deepening our lives and giving substance to our thoughts. As our society surrenders more and more to the high-tech life and to the transformation of the soul's solid pleasures into thin entertainments, we become a people without character, incapable of marriage, family, and community because our hearts have not been initiated in the crucible of humanity. The denial of death that Mike writes about so forcefully, following the lead of cultural anthropologist Ernest Becker, is born of our cultivated superficiality; it is not separate from our numbing and avoiding way of life.

And so I see this enlightening book not only as a support and guide for medical professionals and others in the so-called helping professions, but also as a wake-up message for us all. Hospice work is one of the great inventions of recent years. I admire those like Mike who have developed it into a sophisticated practice and those who simply labor at it during the late hours of night. In my travels I find that hospice workers more than any other group understand my descriptions of the soul and can readily distinguish care of the soul from traditional psychology. And yet, the fact that we need hospices at all is a telling judgment on modern life. As Mike points out, we give death over to the experts and from the very beginning dehumanize the most human of all creative activities—dying.

I suggest that the reader take up this book not as a manual for hospice workers and others who have to deal with death and dying, but as a guide to living. If we don't live our dying, to use Mike's phrase, then we don't really live, and life becomes a sleight-of-hand maneuvering that gives the illusion of vitality but is actually a clever way of pretending to be immortal, something other than human. The lessons of death are available nowhere else but in the vicinity of dying. That is why Mike's good words are of immense value to a society that considers both life and death too cheaply and is therefore unfamiliar with both.

With remarkable clarity and personal authority, Mike takes us from lessons on dying to suggestions for living. Death, with all that surrounds it, is the best teacher on how to make life worth living and how to live compassionately with others. From his hospice work Mike has been able to fashion workshops, programs, and suggestions for individual practice that allow us to work out our family conflicts and congested emotions before we arrive at a moment of crisis. Generously, he uses himself as an example and makes it as clear as possible what he means by letting go, living with loss, and working with compassion.

I know first-hand that Mike's suggestions for storytelling, listening, and working through relationship blocks are powerful. They stir up memories and emotions that may have been lying deep and dormant for years, and are not aimed at just the re-experiencing of feelings. They help us re-imagine our lives, especially in relation to those who are close to us. The exercises may at first glance seem rather formal and lacking in spontaneity, but in practice that is far from the case. Their simple but clear structures help a great deal as participants visit old themes and feelings that have long been too thickly concealed to emerge in a positive, creative manner.

As Mike says, the life of the mind is quite different from that of the soul. At the intellectual level we may prefer complicated theories and clear objectives. But the soul progresses more intuitively and subtly. The mere emergence of a long-repressed family story may waken consciousness in a way that is transforming. I have seen it happen, and I have felt it happen within myself, as Mike gently but firmly encourages people to experience their feelings, by making the simple gift of a cherished object, or the plain statement of a previously unexpressed emotion.

There is safety, encouragement, support, and clarity to be found in Mike's methods. I hope that readers will find in this helpful book not just a simple compendium of techniques but an attitude toward living and dying that counters the usual spirit found in professional and family contexts. There is no need to act from fear, especially in areas that are as deeply meaningful as family connection, illness, and dying. Mike gives important consideration to the caregiver too, as he describes how even the professional goes through meaningful moments in the work of helping others.

Our culture is in a remarkable period of decadence, which means cultural death and the evaporation of values—loss of soul. The best remedy for disease always mirrors the ailment. In a period of waning we need instructions on how to die with grace and beauty. If we learn how to care for each other in our dying, we may discover how to be with each other in our living. This is the kaleidoscopic vision Mike Murphy offers in this book of genuine wisdom. Read it and live. Read it and die.

Thomas Moore

Introduction

I never intended to become immersed in the hospice work from which this book arises. My mother died in 1968, and while there was much unfinished business between us that was not addressed before she died, that experience was the seed that inspired me to begin this journey.

At around the time of my mother's death I was involved in the development of a new psychiatric hospital that was to embody all the well-meaning tenets of community psychiatry. But times change, and since mental health is far from being a science with clear ideas about cause, effect, and management, the treatment in vogue at any one time tends to be heavily influenced by the political and social climate. In the mid seventies, in the wake of a more conservative era, money for community mental health became scarce, and more restrictive practices with reliance on the use of drugs again became the most acceptable mode of treatment.

In 1978, when this change in the direction of the profession caused me to look elsewhere, I registered for a workshop on death and dying given by Elisabeth Kubler-Ross. While there are no accidents, I am quite unaware why I signed up for something that sounded so depressing. I had no great desire to learn about death and dying and did not particularly enjoy the workshop, but I became friends with Elisabeth, and it was she who first gave me the idea of working in a hospice.

Since there were very few hospices in the US at that time, I had no conception of what they were about. The modern hospice tradition has its historical roots in Britain, but during my general practice years in London and medical schooling earlier in Dublin, hospices as we know them now were not much in the public eye. Indeed, death was even more dark and taboo a subject than sex. Despite my naiveté, I took a chance and asked the director of a local hospital whether there might be interest in starting a hospice. I found myself in the right place at an auspicious time.

After one year of planning, the hospice was launched, with myself and a priest as the only staff. We had little idea of what to do.

Before the opening, I visited England to get a firsthand view of established hospices. The modern hospice movement is generally credited to have been started in England by Dame Cecily Saunders, so I was returning to my roots and the roots of the modern hospice. Saunders was a powerful woman in the tradition of Hildegard of Bingen, a visionary Benedictine nun of many talents and great influence who was born in Germany nine centuries ago. Missionary, nurse, social worker, physician, and visionary, Saunders sought to bring real care to the dying. Her name is associated with St. Christopher's Hospice, which was opened by her in 1967 and is still the shrine of the modern-day hospice movement. Saunders combined excellent management of discomforting symptoms with efficiency and compassion, reviving the hospice as a place of care. Through her efforts, the hospice model, first seen a millennium ago around the time of Hildegard, was brought into the public eye and into the mainstream of caregiving life.

In preparation for my venture I visited St. Christopher's Hospice in London, as well as hospices in Oxford and Leeds, and found each to be well run, with staff focused on their mission to pay attention to every discomfort in their patients and give warm and compassionate care. In each of the hospices there was a general air of serenity, and it was clear to me that these institutions were comfortable places for patients, visitors, and staff. However, while the medical and nursing attention seemed to be of the highest caliber, and quiet efficiency reigned, I did not see as much family involvement as I was later to advocate for in our hospice.

Since we were breaking new ground in the US there was no training available to us; my colleague and priest-friend John and I could do nothing more than believe that our professional backgrounds equipped us fairly well for our work, even though in fact neither the priesthood nor medicine had prepared us for what lay ahead. We recruited nurses and a wonderful young secretary, Colleen, who became our eyes and ears and fount of solace, and together set out to provide home care to patients who were dying of cancer. Looking back I would say that the only difference between ourselves and any other agency which provided nursing care in the home was that we had plenty of time, innumerable questions, and a need to do it right—even though we did not know what "it" was. Regular nursing agencies are task-oriented, with the nurse having barely enough time for changing dressings and checking medications before needing to hurry off to the next case. There is very little time to sit and listen and become woven in to the fabric of the family. Early in our work John and I discovered that we needed to become trusted if the family members were to expose their fears and vulnerabilities to us. Traditional medicine and nursing make no time for sitting silently as witnesses to the memories, stories, and concerns of patients and their families, and yet this is what each family needs when death is preparing to spirit away one of its own. While we received some crucial professional support, many colleagues in the medical profession were skeptical of our venture; others were waiting for us to fail, either because they believed that they did not need us or that we would expose their shortcomings.

In those early days we were guided by John's pastoral experience and wisdom and my analytical, psychological approach to dying, the two of us believing that there were stages to be gone through and insights to be imparted. Another major focus for us was the activities surrounding pain control. But we also had plenty of time, so we sat and listened. We heard many stories in those early days of the hospice—short fragments of experience and full-bodied sagas filled with pain and sorrow. There were tales of ancestors and many remembrances bubbling with humor. Some people seemed to be stuck in one story, lamenting endlessly about how awful everything was and how glad they would be when it was all over. Despite the malignant evidence in front of our eyes, other recitals would focus on how wonderful everything was and how marvelous the family had always been. There were many families brimming over with loving tales of the vibrant ups and downs of their lives, some of which were encrusted with pain while others exuded joy and laughter.

We began to appreciate the importance of these stories, and soon came to recognize that we were part of something we had never paused to witness in our everyday personal and professional lives. As we listened and felt the feelings that these stories evoked in ourselves and the people all around, we were deeply moved by the powerful and juicy living that is the vital force of dying. Years later, conversing with and reading the writings of my contemporaries James Hillman and Thomas Moore, I began to think of this vital force as soul: the soul of the individual and the soul of the family. In the early days in the hospice we barely spoke of soul, since it was uncomfortable to mention the word in medical or nursing circles. Soul seemed to be the exclusive province of the clergy, and we took it for granted that John and other ministers would take care of that.

After one year of home-based work the staff of our hospice decided that we needed a special place where people who were dying could stay if they were no longer able to remain at home. A growing community consciousness regarding the needs of the dying supported us in raising the necessary funds to reconstruct a floor in the hospital. A 30-bed surgical floor in St. Peter's Hospital in Albany, New York, became the 10-bed Inn at St. Peter's. We designed the Inn with all the senses in mind, paying considerable attention to the visual impact of color, lighting, pictures, and furnishings, all of which were enhanced by objects brought in by our patients and their families, imparting to the bedrooms a greater sense of who was there. A kitchen was available for cooking and open to all. There was plenty of space for families to feel at home, and they were most welcome to stay overnight. There was none of the cacophony of a hospital, no banging of carts on linoleum floors or rude interruptions by the insistent paging of unknowns, and there was no Muzak. Instead, in stark contrast to the impersonal and chaotic nature of a hospital, there was a palpable harmony of place. The name and the warm decor of the Inn were part of a conscious attempt to counter the prevailing attitude toward dying, which was that it was a medical abnormality that required hospital treatment to fix. We instead regarded dying as a normal state of life, one that requires loving attention, usually at home but occasionally in a special place of hospitality like the Inn.

In the days when hospices were places of rest for pilgrims, the task of the hospitaler was to take care of the physical needs and comforts of the pilgrims and generally make them welcome. The curate, who was also in attendance, took care of the soul with prayer and counsel. Comparing hospitals of today with hospices of centuries ago, we see that the hospitaler has been displaced by the business agent. In these days of industrial medicine there is little by way of welcome, care, and comfort, and not much more than the token presence of the curate.

The Inn became, and still is, a most sacred place. Sometimes it served the function of a temporary place of respite, giving patient and family a short breather from one another. At other times it was used as a comfortable place in which to ameliorate symptoms that were difficult to manage at home. Some would enter the Inn to die when family fragility or aloneness made staying at home impossible.

In the first months of its existence the Inn was fully staffed but not fully occupied, so the staff had time to share food, worry together, and bond. The worry evaporated in the warmth of experience, and the bonding that is present among the staff to this day is fueled by their willingness to spend time telling each other about the joys and sorrows of what they have seen and heard and been touched by at the Inn. Even now in the Inn there is little evidence of the burnout that so often occurs among critical-care providers as a result of grief unmourned and stories untold— pressures that, when compounded, create an emotional burden and physical exhaustion that eventually becomes too great to bear.

Those early days in the hospice were a foretaste of what was to come. Witnessing and experiencing what needed to be done for our patients gave a clear picture of the possibilities for healing at the time of dying, and led to the simple conclusion that we do not need to wait until we are dying in order to make deep connections with those with whom we share this life. It also led to ideas about attitudes and intentions in caregiving that are relationship-centered in an age when medicine is becoming less and less personal, and has little interest in the emotional experiences of either staff or patients.

The relationship-centered approach of the staff in the hospice Inn created a climate of trust and love, a place where it was safe for those in our care to simply be. This was in contrast to the usual impersonal hospital atmosphere, where little attention is paid to the personal feelings among staff—an attitude that filters down to patients and their families. Caregivers need the time and encouragement to take care of themselves and each other; this mutual care is a necessary prelude to the creation of a loving place for patients. Being relationship-centered in its approach, the Inn paid considerable attention to the well-being of the staff through training that focused on their personal and collective feelings and the reactions of caregivers to the amazing experiences of the patients and families in their midst. This in turn led to the staff members recounting their own stories of loss and grief and redemption. A staff that is not encouraged to tell such personal stories cannot create a climate in which patients and families will feel encouraged to tell theirs.

In the Inn and in our work in patients' homes, we learned firsthand the importance of witnessing the emotions, truths, and reminiscences of the one who is dying. The witness is much more than an active listener whose mind is running fast in the processes of thinking, analyzing, and judging. The person who is dying needs someone who will listen *without judgment* to all that is uncovered at this time, accepting all that is said. The storyteller may not be speaking in words, as with the small child or one who is in coma, but all who are passing between worlds need to be witnessed. Witnessing is the expression of our interconnectedness, and stories are threads from the soul that are woven between us. When we are witnessed, it becomes safe for us to pass on because we have felt the connection, soul to soul, and it is also safe for the witnesses to let go. When there is no witness, there are no stories— the process of storytelling includes the witness. And if there are no stories there are no manifestations of soul, because stories are about the soul.

This book is about the storyteller, the witness, and the guide, the three forces needed for a story to be fully told. It is about the giving and receiving of care, essential practices for the well-being of body, soul, and spirit. It is about families and the miracles of healing that can occur around the time of death, despite years of pain and dysfunction. It is about intimacy and the soul, and rituals that celebrate both. We live in an age when there is unlimited information available about everything imaginable and unimaginable, but there is a shortage of wisdom that sorts the information and distills the essential.

Dying is an impeccable distiller, separating the essential from the nonessential. There is no source of wisdom for living lives of meaning and vitality that is more bountiful than that which is available around dying. If we have the courage to sidestep denial of death with its preoccupation to keep busy and productive; if we will face sadness and loss and not attempt to step out of its way; if we will look in the face of the one who is dying—whether it be ourselves or another—or simply imagine our own death or that of one we love in a guided visualization, then we will see that the only vitally important purpose in life is the giving and receiving of love. When we are able to look into the face of impermanence, give thanks, and say "I love you," we will be in touch with all the wisdom we need for a life of meaning. We will not need to be rich and famous or even reborn, because in the moment of looking life in the face we will discover that we have all we need. When all is said and done, we discover that there are very few essentials in this life. Perhaps there are only two: love, and letting go.

The wisdom of dying urges that the roles and masks of everyday life be set aside before it is too late since they often obscure the giving and receiving of caring and love. From lessons learned around dying come practices for living that enable us to love and to live lives of quality and meaning, and these are the practices described in this book: a curriculum for living that emerges from the wisdom of dying.

CHAPTER 1

The Universal Story

In an age of specialization and reductionism in medicine, it is easy to forget the total being. Imagining an endless array of diseases as we are put through the paces of medical school, it seems impossible to us physicians that we could ever understand the whole. We believe instead that our sanity and ability to master medicine depend on selecting a small part of the body about which we become expert.

While this goal seems to make sense, in the realm of animate nature specialization has major limitations, because the whole is there in every part. The whole being requires attention if it is to be in balance. Tinkering with and even "curing" a defective part may throw the body into an even more precarious state of imbalance.

In the same way that every cell in the body is a distinct entity, at once engaged in specific functions and carrying a blueprint of the genetic inheritance of this particular collection of cells, so it is that any one being, any one individual or personality, contains the collective genetic makeup of our species. In this way each of us, while appearing distinct, is fundamentally the same as every other being, with a tendency toward similar strengths, flaws, and eccentricities.

Jean Cress taught me something about this, and that is why I will be telling her story in some detail. If we can sense, imagine, and witness the essence of one such as Jean, we are sensing, imagining, and witnessing our own story and the universal story. In Jean's own words I heard the denial of death, her myriad activities keeping that denial in place. Through the progression of a debilitating cancer I saw her look in the mirror and face death, pain-filled and frightened at first, then becoming lighter and more free as she unburdened herself of all the preoccupations of her life. I could see, feel, and hear her soul, and when all was said and done, I witnessed her death and her delivery.

Jean Cress became a patient about two years into the life of the hospice. She was for me like one of those magical teachers remembered from the distant haze of childhood, with a loving, warm, humorous, and lovely face that inspired courage and purpose. When I first met Jean she was lying in bed, face to the wall, in the tiny spare room of her son's apartment. She looked uncomfortable and depressed, and had little to say other than that she was in severe pain and that the morphine that had been started during her recent hospital stay was not very helpful. Jean knew that she had only a short time to live, and wanted, in her words, to get it over with as quickly as possible. Over the course of the next few days we tried adding some new medications and increasing her morphine, but there was little change. Jean had moved in with her son Ben and his wife a couple of weeks earlier, following a month-long stay in the hospital. Ovarian cancer had been diagnosed three years earlier, and despite three operations and extensive, debilitating chemotherapy, Jean had managed quite well, living alone and generally remaining in fairly good spirits. The month in the hospital, however, had been precipitated by pain, weakness, and an overall sense that she could no longer cope.

The hospice Inn had just opened a few weeks earlier, and I thought that a few days there might be helpful. Jean agreed. She lived for six more weeks. In the first few days her pain was considerable despite large doses of narcotics and other medications, but she began to talk, and we, her caregivers, listened.

She told of marrying her husband, Frank, 45 years earlier. He was a warm, fun-loving man, very much accepted by her family, and their early days together were delightful. Both of them worked for ten years until the birth of their only child, Ben. After the birth, Jean stayed home to care for their son and the running of the household.

Frank was very present in Ben's early years, but business success led to more and more hours and days away from home. His business and his absences became an increasing source of conflict, a conflict that was resolved, forcibly, by a massive stroke. This had occurred 17 years ago, and at the time Frank was not expected to survive. Many weeks in intensive care were followed by months of rehabilitation, and Frank was still alive in an institution, quadriplegic and miserable, when Jean was in the hospice Inn. While he had obviously suffered some brain damage from the stroke and had difficulty with words, Frank always recognized Jean, and from the beginning had vented his rage, helplessness, and frustration in her direction, although the volume had abated somewhat in recent years. Over the last 17 years Jean had visited Frank for several hours nearly every day, attempting to give comfort, support, and love to a man unwilling or unable to absorb it. She had received very little affirmation and thanks except from staff in the institution. Respite came only during her dark times with cancer.

We asked Jean if she would like to visit Frank to say good-bye. Initially she said she would like to go, and so we arranged for an ambulance to take her to him. However, after wavering back and forth with her decision, she changed her mind. Instead of the visit she wrote a short note thanking Frank for the good years and wishing him well in his troubles that she would no longer be able to share.

Her second story was about Ben. As a child he was her delight, and they maintained closeness and friendship even through his adolescence, which was also the time of her fading relationship with Frank. When Ben left for college Jean wrestled for two difficult and painful years with depression, for which she sought help. Ben met his wife Joan while they were in college, and Jean was cold and miserable to Joan when she and Ben were dating. Their marriage was not received with grace, but the arrival of a grandson, David, led to an uneasy peace that had been maintained ever since. Jean admitted to me that she had always held on too tightly to Ben and had been an interfering force in their marriage.

Jean and I agreed that we needed to meet with Ben and Joan and the ten-year-old David. It was a most powerful and moving gathering, laced with stories, tears, and laughter. Jean told them about her marriage and the awful frustrations of recent years from which she had been unable to release herself except through cancer. She spoke glowingly of her parents and of a childhood filled with love and books. Both grandfathers had died before she was born, and there were not too many memories of the grandmothers, both of whom lived far away and had died when Jean was a child. Both of her parents had died of cancer, her mother 15 years ago and her father two years later. Jean was very involved with their care, but her regret was that all three of them were closed off from one another during the illnesses, each trying to protect the other. They never spoke of their fears and concerns, and Jean never voiced her thanks to them or said good-bye.

Jean acknowledged that she had been too possessive of Ben and had meddled in their marriage, and she asked for Joan's forgiveness, saying that she had been a wonderful mother for David. There were also many tears as she spoke lovingly to David, and they shared many warm reminiscences.

Ben spoke with much love and gratitude to his mother, and had many stories to tell. Joan said that she had always felt awkward as a daughter-in-law, and that her feeling of distance from Jean had always pained her. She told of a very poor relationship with her own mother, who had died without there being any healing between them. Joan also thanked Jean for Ben, and for being the best of grandmothers, and for this opportunity to speak. It was a most intimate gathering.

A third story concerned Jean's lifelong pressure to please others and to look good. As a girl, Jean enjoyed bringing home good grades, in this and many other ways pleasing her parents, who were easily pleased by her. Yet Jean never felt she was quite good enough; perfection always eluded her. This thread of Jean's personality was woven into her marriage as both blessing and curse. She knew that she was a good wife and a good mother but she had great difficulty letting things be. When cancer visibly entered her life, it was not the life-threatening nature of the situation that appalled her but the loss of hair as a consequence of chemotherapy. This was a concern she had been unable to share with anyone, and to this day Jean reported that she would not be seen dead without her wig.

A few days after Jean had met with Ben and his family, had told about her life with Frank, and had written the letter to him, her pain diminished. In fact, the medication was reduced to a fraction of the dose she had been taking when we first met. Also around this time she put aside her wig.

Jean lived for another three weeks, calm and serene most of the time, eating almost nothing and drinking only a few sips of water. Initially in those last days it was difficult for me to visit her. I was at a loss for words, and that often makes me uncomfortable. It is traditional to ask patients how they are or remark that they are looking a little better, whether or not it is a lie. But Jean and I both knew she was comfortable, and that appearance had no meaning for her or for me. Family is usually a topic of conversation, but she had said all there was to say and let them go. So over the next days I simply sat with her and said almost nothing. I noticed that when I was with her my mind would still. I commented to the nurses and others how peaceful was this meditative time, and how refreshed I felt on leaving Jean's side. It was obviously the same for Jean. She would smile a greeting. Our hands would touch occasionally, and after a while, when it was time to leave, she would warmly and easily let me go.

Jean died one Thursday morning, conscious until shortly before the end. Her shallow, gentle breath was simply there one minute and gone the next. Ben, Joan, and David were at her bedside. After she died we reminisced for a while about the unfoldings of the previous weeks and spoke of how it had been for each of us. Finally, we each lit a candle of thanks, for Jean and for ourselves, and after pausing in silence for a few moments, we left the room.

When I think about Jean, as I often have over the years, I almost always start at the end. I see her lying in bed, wasted beyond imagining and with no hair, yet peaceful, receptive, light, and uncluttered. None of the pomp and circumstance of ego: that had all been shed, layer upon layer. Jean had nothing more to say at the end and yet there seemed to be no great hurry to leave, for her or for us, and her presence invited peacefulness in all who would sit with her in witness. All this was in stark contrast to Jean's frantic pain and wish to die six weeks earlier. I wondered what might have happened if physician-assisted suicide had been more in vogue in those days.

Jean gave me the opportunity to see and hear and feel soul as I never had before. With the noise and clutter with which most of us lead our lives, soul is seldom glimpsed, in ourselves or each other. Peeling away the many protective layers with which we invest ourselves seems so difficult, and we often wait until the last minute, if we do it at all. We need a safe place in which to expose ourselves, and a hospital is not a safe or conducive place for that kind of opening up.

Storytelling is so important, and Jean told her stories. Stories need not be understood, and like dreams, they may only be fragmentary images, but they need to be told out loud to nonjudgmental witnesses in order to be released. Stories are a blend of fact, feelings, and imagination, and those that are deep and moving seem to arise from around the center of the soul. I have imagined these stories as being like the clouds, gases, and dust that surround Venus. The stories are not the soul, just as the clouds are not the planet. The stories might be imagined as colorful and dark reflections from the soul that, when told, move out of the way so that the being or inner core is clearly visible, as it was with Jean. Family members need to hear these stories and tell their own if they are to experience the feeling of being-as-one that occurs when all that needs saying has been said.

Finally, Jean received the best of care. We imagine that hospitals and other facilities with the word care in their title do actually provide care, whereas in reality most institutions provide, and are reimbursed for, only the basics of bodily attention—feeding and washing—and the provision and follow-up of tests and procedures. Caregiving for body and soul at the time of impending death requires so much more, its goal being to create a loving atmosphere of welcome and comfort for patient and family alike in which it feels relatively safe to be vulnerable. Jean received this, and so was encouraged to do what she needed to do before she died.

What follows in this book is an unfolding of some of the themes portrayed in this universal story. Jean's gift to us—and it is the gift of anyone who dies consciously and witnessed—is the example of ways in which we might attend to dying when it is our turn or that of one or another of our family for whom we care. Jean died having become more conscious of her relationship to herself by being less critical, demanding, and judgmental, adding compassion and love. She made her peace with her family, and this spread out to all her caregivers who felt blessed by her. Jean, her family, and all who provided care were in a loving relationship with one another—this is what made an inspiring difference to the quality of Jean's life and death. Jean's experience, and the stories of others that follow in this book, offer encouragement to look at values and priorities that will be helpful in living a more conscious life, reminding us that we do not need to wait until we are dying in order to live well.

CHAPTER 2

Dying and the Soul

There is a yearning in our society to embrace a working definition of soul. The wide popularity of the recent writings of Thomas Moore on soulfulness in the individual and in the world provides sound evidence of this longing. Something fundamental is felt to be missing in the way we live our lives in this world governed by science, technology, consumerism, and the bottom line.

The word soul is a familiar one, yet the notion of soul is one we seldom address in everyday life. The Oxford English Dictionary has some two dozen notations on soul, defining it as the seat of emotions and feelings and the center of intellectual and spiritual power. Traditional religions speak of soul but most believers fail to act as if it were the driving force in life, both in themselves and in nature. Instead, religious teachings focus almost exclusively on the soul in relationship to death, dwelling on their particular vision concerning the temporal relationship between the moment of death and the time the soul leaves the body, and by what criteria the soul is judged and then rewarded or punished with redemption or damnation.

For all of the religious focus on the soul and death, the soul is also said to be the vital principle in all living things. This was the way in which soul was experienced by our ancestors, who attributed consciousness and soul to everything in nature. Trees were more than sources of wood to be harvested and measured in terms of board feet. They were alive, to be danced around, talked to, and honored as part of life. The forest abounded in magic, fear, and wonder, and there lived all manner of spirits to stir the soul. Native Americans carved totem poles for worship; some tribes decorated a small piece of the parent tree. Known as the Talking Stick, it was passed around from person to person during tribal gatherings and bestowed upon the holder the right to speak from the heart and be listened to by all the rest. Mountains, rocks, rivers, oceans, and all creatures were held sacred, deserving of the greatest respect. In those times and cultures that preceded Western civilization, soul was experienced everywhere, and this appreciation and honoring of the life force was a veneration of the sacred in nature. When there is no appreciation of this life force or soul, nothing is sacred.

The soul might be likened to the cosmos. We look at the skies with the naked eye or with our powerful technology and see stars, planets, and galaxies. The visible appears to be vast, and its study could occupy whole lifetimes, yet it makes up but a small percentage of the whole, perhaps 2 or 3 percent. Most of the cosmos is dark matter about which we know little or nothing. However, when acted upon by energy in the form of light, that dark matter has the potential to become visible.

The soul also has a visible, conscious side, with awe, wonder, imagination, self-consciousness, and appreciation of our planet as parts of this galaxy. But like the cosmos, all but 2 or 3 percent is dark matter or the unconscious, containing within its confines both the potential for greater awareness and the apprehension of chaos, lack of control, and terror of death. This dark side of the soul contains the ingredients for enriching and expanding consciousness, but there is a demon guarding the gate to this rich underworld. It takes the form of terror of death, and unless that demon is confronted, it is impossible to enter and go deep into the realm of the soul.

The tales of the Greek pantheon are timeless and universal myths that serve as metaphors for the myriad facets of the soul. The story of the rape of Persephone has been a guiding metaphor for me in understanding the terror of entering the unknown underworld of the soul. The rape in this story does not refer to sexual violence, and, as in all Greek myths, the young maiden, Persephone, could equally well be imagined as a young man. The rape concerns the loss of innocence, which Persephone imagines is hers as an inalienable right. This innocence has her believe in her own immortality and perpetual youth, with no possibility of her ever being thrust into the turbulent realm of dying.

Persephone was a young goddess of great beauty and innocence, the daughter of Demeter, goddess of the harvest.

Persephone's father was the all-powerful Zeus. One day while gathering flowers in the garden, Persephone picked a narcissus. Gaia, the goddess of the earth, had caused this flower to appear at the request of Hades, king of the underworld. Persephone, unable to resist its wonder, bent over to pick the flower. As she did so, the earth opened up and the mighty Hades emerged in his chariot and swept Persephone off into the underworld to be his queen.

Hecate, the blind goddess of the dark side of the moon, heard what happened but said nothing. Demeter heard her daughter's cries of terror but was unable to find Persephone, and it was only after nine days of worried searching that the Sun told Demeter what had happened. At first Demeter became depressed and then, consumed with anger, she vented her rage on the earth, causing all living things to wither. The great gods became alarmed. Zeus, who knew that his brother Hades had abducted Persephone, sent Hermes to secure her release. As a traveler and messenger of the gods, Hermes was familiar with the territory of the dark underworld. He was able to secure the release of Persephone, but not before the underworld king had enjoined Persephone to swallow a pomegranate seed, a rite that ensured she would spend one third of her time with Hades in the underworld. So was Persephone reunited with her mother, and from that time on continued her life in the two worlds.

The Greek gods are metaphors and images for soulful characteristics of ourselves and our world. Sometimes we are like Hades, wanting to repossess the feminine in our own depths. Or we may find ourselves like Gaia, that older and wiser goddess of the earth who knew the importance of humility as she conspired to bring Persephone down into the place of surrender and loss. And yet again we may find ourselves like Demeter, also an earth goddess but an inconsolable one, who viewed the world as empty and meaningless when she lost the object of her love and desire. Or, like Hermes, the guide of souls and messenger of the gods, who was deft and articulate, at home in the underworld of suffering, grief, and loneliness. Perhaps we are all like Persephone, innocently living our lives in ordinary consciousness, unaware of a darker side to ourselves and blind to the certainty of death.

We often expend great energy ignoring our own inner truth

until some catastrophic or life-threatening event drags us, kicking and screaming, into that dark reality. While this underworld is frightening, it also contains a vast gold mine awaiting discovery. (From this stems Hades' other name, Pluto, a Greek word for money.) Hades is not evil, nor is his underworld bad, even though many religions have associated Hades with the devil and the underworld with hell, and urge that both be banished from the lives of their followers. On the contrary, Hades' unique and vitally important gift can help to add breadth and depth to the soul of the innocent.

Demeter, Earth Mother and goddess of nature and nurture—how we need her if we are to survive! The Demeter in us wants to protect the innocent child from the terrors of living. She calls on the police, physicians, technology, and the gods to prevent these terrors from happening, and stumbles between depression and rage when they do anyway. Demeter is a strong force in all of our lives, and we cry for her when we experience life-threatening illness with its attendant underworld terrors of loneliness, helplessness, and fear. She helps us in our attempt to find a cure and so relieves the dark threats emanating from our imagination. But if cure is impossible or the cries of our frightened Persephones persist, the Demeter in us may be too quick to tranquilize so that she no longer has to hear our screams and deal with her own feelings of helplessness.

What is necessary at that moment is that we expand our role to include that of Hermes, the underworld traveler-god. Hermes is the friend of man and a willing travel-guide for those who ask him to accompany them on the odyssey that we all must make when faced with loss, change, or death. Hermes will stay by our side, encouraging us to face our fears and worries so that we can become more loving and compassionate with ourselves—a necessity at all times but especially when confronting the unknown. However, this role is unfamiliar to most of us, who may be as frightened of both death and the underworld as are our loved ones. We will only become more comfortable with this role if we consciously face our feelings when either we ourselves or our own family members are dying, and when we begin to look at images of our own annihilation. Hermes will guide us and pilot us through the darkness and fears of the underworld, pointing out the sights—the rocks and canyons of our fears and worries—along the way. As we view these peaks and valleys of our feelings and imagination we will be able to glimpse our complexity, and become aware of a little of what was hitherto unconscious. Hermes' help and his skills in navigating through the underworld are essential if we are to gain new insights and enlightenment as we learn about the soul.

The glimpse we have of Hecate in the myth of the rape of Persephone suggests the presence of the perfect witness, one who listens and absorbs but is neither judge nor interpreter. We need such witnesses to our birth, our death, and all the life-shaping challenges in between. This kind of witnessing breeds a connectedness and feeling of belonging that seems to have been lost in this technocentric world. Very few of us take the time to sit still in a place of nonjudgment and be witness to the self, another, or the world around. Yet this is simply the art of a human, being; we are much more comfortable in the role of a human, doing. The trouble with that role is that we often are so busy doing that we miss the incredible feeling of being connected to another, soul to soul. We need some of Hecate's magic if we are to become fully present human beings, in attendance at life and death, rather than frenzied human doings who are asleep to the soul.

Persephone, that innocent aspect in all of us, the one who is still so attached to and protected by her mother, Demeter, never leaves the garden, never willingly takes the risks that are required to discover the riches of the deep. It seems risky because in this underworld we are obviously not in control, whereas in the garden we can have an illusion of safety. Yet it is only in the underworld, where we experience the ineffectiveness of ego and armor, that we can experience real connectedness. Most of us will have experienced the connectedness that occurs at the time of a national disaster, such as an assassination or an air crash. For a few moments we speak to anyone who will listen, and all the usual social barriers disappear, allowing a sense of intimacy with strangers. But this kind of intimacy is in fact available at any time if we are willing to shed ego and be vulnerable to the loss of self. It was Persephone's innocent nature and her love and appreciation of the beautiful that caught her off guard and allowed her to be inducted into her own depths, and it was precisely this vulnerability that offered her the opportunity for healing and rebirth. She needed the ingenious guidance of

Hermes to realize that she could find her way around in the underworld and, like the shaman, return home from there to be master of two worlds. She was to return to the underworld to spend one third of her time with Hades, just as we spend one third of our time each day in the underworld of sleep, where our dreams provide images and ways of knowing not usually available to us in ordinary consciousness.

Of the thousands of families I saw within the hospice program, one in particular offers a modern-day version of Persephone's story. Joe was an aggressive businessman I met within a month of his death from lung cancer, which had only recently been diagnosed. He was bed-bound, so we gathered in his home. Joe's second wife and two daughters by his first marriage were also present at our meeting.

Joe greeted my questions about his worries and his family with a belligerent challenge of my credentials and an attack against my insensitivity at asking personal questions. It was as if he saw me as Hades himself. He then attacked his wife, driven by the perception that she wanted to deprive the children of his first marriage of their inheritance. In the uproar it seemed as though their relationship of ten years had been a disastrous failure, and that in some way she had betrayed him. In fact, before the diagnosis of his cancer their marriage had been a warm, intimate relationship filled with much activity and humor. In his hellish experience of cancer he seemed to perceive his wife as Demeter, one who had failed to protect him from the fears and terrors of his illness, and so he vented his fury at her.

We were not driven away by his rage, and after a while Joe was able to listen to his daughters, who sang his praises as father, hero, and wise man, protecting them, they imagined, from innumerable disasters. He was able to listen, like Hecate, to their heart-rending lamentations as they saw him being torn away from them. He was able to listen to his heartbroken wife as she told the story of the sudden death of her fun-loving first husband and cried that she was once again losing a male source of security, love, and excitement.

In his witnessing of the grief of the women in his life, Joe provided them with comfort and himself with the warmth and peace of being connected to them. As he listened, his rage and terror dissolved, and he was able to speak of his sadness that

13

he was not present at the death of either of his parents and wished he could have said good-bye to them as he was now saying good-bye to his family. My presence in this gathering as a hermetic guide who kept them focused on their fears and concerns made possible what would otherwise probably not have happened. It was only by going into the darkness of their secret worlds that they were able to experience greater connectedness and intimacy.

In terms of relationship-centeredness, Joe transformed himself from a judgmental non-listener to an impeccable witness, listening both to his own heart and the hearts of those who loved him. The intimacy between storyteller and witness is at the center of loving; being in loving relationship allowed Joe to die in peace and his family to feel loved and blessed. My role as hermetic guide was to encourage all in the family to make this deep connection at a time of great pain and terror. My presence allowed the storytellers to say what they had to say and the witnesses to listen in silence and really hear. I experience these moments as times when the storytellers, witnesses, and guides are in truly soulful relationship with one another.

Like Jung, James Hillman, Thomas Moore, and others, I have found it useful to imagine some distinctions between soul and spirit, with the indivisible pair together making up the whole inner being. Stories of the soul relate to our earthy and earthly attachments and detachments, whereas those of the spirit are celestial and otherworldly. The soul dwells deep in the valleys and experiences of everyday life. It is feminine, moist, and full of feelings. The spirit resides on the mountaintops, has a masculine flavor, and its lofty concerns are for meaning, the connectedness of all things, and life after death. The creative, imaginative soul craves connectedness with others and with our world; the spirit teaches detachment from earthly concerns. Philosophers and theologians may not be in touch with their own earthy and earthly natures and so extol a spirituality that seems to be above matters of the soul. They may be so uncomfortable or unfamiliar with their feminine or anima natures that they will not deal with feelings and imagination, even though they claim to be in the business of saving souls. Many of the professional purveyors of spirituality are male, and are therefore likely to be more familiar and comfortable with masculine images of the heroic, and the death-defying and death-denying than with feminine images of feelings, death, and birth.

If soul really *is* vital, and if we need to expose our terrors and sorrows to gain entry into this arena of feelings and imagination in order to connect with ourselves and those we love, it is curious that we pay so little attention to soul in everyday life. Few of us pause and listen closely to our fears and feelings in our daily decisions, not to mention the life-changing ones. We live in soul-destroying jobs and relationships, deaden feelings with drugs of all kinds, and are too busy to sit quietly like Hecate, the blind goddess of the dark side of the moon, and attend to our bewildered Persephone. We have little idea of how to engage ourselves at this level; it is not a sensibility that most of us are encouraged to develop as children, and we see little of it in our parents and our teachers.

Yet there is an innate wisdom that is apparent in young children before it is suffocated by the knowledge and directions of the prevailing culture. Children know about soul and the vibrancy and wonder in life, at least until it is schooled out of them. Our rational and functional approach to human development says that we grow up, moving from childhood into adolescence and on into adulthood and old age. We are expected to "act" our age, leaving earlier stages of development behind, since they are in the past. But at the level of soul there is no time; development is a nonlinear process that incorporates all that has been before and all that will be in the future. The past is present and the child is always now, living within us. If the child, custodian of soul and innate wisdom, has been stifled, neglected, or abused, he or she will need acknowledgment, witnessing, encouragement, and love at some time during life if soul and wisdom are to reappear. This can occur at any time and at any age. I have often guided and encouraged the dying to recognize and embrace the child-self within. This is often the prelude to a peaceful death—and to a peaceful life, if it is done earlier.

While innate wisdom is within us all, acquired wisdom is difficult to come by in these times and receives very little respect in our culture. Wisdom suggests considerable knowledge tempered by compassion and good judgment, and is developed through living life. The wise man or woman can be likened to a fine wine: coming from the best stock, full-bodied, lovingly aged and matured, and perhaps containing a little sediment. Wise men and women are quite knowledgeable, but knowledge when tempered by wisdom is humble and much given to brooding and pondering. It is as if the wise allow the insistent chatterings of the mind to mature in a vat of silence.

Our rational, mechanical age is powered by knowledge and information. It sees the planet as inanimate, a vast resource to be exploited and developed. It sees people as consumer machines, customers to be seduced into buying all manner of products and services they do not need, as well as machines with a whole host of bodily parts to be fixed and replaced by an army of specialists. This death-denying attitude may mute the terror of death for a while by keeping us shopping, but it leaves little room for soul and the appreciation of the sacred.

Centuries ago in Europe there existed many sacred shrines to which pilgrims traveled in order to give honor and thanks and receive blessing and renewal. The journey was as important as the destination. They traveled light and often on foot, and may have prepared for their venture with prayer and fasting. The pilgrims depended for food on fellow beings along the way and there were hospices in which they could rest, where bodily needs were met by the hospitaler and care of the soul was attended to by the curate. The difficulties of the journey and the meetings and caregiving along the way were as integral to the pilgrimage as was the pilgrim's destination.

With the development of the tourist industry, the pilgrimage has all but disappeared in the Western world. The goal of most travelers now is to journey as comfortably and rapidly as possible, with all arrangements made by the travel agent. There is little preparation necessary, and discomfort is something to be complained about. Photographs are taken and souvenirs bought. In trying to pack too much into a short period of time, many tourists return home feeling tired rather than refreshed and renewed and may complain that the tour was not quite what they were hoping for.

Death and birth are two clear destination points in life. We can imagine the journeys leading to these destinations as animistic, soulful events or as logical, rational steps to be taken as efficiently and comfortably as possible.

If we were to consider death as the sacred destination of a pilgrimage, we would prepare for the journey with much prayer and reflection. We would give loving thanks, say our tearful good-byes, and bestow and receive blessings from those near and dear. There would be those who would try to pull us back and others who would attempt to distract us from our purpose along the way. But the journey, like the way of the cross to the crucifixion, is an essential part of the whole, and in order to arrive conscious and prepared we need comfort, compassion, encouragement, and hospitality on our travel. We need companions for the journey, and Hermes as friend and guide would make the way so much easier, and the destination might be imagined as the delivery of our soul.

We might also imagine birthing soulfully, with delivery of the baby as arrival at a sacred destination. The fetal pilgrim is cradled and comforted in the mother during the nine-month journey, and the vulnerable traveler needs the loving attention of both parents as they sing, talk, touch, and make welcome. Friends as living witnesses and a hermetic accoucheur as guide make the way more comfortable, and they would consider their participation a privilege.

Neither death nor birth is imagined so animatedly in these rational and functional times. Death is not to be spoken of, and good-byes are too painful. Everything possible and impossible must be done to keep the patient alive, so that death often occurs in painful loneliness amongst the anonymous machines of the intensive care unit. Birth as well is most often a clinical and mechanical event. Even birthing centers are more like an expensive hotel than a soulful home, and can be seen as both a public relations promotion and an attempt by the medical establishment to maintain their hold on birthing. The whole family, including children, are not often involved as witnesses to the sacred event of birth, and the nine-month journey of the fetus may receive little more attention than what we imagine as necessary for good antenatal care. Weights, measures, vitamins, and diet are all of great importance, but vital care involves time and attention to the souls of the parents, family, friends, and assistants, as well as to that of the developing child.

It is odd that we exclude children and friends from the events of birth and death. They may visit when everything seems to be once again under control after a birth, with the infant bathed and swaddled and the mother once again in charge. To hear her cries and groans, to see her naked body seeping fluids and blood, and to witness the crowning head of the emerging child is usually taboo. Like death, it is too personal; it is too frightening and out of control. Yet it is part of the miracle, beautiful and amazing to behold.

At death children may attend the brief, staged wake in the funeral home. The person they have loved in life is made up to look good and is laid out in an ornate box, surrounded by masses of regimented flowers that look as unnatural as everything else. If we really believed death to be part of life and not an obscene interference in our illusions of immortality, we would hold wakes for the dead where they had lived, at home. They would be laid in a bed in the living room and friends would arrive with flowers from the garden or food and drink. There would be greetings and tears, laughter and condolences, all woven together with bittersweet memories.

When death is obscured by hospital technology and painted over by morticians, and some of the difficult and personal sides of birthing are kept hidden, it is not surprising that the dark side of the soul should remain secret, ominous, and frightening. If both death and birth were brought out into the open and seen as sacred events we would become more familiar with this hidden unknown. In adding this light and depth to the soul there would be much less to fear at the beginning, at the end, and at all stages in between.

Looking back over the years since my friend Brenda died, I now conceive of her as having transformed herself from living the life of a successful tourist to becoming an alert pilgrim on a sacred journey that ended in her soulful delivery. Brenda, an excellent counselor and spellbinding speaker, was witty and full of life. Her religious faith was most important to her, and was brightly woven into the fabric of her life. Her diagnosis of cancer, which profoundly altered the way in which she lived her life, was also an influence in my own change of direction. I started pondering over hospice work a year or so after her diagnosis, and remember thinking that it would be so reassuring if there were a safe place for Brenda to be when she was dying, since she lived alone.

We had many conversations over those last years. At first Brenda spoke of the cancer as if it were happening to someone else, and while she was preoccupied with the details and effects of surgery and chemotherapy, she continued in her upbeat role of leader, mentor, and speaker. At this time she spoke of her faith, and said that she was full of hope that the progress of her cancer would be stayed. Her denial, my denial, and that of her physicians and friends all around was such that no thought was allowed to emerge nor word escape that might be considered negative. No consideration was given to the possibility that all the wishes and efforts would not lead to a cure.

The cancer went underground for a couple of years, as it often does, and all seemed to be well, but then it re-emerged. It was only at that point that Brenda began to peel away the layers that had served her well—if social and professional success is the index of being well-served. She talked about the fear of dying and the need to cut back on her work, and began to pay more attention to herself by traveling less, reading more, and finding the time to be with friends. She was then able to say that she felt more peaceful and had really accepted her dying. That lasted for a while until new symptoms arose, and Brenda had to peel away another layer, again facing her fears of death by cradling the being within and further reducing the demands she made of herself.

A couple of these unwrappings took place in the Inn. One in particular I remember as being quite stormy, precipitated by very discomforting symptoms that were difficult to manage, accompanied by much fear and angry, demanding behavior that was "not like her." This obvious, uncontrollable emergence of energy from the shadow side of Brenda's being seemed to offer balance, and her acceptance of both dark and light was the prelude to a more peaceful end.

Brenda never returned to the Inn after this stormy emergence, apparently having no further need for the safety and protection the Inn provided. She stayed at home in her apartment, and I was there early on the day she died. She was very weak but fully alert and peaceful, free of the terror of death that had plagued her during recent months. Several friends were present, sitting quietly in witness, sharing an occasional story. Her friend Susan was lying by her side on the bed, and sometime while I was there Brenda and Susan quietly began singing "Row, row, row your boat, gently down the stream." The peace in the room was palpable.

Brenda died later in the evening, attended by friends.

CARE FOR SOULFUL LIVING AND SOULFUL DYING

The receiving and giving of care is the vital, loving energy that connects us all. It is relationship. If we neglect care, the soul will lose its vitality and the quality of life, which depends on the vibrancy of soul, will plummet. If we neglect care, the spirit will also wither, and the neglected spirit leads to a universal sense of apathy and disconnectedness. It is this inattention to care that is a major component of the poor quality of dying and the poor quality of living in our present time.

We need a constant supply of care for the well-being of body and soul. Just as the circulation of blood needs to be steady and enduring, so also the receiving of care needs to be ever-present and reliable. In our day it is considered selfish or sinful to think too often of our own needs; the selfless, ever-giving mother or the dedicated super-nurse is held up as a model of caregiving, regardless of the fact that they all too often fail to take good care of themselves, brushing off their own needs for care. Invariably their failure to ask for care becomes painfully burdensome for others. It seems as if care is something we are allowed only when we are sick, and even then it is often in very short supply. The essence of care is loving ourselves and being loved. Without it the soul withers and the body ails.

The giving of care used to be associated with the word charity, which was derived from the Latin words *caritas* (affection) and *carus* (dear), indicating that the root of care was love and affection. Now the word charity has become immersed in social judgment; there is an element of shame in receiving charity, for one should be independent, self-reliant, and have a job. But the origins of the word have to do with the very personal giving of love and affection. The body and soul need charity at all times, both from ourselves and from others. In medical and nursing circles, there is no mention of the word love except as something to beware of because it leads to sexual involvement with patients, so it is understandable how this dangerous but absolutely vital commodity has vanished from professional "caregiving," especially since it may seem easier to become involved with the doings of medical technology than with the uncertainties of personal involvement.

While the body and the soul need to *receive* constant care for their vitality and well-being, the spirit needs to *give* care, both to self and others. Spiritual well-being, grounded in relationships, requires that we connect with ourselves and others, expressing love and giving care. Not only does our personal wellness depend in great part on this exchange. The spiritual well-being of communities and nations depends on the free-flowing movement of our loving energy in this way too, without which we are doomed to an ever more solitary future.

THE EGO AND THE SOUL

Hildegard of Bingen was born 900 years ago in the Rhineland. Visionary, mystic, teacher, preacher, musician, painter, and writer, she was an extraordinary woman for those or any other times. She wrote of her work as being done "in the shadows," which I have taken to mean that she was an illuminator of dark matter—one who, like Hermes, was not afraid to travel deep in the underworld.

One of her mystical paintings, entitled "The Egg of the Universe," is a mandala of great beauty depicting the universe as egg-shaped, containing a globe which itself contains symbols that seem to be an embrace of anima and animus, masculine and feminine. The whole radiates with the essential elements: fire, water, earth, air, and space.

This image of the universe as egg was not unique to Hildegard. It had also featured in earlier traditions, such as the Egyptian and the Celtic, but Hildegard's visionary illumination—with the organic universe containing within its womb our vibrant living planet, which itself contains within its womb the individual with its masculine and feminine natures together with all other creatures—has been an important inspiration for me: a giant cosmic cluster-doll.

I have visualized each one of us as being like an egg. Deep within lies the ovum-like soul surrounded by a nourishing yolk. This yolk or soul food derives from the warmth and love of relationships, and when it is there in abundance for the child, the soul will flourish, along with its wisdom and vitality. When the yolk is rationed or nonexistent, the soul will addle. The shell of the egg is there for our protection, but for nourishment to enter from the outside, from relationships and from nature, the shell needs to be permeable. Yet fear causes it to become thick, cutting off this deep

21

connectedness with all around. The fear stems from the dark matter of the soul, and it also arises more consciously from violence in both the family and society at large. War, the rumor of war, murder, rape, incest, and muggings are met with a strong militia, bulletproof vests, locks, burglar alarms, and lawyers, together with a personal thickening of the shell or armor so that fear, vulnerability, and other feelings are invisible.

Preoccupation with safety, immortality, and the need to thicken the shell leads to obsession with the need to be strong, collectively and personally. A strong nation becomes dependent on its military and its police. A strong individual becomes as solid as a rock, looking good from the outside, displaying no emotions, especially tears. The problem is that we *do* have feelings, hearts *do* break and emotions are constantly on the move. Failure to acknowledge this leads to headaches and heart attacks and a soulless world.

We are absorbed with the development, strengthening, and beautification of this shell, which we also know as character or personality or ego. I have imagined the ego or shell as that part of the soul that exudes cover stories, and we often believe, and would have others believe, that we *are* our cover stories We decorate the ego-shell with baubles and gold, festoon it with children and other possessions, aggrandize it with rank and status. When pleased with the colorful shell, we may wear a satisfied smile, at least until the novelty wears off. When we despise that shell, we tear ourselves apart in self-hatred.

The result of the bulletproof, bejeweled, bedecked, and storied shell is that the inner soul gets cut off from the outside nurture that it needs. If the shell is too strong to break, delivery of the soul at the time of death is painfully difficult. Making the ego porous allows for the soul to touch and be touched. Dying is the ultimate confrontation of the denial of death and it also exposes the fragile futility of the ego. When death can no longer be denied and the ego becomes porous, having let go of its posturing, the vulnerable soul is exposed, ready to pour forth its stories if there are witnesses to listen. Personality and character are important but they are not to be taken too seriously, since they are simply our cover story and nothing more. The body, as part of the shell, is important and needs to be cared for lovingly, but in time it needs to be relinquished. Dying will either be accepted as a necessary part of life for the birth of the soul or, in a world without soul, it will be the occasion of a heroic battle to the death.

Just as a grain of sand irritates the oyster to produce the glamorous pearl, so also the terror of death stimulates the growth of the many-layered shell that surrounds the soul. When the integrity of the shell is given importance over all else, the king's men are going to try to glue Humpty Dumpty together again, regardless of cost. Peel those layers away—and this requires trust in God or the Universe—and paradoxically with them goes much of the terror they were erected to stay. Exposing the soul layer by layer requires that there be a safe haven in which this can occur. It requires stories to be told and witnesses to hear. It requires guides to assist and encourage, and celebration when all is said and done.

CHAPTER 3

Storytelling

Storytelling is the expression of the warmth and darkness of relationships and connections, both intimate and more remote, in the world and beyond. The substance of these connections are our stories, which might be thought of as soul food.

Poets of the soul record the connections and intimacies of their lives in evocative brushstrokes that lay bare their truths and perceptions about this experience called life, inviting readers into the worlds of their souls. The 1971 Nobel Prize winner for literature, Pablo Neruda, wrote passionate poems of soulful love, and the wise, blind seer Jorge Luis Borges wrote mostly of the spirit, as in his story of the wizard who dreamed up a son, which is told in the next chapter. We need wise role models for the expression of soul and spirit—the likes of Neruda, and Borges, and of James Hillman and Thomas Moore—in our present day.

We need to give our story a reading before witnesses. Our story is like a weaving with some of the threads drawn from memories of our experiences and others created and colored by our imagination. The story changes like a kaleidoscope with each telling.

Original stories are crafted from much more than our own personal experience and imagination. A first love, for instance, has threads from the beloved and from ourselves, but there are other threads from archetypal love stories—the birth of Eros who emerged from the union of Chaos and the Night, or the love of Tristan and Isolde. These legends give our own love story an eternal power and freshness that impels the witness to the story to cry for an encore. Our original stories are family myths; they are deep transpersonal tales that give the family meaning and are therefore ones that we never tire of hearing. So many families fail to tell their stories, and it seems to me that these untold stories emit a sense of dark foreboding in the presence of death; it is the silent family that feels so heavy and doomed, while those that have heard from one another appear free of this terror of ending.

The memories that make up our stories are like the patches of a patchwork quilt; they can be sewn together in endlessly differently ways, each giving a different picture so that, with each telling of the story, there is a different emphasis and a different configuration. Using an analogy from music, the quilted composition would be considered a series of variations on a single theme, each variation as valid and true as it is unique. Sometimes there are stories composed of patches that are always in the same pattern, and after a while these stories become devoid of life and soul, iterated from a place of neurotic mire that inhibits any change.

Memories associated with loss of innocence—that is, with radical change, such as when Persephone was abducted into the underworld by Hades—make for the most compelling stories because they are the myths that speak of our fragile humanity, which is the linkage that connects us all. And so the guide might ask the storyteller to tell of the time his father died, or of the birth of his first child, or the time when he learned of the diagnosis of his life-threatening illness. Each of these incidents spawns an endless series of variations on the theme, making a wealth of stories available that plumb the depths of the soul. These are the stories that the storyteller yearns to tell and the witnesses love to hear—original tales of love, connectedness, and loss.

Life, or at least our conscious vital living, depends on the telling of stories as Sharazad knew only too well. Without them we are dead to the soul. King Shahriyar was very much in love with his queen when he discovered that she was plotting to kill him. In a rage he killed her with his own hands, and vowed that henceforth he would marry young maidens and behead them the next day before they had a chance to betray him. Many queens were beheaded, and parents with daughters soon began to flee the country with their families so that after a while few eligible maidens remained. The king was enraged and told his chief minister the Grand Vizier that he would be beheaded if he failed to produce a maiden for the king to marry. The Grand Vizier was terrified and distressed, but his beautiful older daughter,

Sharazad, who loved him very much, came to his rescue, saying that she would marry the king. Sharazad's younger sister promised to come to the palace in the morning before daybreak with soothing sherbet for the king, at which time Sharazad would tell him a story. This ritual was repeated day after day, and the hermetic trickster Sharazad would always end her story at sunrise, at a point where there was great suspense and uncertainty regarding the outcome, so that the king would want to hear more and spare her life for another day. Stories of Sinbad, Aladdin, Ali Baba, and many more were recounted for one thousand nights. On the following night, Sharazad finished her story just as the sun rose, but by this time, the king was in love with her and so spared her life, renouncing all further violence.

All our stories need to be told, not simply the ones that we deem to be light and happy. I sometimes imagine our inner stories as landscapes filled with color. Some parts are readily discernible, light and pastoral; others are more dark, obscure, and menacing, and perhaps these parts attract the gaze and the imagination because of their mystery. If we covered up those parts of a canvas that we found disturbing, the painting would appear very odd indeed, and the viewer would focus on what was underneath the cover rather than what was visible. Many people fear that if the whole picture is seen it will be judged unfavorably, and the devastating consequence will be loss of love. As a result of this fear, many spend considerable energy in life covering up the pictures of themselves and their ancestors or even denying the importance of painting pictures and telling stories. Both choices are soul-destroying, for it is our secrets and untold stories that devastate the soul. So many times I have heard families say that they have no idea of the story of their parents or grandparents who came to America from some unknown place in Europe. They had perhaps escaped the Holocaust or emigrated from Russia, had experienced events so painful that their story was never told. This leaves a void in the family story, a void filled with pain or silence or shame or grief that then becomes part of the family myth that can never be spoken.

Michael was a man in his mid-seventies who was referred to the hospice about one month before he died. He lived alone in a run-down apartment devoid of most creature comforts, and had little to say except that he had recently been in the hospital and was diagnosed as having lung cancer. Initially, no family was present;

26

all the visiting hospice nurse saw was a quiet, withered little man who had been an alcoholic and obviously had a short time to live. Four of his five living children agreed to meet in Michael's apartment, and during the next month there unfolded a story that curdled the imagination for the breathtaking suffering incurred by each one in the family.

Michael had been an alcoholic for as long as each child could remember. He was extremely violent when drunk, and their mother, who had died three years before, was repeatedly admitted to the hospital with bruises and broken bones. Arrests and evictions were commonplace. One evening while he was drunk, Michael had fallen on top of his infant daughter causing brain damage that was still evident in her physical disability 30 years later. Both she and the two youngest sons had been sexually abused for years by family members, and all five of the living children were alcoholics. One child was in jail, and a sixth had died in a motor accident that was probably both induced by alcohol and suicide-related. The younger boys, now in their early thirties and sober, said that the only feelings they could ever remember in association with growing up were shame and rage.

It became very difficult to manage Michael at home in the last few days of his life, especially because his home was devoid of anything of comfort, so he agreed to go into the hospice Inn. The children spent many hours at their father's bedside, and were visibly closer as they told more of their family story. Very little was known of Michael's early life other than that he was abused as a small child, abandoned by his mother at age four, and spent his childhood in a series of foster homes. As we talked around his bed we reframed his story, developing the image of a frightened little child at age four putting on a ferocious Halloween costume with which he could scare everyone. The costume would stay on until the following Halloween, when the little boy would exchange it for another. Year by year, each costume grew more fearsome than the last, and Michael lived his life frightening everyone and attacking anyone who might try to come close until, at this time, with his life almost spent, the costumes fell away, and the vulnerable little child was once more exposed. This story resonated with Michael's children in a place beyond hatred and shame, and with the exception of the oldest son, who was unable to acknowledge either his own alcoholism or his connection with his father, Michael's children were able to tap a well of compassion that is often obscured in much less traumatized families. The jailed son was present both at a family meeting when Michael was conscious and at the time of Michael's death.

The death itself was quiet and peaceful for all, in stark contrast to the death of Michael's wife in a hospital three years before. Michael's children told me that at the time of their mother's death, they were all frightened and upset, enraged at Michael and quite unable to be present in the room with their mother as she died. The daughter, who best exemplified the neglect, abuse, and self-hatred in the family, ran screaming through the hospital after her mother died; she drank heavily and was quite depressed for many months thereafter, requiring a six-week stay in a psychiatric ward. At their mother's death the family was overwhelmed by the chaos, fear, and loneliness of the whole family, all of which lay so close to the surface but was not to be voiced until shortly before Michael's death. The family story had never been told before; this time the fearful gaps in their family life were named and witnessed. In the telling, the black hole of shame, rage, and abuse, which had continually drained the life out of each family member, lost some of its force.

It is quite understandable that a family wishes to avoid or repress painful stories, since such stories often receive little respect from those to whom they are told. The Latin root of the word respect means "taking another look at" or "revisiting." Since most listeners find their own family stories too painful to hear and revisit, they block the retelling with interruptions and alterations. Because the story is never fully heard, it is never changed or reimagined, and so the pain is revisited each time the story is aired. A story will change only when told to a witness who gives it complete attention. In the retelling the story shortens, the painful effect lessens in intensity, and what remains is an imprint in the imagination, or soul, that then becomes part of the life-painting.

Children thrive on stories that are warm antidotes to the terror of death. Children who live in fortunate circumstances may have an evening ritual that includes some variation on the theme of a warm bath, choosing pajamas and a favorite stuffed animal, being snugly tucked into bed, and then being told a story. The perfect time for storytelling is when the soul is open and vulnerable, which is especially likely when we are drifting off, and children's stories are sedatives that help to ease them through the fearful gateway that guards the underworld of sleep.

Children's tales tell of magical peers, often a boy and a girl or twins—perhaps representing the spirit and the soul or the darkness and the light—who set out along some adventurous life path. They are confronted by trials and dangers which they sometimes overcome by masculine fearlessness and strength or at other times by feminine knowing, patience, and wisdom. The witch, who represents the underworld challenges, including death, may seem to prevail as one or other of the innocent is turned to stone or poisoned with an elixir that causes endless sleep, but in the end a kiss or touch of love awakens the dead, and all is well again.

Children may beg for the same story to be read over and over again, and if the storyteller wanders from the familiar theme, corrections quickly follow. It is as if the children are asking every night whether it is really safe to go to sleep, and if they have a guarantee that they will awaken in the morning. They are begging for the reassuring story with the happy ending, since many will have heard that their dog was put to sleep and never woke up, or that grandma died peacefully in her sleep. Some will also know the prayer that articulates the terror of death and includes the line "If I should die before I wake, I pray the Lord my soul to take." Later in life, around the time of death, many will be deeply afraid of going to sleep for fear of not waking up. This is especially so when there is terror in the family of any mention of the word death, and there will be a concomitant insistence that everyone surrounding the dying person give only positive, hopeful utterances.

Mary, a young woman in her early thirties, lived in the country in a fairy-tale house with every possible comfort. I had been warned that Mary would only allow the positive into her house. She had dismissed two housekeepers because she considered them negative and refused to see most relatives and friends because they were too weepy and downbeat and not hopeful.

Her anxious husband, Pete, greeted the nurse and myself at the door with urgent whispered reminders not to mention anything unpleasant. I had requested that Cindy, their four-year-old daughter, be present, but Pete told us that they had decided to send Cindy to grandmother's house for a few days. Mary was in bed in Cindy's room, saying that it felt brighter and more cheerful than her own bedroom. I shall never forget the ghastly scene of this emaciated, dying woman propped up in her daughter's bed surrounded by hosts of Cindy's beautiful toys. She beckoned me to the chair by Cindy's bed and whispered a brief litany about how things were not too bad. I felt soul dead myself in this nightmare wonderland, and any attempts I made to be a little real were stifled by Mary or myself. She died in her sleep a couple of nights later, and Cindy was kept away.

For Mary, neither the tranquilizers she had been prescribed to mute the terrors of the underworld nor the nursery setting of her dying were able to still her palpable anxieties. Since she had banished any mention of death, Mary's terror remained to the end. She was totally isolated and unable to say good-bye, leaving a nightmare legacy that would continue for Cindy and others in her family.

When denial becomes almost impossible for some of those who are facing death, fairy tales lose their power, although religious tales may be very sustaining. For the one who is unable to sleep, a story is usually of little help, and the family often urgently requests sleeping pills. If the terror of not waking up is the major precipitant to the fear of going to sleep, then the sleeping pill can compound the terror, as the dying person attempts to ward off the effect of the pill and stay awake. A gentle reminder to the one who is dying that so many of us have heard since childhood about dying during our sleep, followed by a question as to whether or not this might be a worry, often evokes a sigh of recognition and the voicing of mixed feelings—of wanting to die quietly during sleep and feeling the urgency to hold on. Simply naming this worry often allows letting go into sleep.

Ellen was terrified of going to sleep. Some 20 years before she died she had written a short story for children that she entitled "Ain't Never Goin' To Go," about a little boy who had always been scared of the school principal and quaked with terror at the thought of ever having to appear before her. One day, after the summer vacation, the children were asked to draw a picture of their experience; the teacher particularly liked the little boy's drawing and asked him to take it to show the principal. A wonderful description followed of his heart-pounding, foot-dragging crawl up the corridor to the principal's office. Gingerly tapping at the door, he found himself greeted by a warm, wonderful woman who was enchanted by his picture and offered him gum drops, making him promise to visit again.

Ellen was a teacher who never married but had the warmest of relationships with nieces, nephews, and her students. There was an abrasive, angry, self-critical side to her, and this, when blended with a firmly held set of traditional religious beliefs, caused her great agony. While intellectually she believed in her religion, her soul was petrified by the thought of a vengeful Judge, and this was manifested by considerable agitation and refusal to acknowledge or voice her worries, including the fears related to her life-threatening illness. She had never connected the story of the little boy and his terror of the principal with the story of her own inner child who was terrified of her critical Father, whom she felt she had never pleased. Recognizing this parallel, Ellen was amazed and relieved. The insight was an important release, and Ellen became able to talk more openly about her fears in the week or two before she died. Her death was a peaceful one.

We in the Western world have an unending supply of sustaining mythologies that help us to live life. These myths are traditional stories from a timeless past involving soul and spirit, and are often regarded as insubstantial and fanciful and therefore not to be taken seriously, yet they are of the greatest importance in connecting us to one another. In this rational and functional world with our passionate search for security and control, we look for the truth and dismiss as trivial or simply as entertainment anything deemed not to have the researched imprimatur of truth. And so we fail to see the sustaining truth in the story of the rape of Persephone and in other Greek myths, and in the life-giving *Tales from the Thousand and One Nights* and the vast number of stories from many different cultures. Many myths are heroic confrontations with death and destruction rather than sustaining stories for soul and spirit. In our North American culture, the "taming" of the west and the stories of cowboys and soldiers slaughtering wild Indians needs a more honest reframing. If that were to happen, the epic would include the rape and exploitation of a fragile, beautiful, and animistic country together with the destruction of a wise culture that could have provided its people with sustaining stories and rituals as well as a love and cherishing of the land. As a result of the devastation we caused, we are left with a culture whose sustaining myths are built on the power of electronic communication and the health of the gross national product, both of which have little to do with soul and spirit.

The extraordinary Native American culture so lovingly respectful of soul and spirit was battered by bullets, abused by alcohol, and, more recently, seduced by the harvest to be gleaned from gambling. The inner core of our nation and its inhabitants needs the old stories and rituals if soul and spirit are to survive; it also needs the wealth of stories and rituals, brought by immigrants from many lands, that has been sadly diluted in our cultural melting pot.

The family has a variety of stories or myths, some of which are lovingly sustaining, such as the vignettes from vacations or holidays long ago, or that are themselves a delicious blend of fact and imagination. Other family myths can imprison rather than nourish. I have often heard the utterance "We are such a close family..." yet the family members know little about each other's feelings and imagination. They have, instead, dreamed one another up. I have also heard "My father was so strong and he was always there for me." But the daughter never got to share Dad's vulnerability, fear, and worries when he was dying, and during her childhood she hardly saw him as he was working two jobs and drinking heavily. Some families say "We don't need to speak of our love for one another—we know" and so they deprive themselves of the uniquely human experience of expressing feelings through language, which leads to deeper levels of soulful connectedness.

THE ATMOSPHERE OF STORYTELLING

Storytelling is a sacred event that speaks of spirit and soul, and while sacred events are beyond time and space, there are some settings that inspire us to open up while others seem unsafe, causing us to withdraw.

Marvelous cathedrals and temples all over the world, many of which have taken several lifetimes to build, can give us pause as pilgrims. The lofty cathedral invites us to look up at stained-glass mandalas and pictures of breathtaking beauty that tell stories we can barely imagine. It is almost possible to see the prayer and song rise up above the congregation, lifting their spirits. The cathedral stretches back over time and contains echoes of all the rituals that have ever taken place within its walls, and we are reminded that it will still be there long after we are dead. This glimpse of immortality and the stories of ages does our spirit good and is reassuring to our denial of death, reminding us that we are but a small part of something larger. The spirit needs cathedrals, whether they are of stone or of ponderosa pine, or in the form of the Grand Canyon or the sea. There we can let go and even imagine that here and now would be a wonderful place to die. The soul is more down to earth and needs a smaller scale in which its story can be told. Receptiveness to the telling and witnessing of soulful stories requires an atmosphere of safety that encourages openness and vulnerability.

Nighttime is perfect for the telling of stories, if the setting is right. From the magic of night, deep in the dark, love is born, and it is love that is the necessary energy for the light of day and the ignition of soul.

At night we are closest to the gateway to the underworld. It is the time when Persephone, goddess of the underworld and of death, returns to her throne. Candlelight helps to set the scene. The candle flickers, giving warmth and creating shadows that seem to play hide and seek with the tales being told. The light from a campfire or home hearth helps to inspire storytelling. We face the fire and the light, and all the fearful darkness is behind us so that we are warmed and ready to welcome the story to enter in and perform its magic.

If stories are to be told, it is important that the storyteller be given the time and space to tell the tale in full. Oftentimes with families, this may never happen. A story begins and there are numerous interruptions and corrections, or someone is watching television and refuses to turn it off, or someone storms out of the room, upset by what has been said. There are families where no one has ever told a complete story, and there has been no practice in listening and witnessing without judgment.

A model for listening and telling stories comes from the Native American culture. At a special gathering of the people, those assembled sit in a circle and the Talking Stick is passed from hand to hand. The sacred stick, which might be carved and decorated, is kept solely for these gatherings. The one holding the stick is required to tell the truth as he knows it; when finished speaking he passes the stick to the next person. The stick continues to go around until all that needs saying has been said, the last complete round being made in silence. There are no interruptions and no judgments; the only sound other than from the speaker might be an exclamatory "Ho" from anyone wishing to acknowledge something of what is being spoken.

I have used a ritual fashioned on the Talking Stick in many workshops, and I have encouraged many families to use this ritual in their homes. It is always the occasion for powerful storytelling. With each round of the stick the stories become deeper and more intimate, eventually ending in silence.

THE WITNESS

A most important role in the telling of our family stories is that played by the witness. The word witness derives from the old English wit or "knowledge." If we have our wits about us, we are supposed to have at least some knowledge about what is happening; when we are at our wits' end, we have lost control.

The witness in court is supposed to bring knowledge of the event in question, and if the truth be told, this knowledge allegedly contains the facts. The classic film *Rashomon* (directed by Akira Kurosawa in 1950) depicts a rape and murder as seen through the eyes of a variety of witnesses. The stories, of course, are all quite different from one another, and the witnesses fall far short of having access to knowledge and truth with the ability to report objectively. Like any other human being, each court witness is influenced by the stories and fictions of his or her past, with the natural urge to judge and compare, and is often coached so that the story that emerges is tailored to fit a larger strategy. The reluctant witness is often angry, frightened, or overwhelmed by the need to rescue or condemn.

When listening to a story it is so much easier to sit in judgment than to be still and silent. The witnesses we need to the tales of our soul and spirit are not required to understand or judge or use their wits, but rather to listen with love, and to hear. In my early training in psychiatry there was much attention paid to active listening. This was the principal tool of the trade, and we were trained to pay meticulous attention, word for word, to what was said. We would then analyze what we heard and occasionally articulate our interpretations. This mental work is useful in helping people to reframe their fictions into something more comfortable, but it is not witnessing.

Witnessing is like being a vast open-armed urn with an ear inside that can contain lovingly and nonjudgmentally anything that is offered. Most of us believe that if we listen to a story of great pain and distress we must say something or do something; this is especially so if we are "rescuers" by nature or trade. We have not learned that there are times, much more frequent than we imagine, when the storyteller is seeking only a witness—a human being rather than a human doing or a fixer.

The witness listens with ego suspended. The ego we have fabricated provides boundaries, defenses, and explanations in order for us to imagine that we understand and have some measure of control. If we suspend ego, we become without boundaries which, for the schizophrenic, may be terrifyingly chaotic, but for others will offer the experience of being connected to all there is, with no need to judge or defend or analyze, no need to *do* anything. In simply being, we become a conduit to the storyteller who, through us as witnesses, also becomes connected to all, and the story becomes part of the picture of the whole, part of the picture of God. In this exquisite state of non-doing presence without boundaries, the witness is radiating love, that which in other contexts has been described as the light of the holy spirit. Thus, the witness, through his limitless spirit, is providing exactly what is needed by the soul of the storyteller.

We need witnesses, especially at times of vulnerability, such as at birth or death, and at many times in between. The family meeting, discussed in detail in chapter 7, is a sacred time for the family to gather when one of their members is dying so that each can tell his or her story. When I first convened these gatherings I was reluctant to invite students, physicians, and others, feeling that the meetings were private and that any guest would be both an intrusion and a dampener on the proceedings. This feeling was partially based on earlier hospital experience when I felt that students often invaded a patient's room to take a history and do an examination, procedures that often seemed like a theft—more in the nature of taking something away from the patient and offering little in the way of compassion or thanks in return. However, when I became comfortable enough to ask families if I might bring visitors, I was surprised that most were perfectly agreeable, and I was even more surprised that the family almost always thanked these guests profusely for coming, even though they said nothing and did nothing. I always instructed the visitors that they were attending a sacred gathering and that there was no need for them to speak; that they were there as witnesses to the family stories. It became clear to them and to me how much we need witnesses and how seldom we have the privilege of their company.

Hospitals would be transformed if witnesses were to gather around a patient's bed after his death and tell brief stories of their involvement with him. Physicians, nurses, and others have opportunities to discuss clinical and pathological details after a death, but there is usually neither the time nor the inclination for the discussion of feelings.

My vision is that when a patient died a code pink would be called that would summon all who had been personally involved with the patient to his room; this code pink would be a priority as important as any technical emergency. The physician whose task it was to perform the mechanics of pronouncing death would not immediately leave but would sit with nurses and family members, and each would take a moment to speak of what the patient meant to him or her and light a candle in honor of the life that had touched theirs, and had just passed away. If it seemed appropriate, a prayer might be said, and then the staff would leave. Such a 15-minute ritual would transform the hospital into a sacred place and acknowledge the importance of everyone present as witness to a sacred event. The physician might acknowledge that he barely knew the patient and felt frustrated by the rushed anonymity of his work, yet as he paused in this moment he might be reminded of his grandfather, who had been so important in his life but who had died anonymously in a famous teaching hospital. The nurses might speak of their pleasures and pains in the giving of care, and the family would voice their thanks to all present. It is not money that we need to transform the quality of care, but simply the imagination to sit, witness, be in relationship, and become a part of what is.

Witnesses themselves need the opportunity to speak and tell their stories. During my years with the hospice, Wednesday mornings at 8.30 was the time for staff to tell their stories about those who had died during the previous week. This was one of the most sacred times in the rhythm of the hospice, and an important part of the ritual was that a staff member would bring in breakfast for the group. The staff members involved with the person who had died would tell their stories and collectively light a candle while the rest of us watched or listened. Sometimes more time would be spent in closure around the death of one person in particular; perhaps an experience in which there was much humor, love, and peaceful resolutions that moved us all, or another in which there was loud discord and raging to the bitter end that left us all feeling at a loss in many ways. Often we would pause at length at the death of a young woman, a contemporary of many of the staff, who left behind bewildered children of all ages. Such a death was more obviously akin to our own, and there would always be discussion of leaving our own children and families. We would also remember the leave-takings in our own past, for which we would light candles. This meeting was a barometer of the spiritual and soulful health of the organization.

THE GUIDE

It is not only witnesses that are a necessity in navigating a soulful life and death; we also need guides on these journeys. We need guides to help us through the passage to birth, we need guides to accompany us to the threshold of death, and along the way we need them when we are dragged into the underworld on the heels of loss and suffering. We also need guides to help us tell our stories.

For the storyteller, the guide is not one who acts as therapist. In fact, the Talking Stick is an excellent guide although it appears to do nothing at all. It simply allows the storyteller to give himself permission to speak and empowers the witnesses to listen in silence. Furthermore, with each round of the Talking Stick the storyteller usually allows himself to go deeper with the stories, closer to the central core of the soul and spirit.

The human hermetic guide might be a friend or a family member such as a daughter who might free herself for a while from the role of witness or storyteller. This may be a very difficult task for one so intimately involved, so it is helpful if the guide is a trusted outsider, professional or not, who is comfortable in this role of friend and who is able to nudge the story along a little when it becomes stuck. If tears seem to stem the flow of story, for example, after a pause the guide might gently say "Go on, say some more," when the general urge might be to go back. Like the Talking Stick, the guide gives permission, keeps order, and encourages greater depth but does not demand it.

Paula, a hospice social worker, was guide, witness, and much more for Joan. Fifteen years before her diagnosis of lymphoma, Joan's husband had died of a brain tumor following several years of unpredictable, paranoid behavior. Joan described this time as one long nightmare, and her greatest fear was that something similar might happen to her. She was involved with the hospice for five months, and at first was very guarded and unforthcoming, expressing great concern that she would lose control and be unable to stay at home since she lived alone. She was an expert quilt maker, and her home was a warm nest lined with her art.

Joan gradually allowed the hospice staff into her underworld, developing a particularly warm and trusting relationship with Paula. Joan's worst fears were realized when she developed metastatic brain tumors. Recovering from a period when she was comatose, during which we thought she would die, Joan recorded some of her thoughts with Paula. The following are excerpts from the tape:

I used to worry about losing my mind—sitting around drooling, not knowing friends. I was at home when I nearly died, and was responding a little but did not quite know what was going on. I was taken to the hospice Inn, and I was losing control, but it wasn't very frightening. I was near death for a couple of days. I didn't know what was happening, yet bits and pieces came back. I was aware of a great feeling of peace and contentment. People held my hand and talked. I remember watching female lions when in the coma. It was graceful and not at all frightening. I didn't see any light at the end of a tunnel. It was not what I imagined—it was low-key, comforting. When I recovered consciousness the first thing I said was "What a miracle, dying!"

From those two days I learned not to fear death; I learned to trust that it is going to be okay to die. I learned that the love and support of family and friends is essential and I was glad to have a second chance to express love to people. I've been keeping a diary and can express my negative feelings there. Once I write it down, I don't resent it any more!

From Paula, Joan received patience, loving kindness, and her willingness to be a nonjudgmental witness—a mixture of Demeter, Hecate, and Hermes, with a touch of the goddess Aphrodite, who is the lover of beauty and a beautiful lover. All these traits were mobilized in the service of Joan, the frightened Persephone, who needed a witness and guide in order to allow herself to move through the fears of the underworld. When she felt connected with Paula and others, she discovered toward the end of her life that even her intense fear of losing control lost its force. Joan died in the hospice Inn three weeks after making the tape.

STORYTELLING AND THE ANCESTORS

The vibrancy of the individual soul depends on the telling of the story that is witnessed, and Joan and Ellen experienced this, as did Michael's family. The vitality of the family also depends on the telling of stories, just as the vitality of mankind as a whole depends on there being a wealth of collective stories or myths.

The family history is not simply a litany of facts or a listing of diseases that is the customary preoccupation of medical history taking. In written versions of medical histories, I have often seen the lone and amazingly inappropriate word "unremarkable" in the section devoted to past history and family history. Only one who is almost exclusively interested in mechanical failures will ignore as irrelevant the soulful aches of losses, heartbreaks, loves, and disasters that are a part of every person's life. A living family history must be concerned with stories that speak of roots and uprootedness, linkages and displacements. If we are as the branches of a tree and our family is the trunk, the ancestors go deep and are the nurturing roots. Having talked with thousands of families when one of the members is dying, it was always amazing to me how many knew little or nothing of their roots. Living and working on the east coast of the United States, I saw many families whose ancestors in the near or remote past emigrated from Europe, many leaving the terrors of Armenia, or the poverty and hopelessness of Russia, or the horrors of Hitler. Few of their descendants had even a remote idea about the stories of those who undertook the unimaginably difficult journey in the "coffin ships" that brought them to America. So often I heard elderly folk who had made such a pilgrimage say that they did not want to talk about it because it was too painful. The emotional ordeals of leaving family and all that was familiar and the physical terrors of the journey itself were, they said, too painful to recall. So the generations that followed were left with a lacuna in their story, and the circulation of soulful tales surrounding their roots was defective.

Silence about history is deadly—for nations, families, or individuals. In our times we struggle against boredom and indifference about reports of injustice and genocide from all corners of the globe. The commonplace abuse of children and the aged, self-abuse, and relational neglect are also largely ignored. Until we discover the importance—the absolute necessity—of telling our story and practicing the storytelling art within the family (which is prelude to a wider telling), we will be unable to tell the tales of nations and so will maintain the illusion of our separateness and differences.

Individual and collective love stories need to be told, as do tales of atrocities and loss, with all the darkness intact. Telling the story along with its violence and malignancies allows the possibility for learning and the development of immunity against the deadly aspects of these histories. This immunity is like the immunity developed against any disease; it is neither denial nor repression but rather a conscious ability to live with the dark side of our nature, developed by means of frequent doses of storytelling.

It is sad that so many people believe only "nice" or uplifting stories should be told. They do not want to hear anything that they deem to be negative—anything that might stir up the imagination and the dark, unknown side of the soul. In the stories about themselves and their illnesses, they want to hear only good news and positive thoughts, for otherwise, they imagine, they would lose hope. In many people's minds hope has to do with a restoration of health and living longer. It is the epitaph of denial of death and has little to do with being honest about both the present and the past. Yet if honesty about our lives and our roots is the foundation of hope we can be hopeful from the beginning of our lives to the end.

People who are filled with pain are also not at all anxious to hear (or speak) the stories of their ancestors. They may not understand that family stories told to silent witnesses lose much of their pain—especially after many retellings—and that what is left is the supportive framework of the story and the awe and wonder of the witnesses as to how all this came about. If stories were not judged as good or bad but simply as essential background for the present, then we would be much more concerned about knowing our ancestral stories and passing on our own because, in some way that is not clearly understandable, they provide nourishment and stability.

It is quite clear from working with the dying that the telling of stories and the opening up of roots breathes life into the family. After some of the secrets in which a family has been immersed are spoken, I often hear sighs of relief—expirations coupled with a knowing "Ah!" I have witnessed that the dying storyteller is oftentimes literally more free in his breathing—and able to expire in peace—after recounting tales of his roots and a few of the joys and pains that went along with them. Knowing this, caregivers need to encourage storytelling and the seeking of connections with a dying patient's entangled roots. But if they are to do this successfully, they will need first to experience the power of story and of the ancestors in their own lives.

Remembering the ancestors would enhance the well-being of all if it were part of everyday life. Each nation has some memorial day set aside for the ancestors, but the observances seem to be largely ceremonial and not very personal. For example, on Memorial Day in America many people go to grave sites to pause and remember, but few sit around the grave and speak of their connection to the one they are honoring, allowing the memories to be plumbed from the depths. All Souls Day is a wonderful time to remember those who have gone before, but few take this opportunity. I have the feeling that many of the ghosts that haunt graveyards and attics are the agitated moaning and groaning of stories untold and people or parts of people unrecognized. If we and they are to rest in peace we must tell their tale or have them tell it before they die. How awful when there is no one who knows and can tell the story, ensuring that the turbulence of words unspoken continues on through the generations.

In America, Thanksgiving would be a perfect day for honoring the ancestors. We might have a celebration after dinner, for it is in the darkness of the evening when the ancestors are most easily evoked. Candlelight offers appropriate illumination for such an occasion, and a number of candles of different colors could be arranged on a table along with family mementos and pictures brought by each member of the family. The ceremony might begin with music and a poem or a reading, and then the family members would be invited to come forward and light a candle for anything or anyone they wish. At the same time they would be encouraged to speak about the intention of the candlelighting and add a story about the photographs or other things they had brought. With more candles than family members, there would be a chance for some to speak twice. When all the candles were alight, after a period of silence there would be an opportunity for reflections about the ceremony, and a round of the Talking Stick would be helpful in encouraging all to speak.

Over the years in the hospice Inn there were many ceremonies of remembrance of the ancestors, both for the staff and for the families they served. The family meeting—which will be described in detail in a later chapter—provides another opportunity for telling stories of the ancestors. This family gathering may be followed up by children or grandchildren interviewing their parents or grandparents, with a tape recording or video to provide an oral or visual history for later remembrances. Many families have framed pictures on the walls of their homes of family members past and present, and these, together with a few story-laden memorabilia, form the framework for an ancestral family shrine where candles are lit on special days.

Remembering and honoring the ancestors is vital for the spiritual well-being of the family, and tapping into stories from the family's roots provides nourishing care for the souls of each family member. These celebrations of connections and linkages are family rituals that celebrate the soul of the family. We need more of these occasions in our time, for it is the absence of rituals in our lives that contributes to a sense of apathy and meaninglessness.

CHAPTER 4

The Denial of Death

If we were each invited to imagine the manner and place of our own death, most of us would decline with a comment such as, "I don't like to think about that. It's too depressing." When pushed a little further, we would probably say that we hope death comes quickly and that we will not suffer. If pressed to imagine the place in which our death occurs we would hope it is at home in our own bed during sleep.

When told that four out of five people die in hospitals or institutions, our discomfort mounts. Visions of the death of someone who was important to us return. Perhaps mother was operated on for cancer, followed by chemotherapy and radiation treatments that were a nightmare for everyone. When the disease revived and she died, we remember her surrounded by machines in the intensive care unit while the family shuttled painfully and disconnectedly in and out of the soulless waiting room. This dark and terrifying memory is not deeply buried, but it has not had much of an airing either, making any discussion of death uncomfortable in the extreme. If this inquiry is pushed further to imagine the role of family in our dying, tears may flow; these are usually greeted with awkwardness and discomfort and taken to mean that the conversation should end. The anxiety raised by the question might also induce rage, with an angry demand as to why the questioner is trying to be upsetting. If we move on further, past the tears and anxiety and anger, we would probably say that we don't want to be a burden to the family and that they need to get on with their own lives—as if our death were not a part of life.

The painful nature of this conversation and the fact that it almost never occurs is an example of the denial of death. We will plan the important events in our lives as well as many moments of lesser consequence, and if we can afford it may even buy "life" insurance, but few of us make any preparation for our dying. Many people draw up a will, ensuring the distribution of their assets, but give no thought to consciously taking leave of those they love. As well, most people make no plan for the management of their care during the last days and weeks of life. A few will make a living will giving written instructions about the wish for no resuscitation efforts should death occur, but this is grossly inadequate since it fails to address other aspects of medical intervention. Even if a more detailed medical directive is drawn up, it is likely that the instructions will be ignored by the attending physicians, most of whom are themselves steeped in denial of death.

The cultural anthropologist Ernest Becker published his Pulitzer Prize-winning *Denial of Death* in 1973, three years before his death. While the book received considerable attention at the time, his work never received the amount of consideration and follow-up research it deserved, its truth—like his chosen subject— having fallen victim to denial. A major tenet of Becker's argument was that an interdisciplinary approach to dying and death is absolutely necessary, for death is not a medical illness, nor is it solely the province of religion, psychology, or undertakers.

Becker suggested that the qualities of being human include some that we embrace and others that repulse and terrify us. On the more acceptable, light side is awe and imagination, both of which allow us to appreciate the world in which we live. In using imagination we are able to make real for ourselves things that do not exist; we are also able to conceive of ourselves, which is a prerequisite not only for language but also for enhanced communication and connectedness. This self-consciousness also results in a dark apprehension that terrifies us. That dark understanding is the consciousness of our mortality and impermanence.

Culture develops to help us see the world in such a way that the anxiety caused by the awareness of death is muted or staved off until death is imminent. According to Becker, our culture has three ways in which it cushions this anxiety. First, it provides meaning and stability in viewing the world. It offers stories about how the world came into being that are based mostly on our wishes and fears, evidenced by the fact that there are so many widely differing stories to explain our beginnings. These stories, and others that emerge from them, provide a sense of law and order, and include guidelines for how life should be lived. All this is an attempt by the culture to provide an anxiety-free environment imbued with a sense of strength and permanence.

Second, a culture confers significance on its members so that they feel they have important roles to play, and in feeling important they are less preoccupied, consciously or not, with issues of survival and the terror of death. In cultures in which power, wealth, and appearance confer the highest esteem, the nature of the implicit hierarchy determines that many people will feel insignificant in relation to the few who have "made it." Low self-esteem will manifest in the abuse of both legal and illegal drugs, the use of guns, and the tendency toward violence, mental illness, and suicide. Such a culture also encourages the emergence of charismatic leaders, political or religious, who promise the feeling of belonging and significance to all who will follow their one true way, a political or religious fascism that often itself oozes with violence. Both terrifying insignificance and messianic grandiosity may be forces that lead to a glut of guns and wars against real or imagined enemies, including death itself.

The denial of death is a third way in which our culture promotes anxiety reduction, encouraging its members to erect monuments, write books, make videotapes and movies, and break records in order to become immortalized. Having children is part of this urge to be everlasting. Belonging to any group or gang offers a sense of permanence, and those that have been the most enduring may seem to offer the greatest sense of security.

Fixed cultural conceptions that keep us rooted in a sense of superiority also ameliorate the fear of death. Any one such conception is bound to conflict with other ideologies and ways of looking at the world. Catholic and Protestant, Muslim and Christian, Greek and Turk—historical examples are endless. When these opposing views clash, there are a number of possible responses. One side may derogate its adversaries, claiming that they are primitive, backward, or stupid. Racism and bigotry of all shades result. Furthermore, one side may attempt to convert its adversaries, a strategy that has long been the way of many religions. This is also the tactic of the rich and powerful, who espouse capitalism as the only path toward economic justice—at least for themselves, in order that they can maintain their riches and power. It is also the way of allopathic medicine, which asserts that it has the one true system of beliefs about ill health and that its heroics can rescue anyone from the jaws of death. Nonbelievers are ridiculed or shamed or, as a last resort, assisted in their suicide. Another possibility is that one side may attempt to annihilate those whose fundamental beliefs are different from their own. This has been the solution chosen by many religions, nations, families, and individuals since the beginning of civilized humanity.

A final option, seldom used but nevertheless possible, is that each side can practice tolerance, courageously seeing ourselves and each other as we really are—similar and unique, shadow and light, each struggling with the darkness of our impermanence as well as the expansiveness of our creative possibilities.

If emotional or physical violence is not to erupt and the energy expended in the denial of death is to be channeled in ways that are both loving and creative, it is necessary for society to provide opportunities for enhancement of self-esteem that will transform anxiety about death. When survival and low self-esteem are basic issues it is less easy to deny death since, in situations of depression and despair, poverty, unemployment, and the rampant use of drugs and alcohol, death is close at hand. The difficulty of creating an enduring yet humane society is clear from even a glance at history. At best, the culture may offer the possibility for a reasonable quality of life, but even that is difficult in the face of cultural decline in a care-less atmosphere. The denial of death needs to be faced directly by the individual and the family if the terrors and anxieties attendant on awareness of death are to consume less energy. This will be effected when the giving and receiving of real care comes to pass, and becomes the guiding principle in everyday life as well as in the management of disease.

MEDICINE AND THE DENIAL OF DEATH

Since society as a whole has developed in such a way as to soften or hide the terror of death, our health-care system has been modeled in the same fashion. The unconscious and the unspoken reign. The living enter the front door of the hospital while the dead are discreetly rushed down to the basement and out through the back door. Whenever death is thwarted—when a desperately injured person is pieced back together or a grossly malformed infant is made functional—the exploits of the hospital are proudly reported. The showpiece of medical wizardry—and the most profitable procedure overall—is surgery on the heart. No matter that much of it is of dubious value or could be done less expensively, it is death-defying surgery on the very crux of the matter: the liminal organ between life and death. Since physicians are empowered and liberally rewarded by a death-denying society to thwart death at any cost, when death does occur it is often experienced as a defeat or failure. It is seldom spoken of by physicians and nurses, nor are their personal feelings about death given the light of day. This code of silence pervades not only our hospitals and clinics but also our teaching institutions to the extent that there is no significant education about death and dying, an omission that guarantees that dying will not be accepted by professionals as a part of life requiring their loving care and attention. It also ensures that many physicians will engage in futile treatment in order to ward off their discomfort with death.

This seems analogous to the airline pilot who refuses to learn about landings because he never wants the journey to end. If we imagine physicians as pilots for the life journey of those in their care, most are present and fairly attentive during the takeoff at birth, and they are immensely concerned with navigation and keeping the engines running during the journey. However, they pay little attention to the fuel gauge, and at some point they let go of the controls, announcing that they "don't do" landings. Furthermore, they may even label their passengers' concerns and preoccupations about "landing" as negative or indicative of losing hope. The crash landings that occur with appalling frequency and at great financial and spiritual cost to both the community and the surviving relatives are, of course, a disaster for the one who dies. She is shocked and terrified at running out of fuel in what she considers to be mid-flight, and often feels betrayed by her medical attendants. She also has no time for the kind of peace-making that is possible when the landing has been anticipated. It is unimaginable that airline pilots would not have detailed instruction about coming in to land and the need for a full debriefing when the journey is over. It is equally unimaginable that physicians would not spend a considerable time learning about the art of facilitating smooth landings for their patients and families at the end of their journeys, but such is the situation in death-defying and death-denying medicine.

The word cancer is synonymous with death, even though there is enormous expenditure on research and a major emphasis on public relations to inject hope into its dark image. The whole approach in traditional medicine toward cancer is belligerent: we have declared war. Oncologists are the medical marines, the heroic elite in the fight. Oncologists never give up, and have a seemingly endless supply of weaponry to hurl against the enemy. Their arsenal includes the toxic drugs of chemotherapy which originated with mustard gas used in World War I. Likewise, surgeons attack with the knife and radiotherapists zap or nuke the offending site with radiation or radioactive isotopes. The patient is urged to fight and never give up; some oncologists will say that the patient "failed" treatment when their efforts are of no avail. While, as in most wars, there may be a sense of unity in fighting the common enemy, there are atrocities and indignities perpetrated on the innocent—in this case, the patients.

Susan, a young woman in her mid-thirties, was visiting her parents at their home in New York state. She had been diagnosed several months earlier with widely metastatic cancer, and while there was no conscious acceptance of the fatal nature of her illness, it was clear that she had returned home from Colorado to die. Pain and discomfort became acute a few days after Susan and her husband arrived in New York, and an oncologist hospitalized her for the next two weeks. Susan pushed herself to eat a little and get dressed, but it was perfectly clear to the nursing staff that she was dying, and both Susan and her husband insisted that the oncologist let her go home, since there was no improvement other than some modulation of her pain.

Susan died two days after returning home. On the evening before she died, her distraught husband and the hospice nurse requested liquid morphine, since swallowing pills was no longer possible. The oncologist insisted that Susan be brought to the hospital, saying that since she had been up and eating two days earlier in the hospital, it was obvious that it was not possible for her to be managed at home. Like so many others, this oncologist had no conscious understanding that Susan was dying and *needed* to be home, and that the medication was mainly for the peace and comfort of nurse and family. The oncologist's cold, distant, unrelational, and totally inappropriate response to a cry for help can be understood only in the context of his own denial of death.

A voice must have whispered that it was unreasonable, unfair, and impossible that a young attractive woman should be touched by death, a force that was beyond his capacity to control.

There is no requirement that oncological medical marines receive any kind of personal familiarization with dying, and this makes them as dangerous to the soul of their patients as a self-styled witch doctor might be to the body. We speak of individuals becoming a victim of cancer, but it would be more correct to say that many individuals are victims of our society's attitude toward death. If the attitude were to change from a belligerent confrontation of death to loving care that is relationship-centered, the atmosphere in which treatment takes place would be much more conducive toward living well to the end. For this to happen, we need to alter our expectations of physicians. We need to tell them that death *will* happen and it is not their fault, so they don't have to fight it off to a bitter and soul-destroying end. We need to tell them that we want to avail ourselves of the benefits of scientific medicine but we need them to blend their scientific skills with warmth and wisdom and not leave us when the technology is of no use. Only then can death and dying become part of the art of medicine. Only then can physicians open up to dying and death— their own and that of those near and dear to them, as well as the dying and death of their patients.

THE FUNERAL HOME AND THE DENIAL OF DEATH

The cultural attitude toward death is nowhere better illustrated than by the funeral home business. Like any business, it initially came into being because of a perceived need, but it has become a powerful and profitable undertaking that shapes the manner in which death is handled.

In previous centuries it was less easy to maintain our level of denial about death; evidence and reminders about it were all around. Life expectancy was much shorter than it is now; infant mortality was high; plagues and pestilence were everywhere. Most people died in their homes; it was there that the family gathered for the wake. No special effort was made to beautify the face of death nor to remove it from the home in which the person's life had been lived. The waking ceremony was left in the hands of the family, and going through each step was important in the ritual of remembering and letting go. Washing, preparing the body, viewing it in the home, telling stories, laughing, weeping—all were part of saying good-bye, a departing that yearns for time, care, and tenderness.

In our modern-day death rituals, the funeral home personnel sweep into hospital or home, remove the body in a black bag, sanitize it, lay it out in the most expensive box possible, and arrange for a viewing of the body for perhaps two or three hours on one or two days. If the funeral home is large enough, there may be more than one viewing occurring at a time; since all the rooms look the same, it is easy for the visitor to go into the wrong room, as I have done on more than one occasion.

Sanitizing death through the funeral home removes it from everyday life, dampens and deadens mourning, and allows us to get on with our lives as rapidly as possible, immersed once again in our denial. The financial cost of funeral-home waking and burial is obscene, but the awful cost to our culture is the enormous contribution this modern-day ritual makes to the deadening of soul.

THE FAMILY AND THE DENIAL OF DEATH

Just as the knowledge of death looms over the individual who expends great energy in its denial, so also the family lives with the certainty of its dissolution. A family may experience the death of its elders as the first assault on its safety, togetherness, and permanence. Later, as children scatter and parents age, many adult children begin to voice their fears that the family will break up after the death of one or both parents.

Families that understand and cherish the sacred nature of their members are powered by tolerance and love. Acceptance of the eventual dissolution of the family and the impossibility of holding it together leads to less energy being employed on appearances and conformity, and the social and religious structures are seen for what they are: supportive and helpful in living life, but means and not ends, and not for everyone. Those families in which there is greater acceptance of dissolution and less impetus to deny death forge linkages that will transcend individual beliefs, geographical distance, and even the death of their members.

Jorge Luis Borges wrote a powerful short story about dreaming of immortality. Called *The Circular Ruins*, the story is about a wizard whose task it was to go down to the ruins of a temple on a riverbank and dream up a son. For three years he lay in the temple, fed and watched over by fearful natives. Eventually he dreamed up a son who was complete in every detail except that he had no life. Fire visited him, announcing that it would breathe life into the wizard's son if the wizard would tell no one. With the breath of Fire the son came alive, but the wizard was afraid his son would discover his origins: "Not to be a man, to be a projection of another man's dreams—what an incomparable humiliation, what madness!" When the wizard became old and was about to die, Fire came; the wizard walked toward it, but Fire did not harm him. It was at that moment the wizard realized that he, too, was the dream of someone's imagination.

Within a few days of reading that story I met with a family in which the father, Robert, was dying. Although he had been a successful businessman, Robert was aloof and judgmental, especially toward his wife and his son Bill. Bill had not finished college; he had been in and out of a number of jobs and was married to a woman for whom Robert had never expressed a word of approval. I remember Bill, in Robert's last days, saying to his father, "Dad, I think I have been a great disappointment to you. Somehow I feel that I have not lived up to your expectations." "You are right, son," was the painful and chilling response. Robert said little else to his son before he died.

This dark family meeting was a gift to me in its illumination of Borges' story. Through witnessing Robert and Bill I realized that many parents dream up their children; they have little idea who their children are and what they feel. Children also dream up their parents and are unable to see the frightened, struggling soul who also happens to be mom or dad. As Borges points out, this is madness and an awful form of humiliation, and it is dreadfully sad to behold. When we dream one another up it is not possible to ever say hello, and if we have never said hello, it is impossible to say good-bye. And so the family dream, or the family nightmare, continues.

If we are to break this endless cycle of dreaming described in *The Circular Ruins* and in the story of Bill and his father, we need to say hello and we need to say good-bye. In those families where coercion and abuse have made pale any expressions of love and esteem, the individuals may well ask why they need to say good-bye—why they should get together as a family and talk of past and present when to do so would most likely revive old wounds and incur new ones. Some in the family will have left home at the earliest opportunity after years of abuse and fighting, believing that it was impossible to live within the confines of their particular family with feelings other than anger, rage, and shame. Yet it is especially vital for the children of these families to say hello *and* good-bye at the time of a family member's imminent death, because the dreaming they have been a part of for generations is a nightmare of violence, death, and survival that makes living a truly generative life impossible. Great energy is bound up in dreaming, energy that is used in shielding, masking, and repressing feelings, all of which conspire to keep the vital force of life at bay. The cycle will only be broken by waking up, saying hello to those who are a part of our lives, acknowledging the hurts, disappointments, and betrayals, letting them go, and saying good-bye.

In Eugene Ionesco's gently humorous play *Exit the King*,[1] the king refuses to take that soulful leave as his death nears, even after 400 years of living. The following dialogue ensues between the king, Queen Marguerite, his mistress Marie, and the king's doctor:

KING: I was full of life, wonderfully full of life!

MARGUERITE: At fifty, you wanted first to reach your sixties. And so you went on, from sixty to ninety to a hundred and twenty-five to two hundred, until you were four hundred years old. Instead of putting things off for ten years at a time, you put them off for fifty. Then you postponed them from century to century.

KING: But I was just about to start. Oh! If I could have a whole century before me, perhaps then I'd have time!

DOCTOR: All you have now is one hour, Sire. You must do it all in an hour.

MARIE: He'll never have enough time, it's impossible. He must be given more.

1 Calder Publications, London, 1963; Grove Press, New York, 4th edition.

MARGUERITE: That is impossible. But an hour gives him all the time he needs.

DOCTOR: A well spent hour's better than whole centuries of neglect and failure. Five minutes are enough, ten fully conscious seconds. We're giving him an hour! Sixty minutes, three thousand and six hundred seconds. He's in luck!

In that metaphorical hour—in the days, months, or years that stretch between us and our death or the death of a family member—we have the opportunity to loosen and soften the defensive shell and the denial of death that encase us and attend to the images and feelings that emanate from within.

On several occasions I have talked to individuals grappling with far-advanced illnesses who expressed the fear that they were losing their minds, when actually they were losing their denial of death. I remember the time a kindly academic physician was wheeled into my office; with one look at him I knew he was close to death. The startling reason the physician gave for his visit was that he was fearful that he was going out of his mind, and he was seeking my opinion and counsel. With a few gentle questions about his illness, fears, and worries, it became apparent that he had never allowed himself to acknowledge both the severity of his illness and the fact that he was close to death. The endless medical tests that attempted to diagnose his advancing illness and the treatment that served to patch up the cracks in his armor were distracting diversions for all, and made it more difficult for this man to deal with his inner concerns. The physician was visibly relieved to recognize that he was out of control in that he could not alter the course of his illness, but he was not going mad, and he was then able to talk at length with his whole family before dying at home one week later.

In fact, this man *was* going out of his mind. We place great importance on the development of the mind. With it we survive day by day, making attempts to understand a little of how the world works and occasionally becoming curious about our bodies and souls. The mind is a wonderful plaything! When our outer shell or armor cracks—as can happen at any time in life but most often as we become aware that life is coming to an end—we no longer need the mind to create stories and attempt to persuade us that we are in charge of our lives. And so we can go out of it, sometimes gratefully with a sense of relief that we no longer need to think or worry, and sometimes kicking and screaming as we attempt to continue to understand and control. If we have never had practice in releasing the mind through an experience such as meditation, we will have never discovered that it can be a great relief to be empty of rational thinking, and so the perceived loss of mind toward the end of life may well be terrifying.

It is odd how seldom I have seen so-called psychiatric illnesses among those who are dying. Nervous disorders might be thought of as defects of the guardian ego which becomes of little importance and is pushed out of the way when we are dying by energies from the soul that demand consciousness. I have seen people who had been diagnosed as schizophrenic sometime during their tumultuous lives whose dying was no more or less remarkable than anyone else's, even though all the people around them were expecting some kind of catastrophic explosion.

One woman had been treated for depression for several years earlier in her life, and after her diagnosis of rapidly advancing lung cancer, was again diagnosed as being severely depressed and referred to a psychiatrist. This depression was thought to exist because she expressed so vividly her imaginings about how the cancer was behaving inside her as well as her fears of what lay ahead. She ruminated about how it might be to die; she spoke also of her loneliness despite two wonderfully attentive children, and the fear she had of losing her mind. All this warm and wise woman needed was a witness who could marvel at her expressions and assure her how ordinary were her feelings and imaginings, but how unusual it was to have someone paint these pictures so vividly. She also needed to hear an educated projection about how it might be for her in the coming months, around and about the time of her death, with a guarantee that she would always be heard and never abandoned.

If we are to be prepared for death and, unlike the king in Ionesco's play, live in its presence, we need to confront it. We need to imagine our death and rehearse it as best we can so that it becomes more familiar and less of a terrifying force that impels our every moment. Confronting death will encourage us to tell our stories and listen to the stories of those we love. Confronting our own death will ensure that we are well prepared to listen to the stories of others and be their witness and guide when they are dying. Nothing less will fully prepare us for being present at all stages of life.

CHAPTER 5

Living with Consciousness of Death

It is amazing to realize that physicians, without having had any real preparation, are expected to attend their patients as they die. Because they have not been encouraged and guided in confronting their own denial of death, they are not prepared with the loving skills necessary to guide and witness their patients and families. Many physicians and nurses have told me that they have seen hundreds of deaths and have "no problems" with it, which is not unlike a passenger in a car saying that he has seen hundreds of automobile crashes and therefore must know how to drive. Little wonder that in the process of dying, when there is often much tension and grief, patient and family feel quite unable to navigate alone and yet may not find the appropriate guidance from their physician or other caregivers. The caregiver may stealthily depart the scene with the aside that nothing more can be done, or retreat behind a wall of drugs, instructing the family to bring their dying relative to the hospital emergency room when they become unable to cope.

Caregivers—that means all of us—need preparation to attend to the dying, and that preparation must be experiential and not theoretical. A few lectures on death and dying and a few clichés about dignity, comfort, and acceptance are not enough. Until we have experientially examined the time of our own dying, the journey may be too anxiety-provoking to be as one with another who needs our assistance at this time. The hospice can present a model of loving kindness and the best of witnessing, but it may be difficult for the caregiver to learn how to become a guide unless he is comfortable being fully immersed in the experience by having imagined his own dying and that of those close to him. Such experience is usually not offered in hospices or anywhere else.

I introduce the following exercise, a guided imagining of one's own death, early on in workshops on dying and death (a curriculum outline for such training is contained in the Postscript to this book). When working with this text as a guide you might wish to make an audiotape of these instructions so that you can follow them alone at home, or with a companion. As the instructions are recorded, be sure to pause between questions to allow plenty of time for reflection.

In the workshop setting the group breaks up into triads following the visualization. In each triad, one person will tell the story of this visualization, another witnesses, and the third acts as guide. Following each 20-minute storytelling all three people relate how the experience was for them. Then after 30 minutes the roles are changed so that each person in the triad has the experience of each role. Following the work in triads, all return to the large group to share experiences.

Before beginning the exercise, find a comfortable spot—it may be sitting in a chair, or it may be lying down or propped up with pillows. The problem with being too comfortable, though, is that you might fall asleep. That is life—too much comfort may well dull consciousness so that we miss out on some important experiences. Or then again we may just be tired and not taking very good care of ourselves by not allowing ourselves enough sleep. A number of people *do* fall asleep during the exercise. If that happens to you, simply try to consider it afterward as part of your experience, without self-critical judgments of how you blew it or missed out. You can always do the exercise a second time, or a third.

VISUALIZATION: IMAGING YOUR OWN DEATH

This is an inner journey, and I will be your guide, so listen to the commentary as I point out sights along the way. Close your eyes, because that helps to shut out some of the distractions that entice us away from looking within. For the next few minutes you will be looking through your mind's eye at your body, gently helping and encouraging it to relax and let down the armor that it may be holding in an attempt to protect you. You will be spending the next few minutes making your cocoon—the gossamer with which you surround yourself—more permeable, so that you will be able to allow in the realization that you, too, will die sometime.

Many of you will have your own way of inspiring this relaxation. This is simply one way, no better than any other. If you are doing this meditation alone at home, give yourself plenty of time for relaxation as you allow body and mind to settle.

Start by looking through your mind's eye at the muscles of your face and scalp. Gently become conscious of the muscles around the eyes and mouth and then quietly tell them to relax ... Move your gaze down to the neck, where there are many possibilities for tension: "pain in the neck" when we are angry; "all choked up" when we are sad. Smile to yourself, bringing warmth and relaxation into these neck muscles ... Now squeeze the tension downward from the shoulders through the arms and forearms like you are squeezing water out of a sponge, letting the tension pass through wrists and hands and drip out through the tips of your fingers.

For a few moments now watch your breathing. If we always remembered how to breathe, all would be well. We enjoy anything inspirational and want more of the same. The trouble is that we want to hold on to our inspiration; then we become blown up, unwilling or unable to expire. When we receive bad news, such as the diagnosis of a life-threatening illness, we gasp and then hold our breath while we wait for the next test to tell us if the treatment is working. It is obviously impossible to live life holding the breath. We need to risk expiration as the prelude to the next breath—the death of expiration is followed by the resurrection of inspiration. Watch the breath for a while, noticing the in-breath and then the relaxed feeling of chest and belly as you expire.

Next, look at and feel the muscles of the spine, from the neck all the way down to the lower back. These muscles are always at work, particularly if we tend to carry "the weight of the world" on our backs. Then go to the muscles of the abdomen, which try so hard to help us not "spill our guts." Give all these muscles warmth and love, inviting them to relax.

As you did with the upper limbs, now squeeze all the tension from your buttocks down the thighs and legs through the ankles, and let all your stress soak out into the ground at your feet.

Having given yourself the time and attention to become more relaxed and open, now take a trip in your imagination to a safe place, a place you have been to in the past. It may be by a particular stream or on a mountaintop or in the woods, or it may be in a comfortable corner of your home. Wherever it is, paint the picture in all its detail. See the colors and hear the sounds. Sense the smells, tastes, and textures. Take your time, acknowledging all the comforting feelings that emerge from that place, if you will only allow yourself to become aware of them. Pause for a minute or two while you experience this refuge ...

And now, sitting in your safe place, close your eyes and imagine yourself going on a visit to your physician's office. You have not been feeling well for several weeks and have had a number of tests. Today you have an appointment to review those tests. How do you feel as you set out on this journey? Are you aware of any fears and concerns? Do you go alone or do you ask someone to accompany you?

You arrive at your physician's office. He is not yet available, so you sit in the waiting room. What do you see and feel as you look around?... As you are ushered into his office, you try to get a reading on your situation from his behavior. What, if anything, do you pick up?... Now you both sit down, and without much preamble he tells you that the results of the tests are not good. You have an illness that has progressed to the point beyond which there is no useful treatment. He says that he will immediately arrange for a second opinion if you wish. Do you choose that? ... He goes on to say that he believes that you have only a handful of weeks to live, and that he will be available at any time to help make you as comfortable as possible. Are you gasping or holding your breath? Are you able to ask any questions?

You leave his office ... Where do you go? Who do you tell first, and how do you tell them? A couple of weeks pass and you are feeling much weaker, with little energy to get up and around. You have almost no appetite but have few discomforts other than this draining weakness. How is this for you?... Do you have anyone around to help take care of you and provide companionship? Or do you perhaps not want to bother other people? ... Are you able to ask for what you need, or do you try to protect others and yourself from your vulnerability? ... Are you prepared to die at home, or would you rather be in the hospital?

A few more days pass, and you decide to invite your family and loved ones to assemble at your home. Who do you ask? ... Who do you not want to see and why? ... Since this is a journey in the imagination, you can ask anyone you like. You can ask a favorite grandmother who died when you were a child and to whom you were never able to say good-bye and thank for all her loving laughter. You can ask a parent who died hooked up to machinery—to whom, in the panic of it all, you were never able to say what you needed to say and both give and receive a blessing. You can ask an old lover with whom you had a falling out, and to whom you have not spoken in years. Take a few minutes now to imagine what you would say to each person in turn, and what they might say to you.

Some days after this gathering you develop pain, and it is quite severe. Do you call your physician, or do you "grin and bear it," waiting until it becomes really bad? ... Then you have bouts of incontinence of bowel and bladder. How is that for you? Who cleans you up?

Your breathing has changed in quality, and you realize now that you are close to death. Who is around you? ... As your breathing changes, you notice longer pauses between each breath. Finally you let a breath out and you do not bring another breath in; you expire. How is that moment for you? ...

Then you find yourself out of your body looking down on the scene of your death. Who is there and what is happening? ...

The next scene is at your wake. Where is it and what is going on? Is it the way you would wish it to be? ... And now you are at your funeral. Imagine all the details, together with the feelings of all those in attendance. Is your physician there? ...

Now you are in the presence of God, or whatever greater power you imagine there to be. You have the opportunity of reviewing your life. What would you have done differently? Would you have chosen those parents and that particular cast of relatives? Are there relationships that you wish you had taken better care of, and did you leave important unfinished business behind? ...

Now, coming back to your safe place, realize that this has been a trip in the imagination, one that has allowed you to review priorities and recognize changes that might need to be made in the present. You can take this journey again, any time you wish. It will allow you to become more personally familiar with death and both clarify and remind you of what is of fundamental importance in living your life.

When you are ready, look around your safe place; thank it for being there and say good-bye. Then return to this reality simply by opening your eyes. Find a spot with your two companions where you can tell your story, witness, and be a guide.

In the workshop situation, when the large group reassembles, everyone is invited to say what they learned or what surprised them in any of the roles. There are usually a few participants who find it difficult to identify a safe place. This leads into a discussion of safety and trust, without which it is very difficult to do this exercise peacefully. On the larger scale, it is impossible to live and to die in peace if there seem to be few places and persons that feel safe. Naming and identifying such an issue is the prelude to its solution, and I suggest to those who had difficulty that they practice the exercise at home without any expectation that they will come up with a safe place. If they settle themselves in a comfortable place and simply witness themselves in this imagery without trying to make a safe place happen, it will usually emerge on its own. Quite often the location of the workshop becomes the safe place to which they can return in their mind in the future.

Notes on the Exercise

The Appointment
The pain on learning about the fatal illness is expressed in many different ways. I remember a workshop participant and family practice resident who, on hearing the diagnosis, refused to believe it and spent the rest of the exercise totally absorbed in this denial, so much so that he heard nothing more. He was not "present" for

his dying, death, and beyond, coming back to life only when he was once more in his safe place! While that does not usually happen in the comfort of the workshop setting, it is a typical response for many on first hearing of their life-threatening illness. They hear nothing of all the explanations, reassurances, and treatment plans, retreating into a limbo of suspended animation.

When faced with a significant appointment like this one, it is interesting to imagine whether we would go alone or with a supportive witness. So often it has been drummed into us that we need to be strong and independent and not bother others. This dreadful attitude, which does not acknowledge either our impermanence or our interdependence, deprives us of available comfort. Independence at this time is a curse.

Receiving Bad News

I have heard many stories over the years of physicians giving patients a life-threatening diagnosis over the phone or in a hospital corridor, or standing up with the escape route planned in advance. What was the manner in which your physician told you the news in this exercise?

To whom do we first tell the bad news on leaving our physician's office, and how do we do it? It is not at all easy. We may try to protect our elderly parents from the information, and tell ourselves that our children are too young to know. I have often met wives who try to protect their husbands who have a life-threatening illness. They are the ones who speak to the doctor, and they are the ones who are told diagnosis and prognosis. They attempt to weave a blanket of comfortable deceit around their man, but before they know it they become entangled in a noose of secrets and lies that strangle intimacy and real support. Physicians often collude with family in order to "protect" the patient; this is bad practice if not malpractice, and certainly not relationship-centered. This information belongs to the patient, not to his wife or the physician. It is *his* life and it is *his* dying. The task of caregivers is to share the information as lovingly and supportively as possible, something that is not easy to do.

Home or Hospital?

Sooner or later the question will arise about whether or not to be in the hospital at some time during the last days or weeks of life.

Choosing to be in the hospital is not usually a matter of tests or procedures that can only be performed there, but it concerns the helplessness of both patient and family in the face of dying, and the physician who feels obligated to *do* something. When all are fully aware that dying is what is happening and have discussed the situation and comforted one another, it is quickly realized that almost everything related to comfort can equally well be provided at home. The hospital does not provide safety and security nor the personal touch that is necessary for body and soul. Yet the majority of individuals still die in hospitals or other institutions. Where would you wish to spend your last days?

The Family
The thought of calling the family together is daunting for most of us. We would most likely want to see each member individually, although we probably have trepidation about talking to a number of them. We imagine that if all the family members were assembled, the usual chaos would reign, only more so. This gathering receives more attention in the next chapter because, in my opinion, it is the crucial forum in which quantum emotional healing may occur. But in this exercise we simply *imagine* what it might be like, what we might say to those assembled, and what they might say to us. It is usually a great surprise to all of us that the experience of speaking to family, whether they be alive or dead, is so authentic—that mother or grandmother or brother really seemed to hear what we had to say—and that it feels so liberating to have been able to say it.

Symptoms and Signs
The feeling of weakness and not being able to fend for ourselves is often a most distressing symptom. Now, like it or not, we are going to have to ask for help. Incontinence for many is a fate worse than death. Most of us were taught at a very early age— perhaps it was even beaten into us—that bladder and bowel control are mandatory for survival if we want to be loved, and so this revisiting by the unmentionable may inspire extreme shame. Loss of dignity may be another feeling brought to consciousness in this part of the exercise. It may be difficult to imagine that incontinence could be well managed by both ourselves and our caregiver with a tinge of humor and much love. The offering of

63

care is actually considered a privilege by most, and the smell and mess of incontinence nothing more than a minor distraction.

When appetite is lost, the family will often want to push food because they have no idea what else to do, and the answer to stress, uproar, or confusion in many families is to feed. It is hard for families and caregivers to imagine how difficult it is to eat when the appetite is gone, and the constant peddling of food may take on the unpleasant characteristics of a life-and-death struggle. We need to remember that loss of appetite may at times be nature's way of easing us out of this world by helping us to let go of that which has hitherto been most life-giving.

The Breath

Vipassana and other practices of meditation teach sharpening awareness of the mind through attention to the breath. When we focus on the breath we are able to see clearly how the mind darts around, thinking of everything but breathing. Returning very gently to the breath, over and over again, leads the mind toward becoming more still so that it is better able to see and hear what is around and within, allowing us to be more present to ourselves and others. We become more aware of the here and now. We watch the mind and all that occurs in our consciousness in the same manner that the vast sky might be imagined to watch the clouds and the ever-changing weather. It does not have to do anything: the clouds and weather will change and pass on their own, and the sky remains tranquil. Clarity of mind leads to the grace of patience, and patience is wisdom. Meditation is the *practice* of wisdom. It is an exquisite way of caring for ourselves and practicing the art of witnessing, and as such could become a vital part of healing. Instruction in meditation has been introduced into the occasional medical school. Meditation seems to me to be at the center of relationship-centeredness. It is very powerful medicine.

In this exercise how did you experience your breathing, and your last breath?

One of the fears about dying is that we might in the end be gasping for breath, and anxiety about suffocating or choking to death is a common concern. It is amazing that physicians still withhold morphine that could relieve anxiety and still the fearful edge of the breath. When dying as a result of heart failure or lung disease, breathing can be quite labored and difficult; that time we can only hope that our physician-guide has the experience and the wisdom to use appropriate medications in useful doses.

In the exercise, the uneven breathing and its eventual cessation cause less anxiety for most people than might be expected. My experience suggests that if someone has been engaged in conscious dying and there have been loving witnesses and guides along the way, the alteration in breathing, coupled with a dulling of awareness, is less fearful. It is as if at this point the person feels safe in other hands. For those who are unprepared and not present to their dying and uneven breathing patterns, the changes often trigger panic in both themselves and those around them.

In the hospital, there is indiscriminate use of resuscitation and an over-ready reliance on the respirator, even when it is obviously not being used as a temporary lifesaving bridge to unassisted breathing. If we are not to give our lives over to protocol and we wish to avoid futile treatment, it is essential that we draw up a medical directive, an example of which can be found in the Appendix of this book.

The principal benefit of having a medical directive is in bringing our wishes about the quality of life into the open so that we can discuss them with our family, along with other soulful matters. The document also gives guidance about our specific requests, should we become irreversibly incompetent to make decisions for ourselves. However, physicians and nurses unprepared for dying are likely to ignore "do not resuscitate" orders and medical directives. As patients we need to be assertive advocates for the manner in which we want to live and to die.

After Death

This exercise offers us an opportunity to look down at what is happening to our family after we die, whether or not we believe in life after death. It allows us to imagine how it might be for them, which could lead to discussion and planning, something that usually never happens because we believe it to be too morbid.

What happens to the body after a patient dies is almost completely out of the hands of the family, although it has not always been this way. If we die in the hospital, the family is moved out of the way for the physician who arrives to pronounce death. Then, after the briefest possible pause our body is whisked away in a closed container—death is not allowed to be seen in hospitals—down into the basement, there to await the arrival of the funeral director, and our bed is quickly filled. At some point our body is zipped into a plastic bag and the funeral director spirits it off to his "home," there to await the decisions of our distraught and often unprepared family. The low-key but insistent sales pressure fueled by ideas of what is socially right and proper leads to suggestions about expensively cushioned coffins, embalming, ghastly make-up and poses to make us look good, regimented flowers, and suitable visiting hours. All this occurs in a sterile environment, the whole event being orchestrated by a funeral director who has little knowledge of the vitality of our soul. The superficiality and soullessness of what occurs in a funeral home becomes ever more vivid when we imagine that it is our own wake that we are attending.

Not long ago most deaths occurred at home, and the body was not handed over to anyone. The physician might arrive in the home as guest, guide, and friend, pronouncing death and giving comfort. The body was washed by the family. This was not a routine bathing for hygienic purposes but rather a loving act akin to baptism. In fact, the ritual of baptism soon after birth might be imagined as a welcoming cleansing of the soul on its arrival into this life, and the washing of the body at death as a ritual cleansing and loving good-bye as the soul departs. This rite of bathing the dead by family has largely been abandoned in both Jewish and Christian tradition, although there is sometimes a ritual bathing paid for by the family rather than performed by them. In the hospice, we invited family members to assist in this ritual cleansing, and while many declined, those who participated were always moved by this opportunity to give love and care and say good-bye.

We are desperately in need of sacred rituals to sustain the soul in times of change. The funeral-home ritual has been sucked dry of soul and designed for convenience and profit. Death is not convenient, and when it happens, lovingly designed rituals help to lubricate grief, allowing it to mature and then fade in its own time. Plastic rituals desiccate grief, preserving it and encouraging it to go underground where it is not seen but where it eats away at the soul.

Would you consider having your wake in your own home? It

may seem most inconvenient for your family, who will have to prepare the space, but that is where you lived, and it is where you are welcome. What about some celebration of your life? That is often left to the memorial service, or there may be a few words at the funeral. But how about a celebration at your wake? It used to be that way, and there was food and drink and endless stories told in the gathering. The wake at home allowed the whole community to mourn; now, in this age of the individual, there is little sense of community. The wake in the funeral home or elsewhere is a lonely opportunity for lines of individuals to pass through without becoming too involved and without feeling the web of connectedness that is so apparent when death is experienced as a community event.

Then there is your funeral. Where will it be and who would you like to preside? Will it be in church or a funeral home, or will you have a memorial service at some time in the future? Will you be buried or cremated?

There had been no cremations in my family until my father's death. He felt strongly that too much land is wasted on graveyards. I disagree with that point of view, believing both that we need a place for the dead and that graveyards can be havens for solitude, but I was not opposed to my father's wish for cremation. The act of his cremation, however, caught me by surprise. He was waked in the living room of the home of Albert, a priest-friend of his and mine. It was a reassuring experience to be with my father's body in that warm place, and comforting to be able to get out of bed and sit with him in a night-watch. His body was contained in a simple pine box, and at the funeral mass this casket was placed next to the altar close to Albert, who conducted a most personal ritual. Following the mass we went to the crematorium, and after a brief ceremony during which I stumbled through some of my father's favorite poems by Omar Khayyam, he was cremated. I was taken by surprise at the sudden disappearance of his pine box during the ceremony. This was in contrast with the slower pace at my mother's funeral some years before. At her burial I carried her casket on my shoulder, along with three others; we moved very slowly, covering a distance of more than 100 yards. I remember that walk quite vividly. It was followed by laying the coffin down at the graveside, and then listening to some gentle words from Albert. Afterward, we slowly lowered her casket into the ground and threw earth on top. That ritual seemed to be at the right pace; the steps I took with my mother's body and the participation in her burial were what I needed. My father's cremation seemed to cut the process surrounding his death too short; there were no steps taken nor burden carried. Ceremonies of this kind should give time for memories, sobs, and expiratory sighs—all part of allowing the reality of death to penetrate the soul and begin the process of letting go.

Re-minding

At the end of the exercise we were in the presence of God, and had the opportunity to reflect on the course of our lives. What would we do over again if we had the chance? Not a very useful question if taken literally, because what is done is done and cannot be undone—we need to let the past go. But a reflection along these lines could be the catalyst for changes in the here and now. For example, in my children's earlier years I was an absent father. This was not a physical absence but rather one that emerged from depression, self-absorption, and emotional distance. I can do nothing now about being a better father then, but I am able to acknowledge what happened, take responsibility, ask their forgiveness, be compassionate toward myself, and let go. I am able to re-member—to put the pieces back together as best as I am able—and, having re-membered, can allow myself to let go of the guilt and shame which would otherwise continue to replay over and over again like a broken record. Having freed myself of these painful feelings related to missed responsibilities and opportunities, I am now a more present and loving father. My relationships with my children are fulfilling, and I am told that this is so for each of them as well.

What unfinished business do we have? Whatever it is—and there is always something, great or small, for all of us—it emerges from being stuck in the past. If we have the wisdom to allow the mind to be still and are not concerned with the whys and judgments related to past events, we can let go, and in injecting love, can transform relationships and the living of our lives.

Summary

An exercise of this nature helps to disperse denial of death and dying. Soulful living is only possible when there is consciousness of death and impermanence, when death is at our right shoulder reminding us about what is important in our lives. Deflating and dispersing denial of death makes us more conscious of the need to give and receive love before it is too late; it is an essential part of self-care.

CHAPTER 6

Care of the Soul

Care of the body usually receives more attention than care of the soul. The need for exercise and reasonable attention to the diet is part of the belief system, if not the personal practice, of many people, but since the soul cannot be weighed or measured it is often ignored. The soul is the vital force or animating principle that makes us alive. It is as if this central core is surrounded and protected by both body and ego that make up a cocoon in which the soul nestles. This protective cocoon needs to be permeable and pliable if the inner soul is to be nourished and thrive. However, many have fabricated an ego that is hard and thick, allowing little access for love and connectedness from the outside. While this may be thought of as protecting ourselves, of taking good care of the self or being self-sufficient, and while there is considerable cultural approval for independence, the soul addles if it is not involved in relationships that are sustaining and nurturing. An impenetrable nature deadens self-awareness. As well, thick and "strong" egos are not very adaptable to the stresses and strains of impermanence and life-threatening disease. The impermeability of the cocoon is particularly maladaptive during the process of dying, at which time it is necessary for both body and soul to allow in a great deal of care and support from the outside. Eventually we need to allow ourselves, and be given permission by those who love us, to leave this protective cocoon, however well we may think it has served us in life.

The ego is often given an importance that goes far beyond its function as a flexible, permeable, and protective container for the life within. It is ascribed value and net worth, and judgments are made related to its beauty or ugliness, strength or weakness, brightness or dullness, all of which distract attention from the inner soul.

Even if we imagine our body as a machine—and our medical system acts as if it is—there is very little preventive maintenance. An annual physical is a bit like a yearly visit to church on an annual spiritual; neither does much for body or soul. Nutrition is obviously not taken seriously enough by most of us, including the medical establishment. If physical exercise was thought of as important, and sports medicine more than repair operations, gyms would become an integral aspect of all medical centers.

If we were to imagine the body as a shrine or sacred vessel that contains the soul, we would treat it very differently than most people do now. We would honor it as a place of sanctuary. We would take care of it physically, and we would also make sure that we took the time to pause often and listen to the soul within.

A visualization exercise that we do in our workshops brings attention to the often-neglected inner being. The exercise is helpful in becoming more self-aware and self-related and is an important aspect of the training for living and dying.

The first part of the exercise involves a guided relaxation. During this phase, the participants imagine a safe haven for themselves in much the same way as they did in the earlier workshop session when they imagined their own death. Once in that place of safety, the group is led in a visualization that enables the participants to come in touch with their inner souls. As before, following the visual journey the group splits into triads to share experiences of the exercise, communicating within the storyteller-witness-guide framework. Usually the storyteller is given 20 minutes to relate her experiences, and then the group takes another 10 minutes for each to say a little about the experience of storytelling, guiding, and witnessing. Then the group members change roles and begin storytelling again. In 90 minutes the group reassembles.

If you are practising this exercise at home, you may wish to tape the instructions or simply rely on memory to be your guide for the steps along the way.

VISUALIZATION: THE CHILD WITHIN

Find a comfortable position sitting in a chair or on cushions, or if you are at home you may wish to lie propped up on your bed.

As in the previous exercise, spend a few minutes focusing on your outer cocoon, encouraging it to relax and become more permeable. Begin by closing your eyes. Imagine a wave of relaxation, like gentle waves at the seaside, flowing down slowly from the top of your head to the soles of your feet, taking with it any tension and stress that has tightened your body. Take a few moments to experience the relaxation created by this healing wave. Now, for a few minutes pay particular attention to the breath, which is itself the connecting link to the soul. When the breath ceases, the vital force or soul disappears. Notice the in-breath as it passes through mouth or nostrils and goes deep within, as if to nourish and embrace the soul. Notice the out-breath and the sense of relief as it passes out through the cocoon ...

Feeling more relaxed and conscious of the flow of life, in your mind's eye take a trip to a safe place. It can be the same one you visited before, or another safe and sacred spot. Take your time to experience this place in all its detail ...

Now that you have spent some moments encouraging the body to relax, soften, and become more permeable, and are in your familiar and comfortable safe place, sit down and look off into the distance. You then notice that far away there is some movement within the stillness of the scene. As you watch it becomes clear that there is a person running toward you. You continue to watch, and soon you realize that it is a child. As the child comes closer, you notice that it seems disheveled and upset, and its clothes look vaguely familiar. Closer still, and you realize with a startle that this child is you; she is you when you were seven or eight years old, and she is crying.

You open your arms and she jumps on to your lap, hugging you tight, her sobbing face buried in your chest. You hold her and kiss her and gently stroke her back and her face. After a while the sobs subside, replaced by a flood of words. She says that you never pay much attention to her. When she is afraid—and she is often afraid—you tell her to be quiet and grow up. "I panic and want to be comforted, and all you do is eat something to try and calm me down." She continues "Sometimes you have a drink or two and allow your feelings to explode, but you never listen to me. I worry about you because you do not take care of yourself—you do not take care of me. You are always on the run, taking care of others. You take wonderful care of your husband, his mother and yours, your children, your colleagues and your friends, but you never seem to have time for me."

There is much more, and you listen. After a while her talking abates a little. In a quiet moment you simply tell her that she is right—that you have paid her very little attention. You have ignored her cries. You continue: "I have been so harsh and critical of you, dismissing your fears and your hurt and your anger, and not even acknowledging your loving warmth and that marvelous playful creativity. Dearest child, please forgive me. I have neglected you out of my own fear of failure and not being loved and I almost killed off the one closest to me." She listens silently, and then she wraps her arms around you and kisses you, and you simply hold one another.

When the moment is right, you tell her that from now on you will create a space each day into which she can enter. You will find a corner in your house where you will not be disturbed and you will sit down, close your eyes, pay attention to your body, and then go to your safe place. There you will focus on your breathing, and, you tell her, on the in-breath she can enter any time she wishes. She looks in your face and smiles, gives you a kiss, and jumps off your lap, saying that she will be back. She heads off lightly, in the direction from which she came.

You continue to watch as she fades from sight and you remember your promise to her, wondering how you will honor it since it is so fragile, and resolutions to take time for self-care have disappeared before in the face of demands by others. You think of a time each day when this would be possible, telling yourself that this is the first step.

When you are ready, breathe in your safe place and then let it go, saying good-bye. Then make the journey back into the room. Open your eyes, find your two companions, and begin to tell your stories. If you are doing this exercise at home with a companion, this is the time to share the story of what occurred during the visualization; if you are alone, you may wish to write about your experience.

Men may find it more difficult to immerse themselves in this visualization, as most are not used to looking within and paying attention to their own lonely and neglected inner selves. In speaking the visualization, I often incorporate into the visualization examples of self-neglect that have been told by participants in the workshop, such as this man's story which relates to insufficient attention being paid in times of grief and fear. In speaking as his inner child he says:

So often you told me that boys do not cry and that I should grow up, but I remember when dad died when I was eight or so and everyone was so upset. I was sent to the neighbors and never saw dad being taken to the hospital; the one visit I remember before he died was scary and horrible. The funeral was a nightmare—all anyone told me was that I would get over it and that I had to be brave, and you forced me to swallow my tears. Then years later when mom died, during the months she had cancer you were so busy trying to relieve everyone else's pain and anxiety that you forgot all about me. I wanted to weep with her and tell her how awful her illness was, both for her and for me, and I wanted her to hold me and I wanted to put my arms around her, but you never allowed that to happen.

To all this he simply listens as the silent witness, and after a while he tells his inner child that he is quite right.

I have spent a lifetime trying to appear strong and knowledgeable, ignoring my vulnerability because men are supposed to know and fix everything. Yes, dad's death was awful. And mom's was heartbreaking, although I never allowed myself to acknowledge the full pain.

Who is the child that we have neglected? It is my belief that it is the soul, and failure to acknowledge it leads to feelings of emptiness and purposelessness. When feelings and the inner soul or vital force are not respected, apathy ensues, relationships become fraught with difficulty, and burn-out or depression follow.

I imagine the soul entering into life at birth. Since it is the body that the parents and other observers see, that is what they pay most attention to. They watch it grow, training it and molding it into a form that is personally, socially, and culturally acceptable. If the child is loved body and soul, it will thrive; if love is missing, the soul will wilt and remain unfertilized and unrealized. Later in life the body once again becomes vulnerable and helpless, and eventually it is shed, releasing the soul.

Both birth and death are times of transition for the soul, times when we particularly need loving guides and witnesses. Religious traditions tell us that we need to be as a child if we are to be in touch with our perfection. This might be restated to say that we need to be as a child or as a dying person—that is, in a state when the ego is not apparent, either because it has not yet developed or because the cocoon is thin. In both instances the soul is exposed, and both times we need the most loving of bodily care. But the essence of soul is within and beyond the body, and it is this essence—this inner child—that needs to be displayed and honored, because it is our essential nature.

In her writings about the sexual, physical, and emotional abuse of children, the Swiss psychoanalyst Alice Miller describes the trauma of abuse as "soul murder." This seems to be an apt description of the numbing and paralysis of feelings and imagination that occurs in many abused children. I believe that there is also such a thing as soul suicide when the soul is numbed by drugs, alcohol, a lifeless job, or deadly relationships. Soul suicide also ensues when dying occurs without stories being told and without the letting go of all the strangleholds of rage-filled relationships, a letting go that could lead to forgiveness, the giving of blessings, and the saying of good-byes—all of which revive the soul in one of its most important passages.

The child we met in the visualization may tell us that she has been neglected, abused, and almost killed off, not by appalling parents or relatives but by us; it was our inattention and disregard that led to her failure to thrive. Many people have suffered awful childhoods and have spent a lifetime recounting all the details, apportioning blame mostly to unfeeling and incompetent parents. Those injuries may have happened, but the perpetuation of this abuse and the failure to receive love in the present is due to self-neglect. I have seen many adult children hovering over their dying mother transfixed and with bated breath, as they wait and hope for an expression of love that never comes. Mother is quite unable to be anything but critical and ungiving, like her mother before her. The needy adult child forgets that she has within her all the love that is necessary for the nourishment of her own inner soul-child. We need to listen to the voice of the soul; we need to listen to the child when she says that she needs our time and our love if she is to be vibrant and magnify our life with her wisdom.

ON POSITIVE ATTITUDES

In fighting competitive wars of all kinds, a positive attitude is associated with winning, and winning is proclaimed as "the only thing." Nothing else is imaginable, and during the war (or the football game), thinking of the "enemy" (the opposition) as people just like ourselves and in need of our understanding and compassion has no place. Biblical exhortations to love our enemy are ignored. So it is in the war on disease. Even if this violent attitude had some ethical merit, disease infiltrates our body cells, and in effect becomes a part of us, so that declaring war on it, together with the attitudes and behavior that go along with this warfare, is also declaring war on ourselves.

What if the attitude were one of "tough love" instead of all-out warfare? What if, instead of storming the disease site, we negotiated. We would say to illness at the outset that its presence in the embassy of our body is quite unacceptable and that it has to leave, and that this is not negotiable. But we will talk, and we will listen to the story of the disease, and we will bathe the negotiations in life; we will provide warmth, love, dance, and laughter, and we will listen. We may hear that the disease arrived in our bodily embassy in the wake of self-neglect or neglect of our environment through smoking, chemically laced foods, and industrial pollution, or that it arrived out of the blue from causes we do not understand. We listen with loving attention but remain firm in our position that it must depart. Perhaps it will simply leave at this point, melted by our love and determination. Disease will do that. There are many stories of spontaneous remissions for which our most rational scientists have no explanation.

I am quite sure that love may melt illness in just the same way that love will sometimes melt any other form of violence and dissidence. If the disease does not leave, we will bring in various forms of coercion while maintaining our loving attitude, and the new and more assertive treatments may cause it to withdraw. If it still remains and stays there to the death, at least during the time it was there life would have been lived as fully and lovingly as possible, and the soul-child would have felt that she had been heard and honored.

SELF-CARE

When the child within asks us to take care of her and when we imagine taking care of the soul, what do we mean?

Many of us were brought up to believe that self-love is bad, that it is selfish and narcissistic. We were told that instead we should be thinking of others, although even that admonition is muted in our present age. The objective of the soul is to experience the connection of all things and this can only be accomplished by witnessing. Witnessing is the energy of love uniting us all, and if we witness ourselves we are witnessing all things. In this way it becomes very easy to love others. This is something I have experienced when I am together with a group of souls for several days in a workshop, and it is also the experience when meditating with a group over an extended time.

Vipassana meditation is the silent and patient witnessing of the stirrings of our being. Practices of this kind are models for taking care of and listening to ourselves. This practice requires doing nothing other than being exquisitely aware of what is coming to pass in the present moment; it also involves being aware of what is happening all around us, because in the realm of the soul there is no boundary between us and everything else.

When leading workshops on dying and death, I began to notice that toward the end of a workshop I would always say that I felt this particular group of people was the most wonderful group I had ever had the privilege of experiencing. It took me a long while to realize that it was really true. Each group *was* the most wonderful because they were all the same. When egos are left aside in a safe environment and souls are able to relate to one another or be one another, then each group really *is* the same, and individual differences vanish.

In the same way, during ten-day Vipassana meditation retreats, which are held in silence, I have spoken to nobody except for a couple of brief periods with the teacher and an hour toward the end of the retreat with a small group of my fellow retreatants. Yet during the retreat and on leaving I feel as one with them all, even though we have not spoken and I do not know their names. Care of our soul includes discovering this connectedness with others. It will happen in love; it may happen occasionally with friends or with groups and most miraculous of all, it can happen in the family setting, as I have seen time and time again.

Additional ways of warming and caring for the child-soul within involve bringing all of the essential elements of care into the relationship with self and others.

We need the passion and warmth of *fire*. We are all taught to be objective and unemotional; we are warned that if we become too involved with others in our professional lives—with patients, students, clients, parishioners, or others in the workplace— we may be burned. As has been discussed earlier, this life strategy is antithetical to caregiving of body and soul for both ourselves and others. If we take good care of ourselves we will be able to take care of others, and while there are no guarantees that we will not be burned, there is no alternative if we are to give care that is powered by a true loving relationship.

We need the life-giving element of *water* without which we are dust, and yet much of what passes as care takes place in climate-controlled atmospheres that are deadly dry, devoid of the healing moisture of tears and laughter. The feminine art of caregiving is, of its nature, moist, and we need lubrication. Tears are *the* solution. If we will risk crying a handful of tears, they become the solution into which our cares can be stirred so that they dissolve. If we are caregivers of any kind, we need not fear crying with the one for whom we care, since the tears are simply a lubricant for the relationship. We can even give our tears as a blessing. One little boy I worked with insisted on putting his tear-stained tissue into his grandfather's casket at the wake.

We need *air*. Each breath we take consists of an inspiration, a liminal pause in the doorway to letting go, and the expiratory out-breath. We need each step, and there may be times when, as caregivers, we need to guide others in breathing. We need to know and to tell others that inspiration is normal, as is the wish to be inspired by good news, but holding the breath for fear of letting the good news go makes living quite impossible. So we must also allow ourselves to expire. As caregivers, we must give those in our care room to breathe. We, too, are unable to hold on, and when it is their time to go we need to let them expire while being there as their witness.

We need to be *down to earth*. Many of us are in the clouds—we may feel safer when we hold ourselves at a distance from problems. Being down to earth is to risk being vulnerable and not knowing the answers to all of what is going on. However, remoteness is not a soulful, comforting or connecting experience. As caregivers we need to ensure that we have our feet on the ground and can be a witness and occasionally a guide when those we care for enter unknown territory.

We need *space*. The crowding, clatter, and fears attendant on urban living are often at odds with our need for space, sanctuary, and room to breathe. And the terminally ill also need to be given space, to be made welcome, along with the message that there are no expectations and there is no hurry, that whatever happens, all will be well.

The inner soul is asking to be witnessed by our mind or ego or personhood. The soul asks that we care for her, which in turn allows the soul to be vitally alive and able to give care to others. Only when we pay attention to our soul will we be able to build relationships with the living and the dying.

CHAPTER 7

Dying and the Family

Early on in my hospice work it became apparent that there was usually much worry, anxiety, fearfulness, and sorrow when a family member was dying, but there was little open recognition of the fact that someone was soon to take leave of the family forever, and that the family needed to say good-bye. Many people claimed that farewells were not necessary or were potentially too upsetting; others declared that words were superfluous because every person in the family knew how the others felt. Sometimes the family facing an imminent death was heavy with secrets: alcoholism, ungrieved losses, violence, infidelity and other betrayals, as well as unfinished business from earlier marriages. There were parents who had not seen their children for years and siblings who had not spoken to each other for decades. In many instances, the dying person would say angrily that if a family member would not make the time to visit him when he was well, he had no interest in seeing them now that he was dying.

I remember a man in the last couple of weeks of his life telling me about his two brothers, the older of whom he had not seen since the funeral of his father 20 years earlier, and the younger since their mother's funeral several years ago. All he remembered was that there was much ill-feeling over their father's will, and since that time they had only spoken a few times on the phone. When I asked if he would like to see them, he was initially dismissive of the idea, but after a few moments he said he would like to make peace, and I encouraged him to call them immediately. He did, and they arrived that evening, one from Florida and the other from Washington for their long overdue reunion, wasting no further energy in the futile exercise of blame.

Occasionally families would meet together without any prompting, but the gathering would often leave those attending with a sense of incompletion and of things unsaid. An upwelling of emotion might cause feelings to remain unspoken, or one family member might interrupt, correct, or judge the words of another, effectively staunching the flow of feelings. The quiet ones in the family would usually stay in their well-practiced roles by remaining silent, depriving themselves of experiencing their own feelings and exposing the rest of the family to this hidden dimension of the soul.

I remember a woman in her forties whose father was dying as a result of far-advanced heart disease. She had a dream a couple of days before the scheduled family meeting. In the dream she was working in a new job. In the course of her duties she opened a door into a room filled with skulls. Opening another door, she found another room with row upon row of skulls. At that moment she realized that she was working in a concentration camp, and became overwhelmed by the fear that she would be required to cut off heads. She initially associated the dream with a visit to Israel some months earlier during which she had been preoccupied with the Holocaust. It was only when she recounted this dream to me after the family meeting that she related it to her fears about what secrets might be uncovered when her family sat down together.

I began to meet with those families who welcomed an outsider, ones who intuitively knew that they could be assisted through the dark underworld of dying by a nonjudgmental hermetic guide. I usually only met with the family on one occasion, and was often asked how healing or resolution could be achieved in just a single session. Conventional wisdom would have it that the trials and tribulations of family life may require years of individual or family therapy to work through the experiences of a lifetime. However, when facing the prospect of an impending death the family is forced to recognize that an ending is in sight; this concatenation of beings linked by birth and life experience is about to undergo an irrevocable shift. The family meeting is a sacred pause, an opportunity to relinquish deadly, soul-destroying stories, to heal and make peace, and it is the last chance. These few moments can be life-changing if we allow ourselves to enter into the spirit of this ritual, both telling and listening to stories and offering forgiveness, gratitude, and blessings.

My experiences with family meetings remind me of the story

about the first of four tasks set by Venus for Psyche which had to be completed if Psyche was to be reunited with her lover, Eros. Venus set before Psyche a huge pile of mixed dark and light seeds with the instruction that she was to separate them before nightfall. Psyche started the task and then quickly realized that she would never accomplish it in time. At that moment an army of ants arrived and separated the seeds in short order, well before sunset.

Likewise, when the family meeting starts it often seems impossible to those assembled that anything will be accomplished. Many times there is neither the atmosphere of trust nor a real interest in knowing the fears and worries of others in the family. The question occasionally asked by a skeptical, frightened, or hostile family member about what I hope to accomplish and why I want to upset everyone at a time like this used to be enough to send me into a frenzy of doubt. In the early years of facilitating family meetings I often had the desire to run from the room, begging forgiveness for being the instigator of unrest. In line with my traditional training, I thought that we needed months to do what needed to be done, and we only had a very short time. But after a while I began to notice that miracles were happening: in just an hour or two, so much was sorted out. As Psyche learned, the "ants" *will* get to work if we let them!

The family meeting is an opportunity to speak from the heart and be witnessed. It is a sacred ritual that inspires healing; it is not a therapeutic exercise for the mind. It is an opportunity to truly recognize another in all his peculiarities and to acknowledge the age-old similarities that exist between any two human beings, not to mention between kith and kin. The family meeting is an opportunity to give thanks for being a part of each other's lives, to forgive hurts, and to say good-bye. The specific nature of the life-threatening illness has little bearing on the family meeting. The prognosis for advanced cancer may be a little more precise than that of late-stage heart or lung or neurological disease, but the issue of the need for a family meeting is the same; it is always necessary, and the sooner the better.

During my first years in hospice work, the courageous families I met with taught me a number of basic truths that gradually became guidelines for all family meetings. I list these guidelines here, and will discuss each at length through the chapter.

- The first speaker should be the one who is dying, if he is conscious enough to be able to speak a little, and he should begin by telling the story of his illness. The "story" as we are speaking of it here is not to be construed as a recitation of facts but more as a series of impressions—a few brush strokes of facts colored by feelings. Although he may have spoken to everyone individually, and some family members might have spoken to the physician, this may well be the first time the person who is dying has told the story of his illness to the whole family (or those who chose to gather), who are present as loving witnesses, all hearing the same thing.

- The usual style of dialogue within a family allows interruptions, corrections, judgments, and other struggles so that stories usually remain incomplete and feelings unrevealed. In family meetings a guide should be present to ensure that only one person speaks at a time, and is allowed to continue without interruption. The guide will occasionally give the storyteller a gentle nudge if the story seems stuck or incomplete, or may need to cut a story short when it seems to be especially long-winded or when the speaker is using up the time to protect or prevent others from having to speak. Most of the stories may only be vignettes, but that is all that is necessary. A guide from outside the family is ideal, especially when it is understood that the role is not to fix or rescue but to be a nonjudgmental friend who is reasonably comfortable with the underworld of dying. The Talking Stick is always available as a nonjudgmental guide, giving the storyteller permission to speak and the witnesses the courage to remain silent.

- Young children and grandchildren should always be present, as they are a vital part of the family. The very young may not seem to understand, or yet have words, but if at all possible— and even when it seems impossible—they should attend and be welcome to wander in and out. Often I have heard adults tell stories about the death of a parent or grandparent when they were five or six or even older, and how they were excluded from the scene in the name of protection. However, even though young children may not seem to understand what is happening or be able to put into words or remember the death, their presence becomes part of the family mythology; the story of the family meeting can then be told over and over again in the years to come, connecting the child with its deceased relative at each telling.

- The one who is dying should be encouraged to invite friends, colleagues, and acquaintances to the family meeting. On several occasions I have had separate meetings for friends because of the large numbers involved.

- The meeting should end with a blessing.

Since the family drama has been long in the writing, there is no script for the family meeting. As guide I simply act as a soul-director who invokes the words that are present but may never have been spoken, helping them to emerge without judgment while encouraging the witnesses to be quiet and attentive. It is of the greatest importance that each family member be a witness to the storyteller, something that may never have happened before. As a person becomes witness to the story of members of his family without interrupting, judging, or correcting, the fragments from the imagination and memory of the storyteller settle into the sounding chamber of the other's soul, deepening connection without any need to change a thing.

As I became increasingly aware of the amazing possibilities for healing when family members gather together and allow themselves to speak from the soul rather than from the mind, I suggested that every hospice family be offered and encouraged to have such a meeting. While there were always a few who eagerly embraced this opportunity to gather, most expressed a greater or lesser degree of resistance to the idea, although it was quite rare that there was an outright refusal to meet. Some family members would not attend, saying it was unnecessary or too upsetting, or giving the excuse that they had to work even when advised that this would be one of the most important gatherings of their lives. Still others avoided meeting for fear they would break down. Having lived for years with the family myth that to be emotional or to allow feelings to escape through the protective shell is to invite chaos, they believed that speaking their emotional truths would cause them to fall apart. These families have never even considered the possibility that the escape and sharing of feelings might be unifying for the family, a soulful breakthrough rather than a catastrophic breakdown.

What follows are images of the family meeting that have emerged over the course of almost 20 years, images gleaned from many hundreds of gatherings in which I have had the joy and privilege to participate. While for the purpose of illustration I use one scenario—that of a dying father—through most of this section the steps of the meeting are the same regardless of the participants' age, gender or relationship to the one who is dying. While cancer was the diagnosis of most patients in the early days of the hospice, the principles of the family meeting apply to any illness, including coma and dementia.

REFLECTIONS ON THE STORYTELLER

The first storyteller is the one who is dying, and he or she speaks of the illness because it is that which is the inspiration for this sacred gathering. If it is mom who is dying, she will tell of how she learned of the illness, what her reactions were, and how she told the family. She will also tell her version of how this is affecting each member of the family—they will speak for themselves later—and will then go on to speak of her fears and her worries. Mythologically, this part of mother's story correlates with Persephone gathering flowers in the garden when she picked the narcissus and all hell broke loose; her fears and worries are glimpses from the underworld into which she was swept.

Women usually find it a little easier to speak of soulful concerns because, culturally and innately, soul seems more accessible to women. However, it is not always this way, and I have often been surprised at how soulfully men will express themselves when given the encouragement and space in which to be heard.

If it is dad who is sick, the story would probably start differently. A father's dying is often particularly difficult for the family to face, since he is the front line in their denial of death and the family feels especially vulnerable now that this denial can no longer be maintained so easily. He is often reluctant or uncomfortable to speak and may ask his Demeter-wife to tell the story, or she might spontaneously begin to tell his tale. The family may never have heard him tell his own story since mom has always been the one to whom the children have spoken, and it is she who usually speaks to the doctor. It is as if mother is the custodian of the soul of the family while father plays the role of guardian against death and other dangers. Mother needs to be gently held back because it is important that father tells his own story and takes responsibility for his own dying; she cannot rescue her husband. His journey needs to be named and spoken of by him if he is to take charge of this part of his life, and it is almost always a great relief for the family when they hear him speak. Mom and the family can be there as guides, comforters, and witnesses, but he needs to listen to the fears and rumblings of his own soul and tell his own tale.

The invitation to father to speak about his worries and fears almost invariably starts with concerns about his family, and particularly his wife. I usually ask him how they met, what she is like, how he feels about her and, in looking back, how he views his marriage. These powerful questions often evoke jokes or nervous laughter sometimes verging on uproar in the family, but gentle persistence often leads to words he has never voiced. The surprise is that when spoken, the disappointments, disillusionments, and resentments can be let go, and room made for the expression of vulnerability, tenderness, and love. When asked about his specific worries for his wife, it usually becomes clear very quickly that she has the practical skills to cope quite adequately with the usual problems of living after he dies, and that his worry for her is actually borne of his own projected fear and sadness at having to let go.

When asked to speak about each of his children, he usually starts by reciting their accomplishments. Listing these, he is in control. He is also in control when he jokingly tells of what he perceives to have been their misbehaviors and irritating qualities. But when he talks about what he has glimpsed of their soul nature, he is less articulate and much less composed. When asked how he imagines that his illness is affecting them, he almost always ventures that they are extremely upset, but it is rare that he has ever asked them how they feel, and it is during the family meeting that he hears of this for the first time. Sometimes one of the family members will interrupt, telling him not to get upset. That is a moment for the guide to interject, reminding everyone how appropriate it is to be upset and encouraging the recognition that this is a breakthrough, not a breakdown.

In the early days of the hospice I was facilitating a family meeting presided over by a Mr. Ryan whose wife, eight children, and their spouses, together with several grandchildren, were present. It was a love fest! He told stories of a wonderful marriage with many struggles, and had something loving and supportive to say about everyone in the room, and they about him. There was much laughter and many tears. After about two hours he was exhausted, as were we all, and I was winding up proceedings by asking whether he had any questions or anything more to say. Mr. Ryan was slumped down on the couch looking drained by this time, but he sat up straight and summoned new energy, saying that he wanted to speak to his five youngest grandchildren who had been wandering in and out of the room but had not been directly addressed. Ranging in age from about six to nine, they sat on the floor in a semicircle at his feet. The following is my recollection of what he said: "Children, I have cancer and it is nobody's fault. It just happens. I am going to die and won't be there to see you grow up, but I want you to know that you have each been a joy in my life, and you will always have my blessing and my love." There was not a dry eye in the room for any of the witnesses to this most precious event. I have repeated this story many times to grandparents and others, because Mr. Ryan reminded us how important it is for grandparents to take leave of their grandchildren face-to-face, if it is at all possible. So often they are best friends and unconditional lovers, and it is an act of betrayal if the grandparent leaves without saying good-bye, delegating the heartbreaking task to the child's parents.

In some magical way the eternal nature of soul is honored in moments such as those between Mr. Ryan and his grandchildren. Such moments celebrate the link of the spirit with the future, and forever weave the event into the fabric of the entire family, to be told time and time again. It is not so much the content or quantity of what is discussed but rather the fact that we consider it important to pause and reflect, to feel the connections with those we have loved and tell the stories of their lives and of their passing. It is a tragedy that we do not understand, as Scharazad did, that our life and continuity depend on the telling of tales.

A man who was born in Turkey was being cared for in the hospice Inn. He had no family, so in a literal sense there was no family meeting, but for an hour or so a nurse and I felt like family as we listened to a whole series of tales of his life: the murder of his father in Turkey; the family flight to Persia and then Lebanon; stories about his mother and siblings and the magic of the paradise that was Lebanon and then his eventual move to Boston. We heard of his loneliness and fears as cancer advanced, and his relief at being safe in the Inn and having two people listen to his story. That is what this man needed to die in peace: witnesses to the brilliant threads of his life.

CONCERNING ANCESTORS AND ROOTS

Reflections about parents, siblings, and growing up often reveal continuing pain from deaths unmourned and loving words unspoken. Bringing these memories and images from the shadow into living consciousness allows some mourning to take place and lessens the deep anguish resulting from holding on. This in turn makes it possible to die in peace, free from the pain of preceding deaths. If this is not done, the one who is dying will expect that the mode of his death will be like that of his own mother and father, with its physical pains and terrors of long ago repeated for him. In his imagination, he re-dies their deaths along with his own. Wounds unwitnessed, unmourned, and unspoken leave a paralysis of soul that is passed on from generation to generation.

John, a man who ran a successful farm, was dying of lung cancer in his early seventies. He inherited the farm in a run-down state at the age of 17, following his father's suicide. He never spoke about the suicide but for a few brief remarks to his four children when they were in their twenties, when he told of identifying his father's body after it was recovered from the Hudson River. His wife and children described John as a loner who never spoke of his feelings. Indeed, at the first family gathering a month before his death he was unable to talk about his worries and his feelings for his family, though he did allude to the ever-present pain related to his father's death. It seemed as though John's unexpressed grief, fear, and intense loneliness around his father's death remained a lifelong barrier to intimacy with his family, and even made it impossible for him to grieve the impending loss of his own life and thus give himself comfort. John's family was very articulate and expressive of feelings and had clearly broken with the tradition of loneliness enacted by father and grandfather. John's wife modeled an openness that allowed feelings to be shared and souls touched; the whole family was able to say what they needed to say to John and to support one another in their grief.

It is vital that we grieve in order to remain connected to the present. When we grieve we allow ourselves to wail, lament, remember, rage, tell stories, and be immersed by waves of emptiness. The feelings of loss simply need acknowledgment and expression, and after a while they will pass. Many fail to grieve or else cut short their grief for fear of being overwhelmed and perhaps going mad or killing themselves. Families often interrupt the grief of one of their family members out of feelings of helplessness. We do not need to shut down our grieving. What we need is a witness to our grief—a Hecate who will listen.

John never exorcised the feelings and images in association with his father's suicide, and so this dark soul-wound was an ever-present dampener in his life. Grieving for our parents offers us practice in letting go of important connections, and is in turn a preparation for letting go of our own lives. When at a subsequent gathering John was able to tell the tale of the distraught, grieving 17-year-old and was listened to with rapt attention by his family, he was then able to hear them, express feelings of love and appreciation, and die peacefully.

REFLECTIONS ON THE WITNESS

When the time comes for the witnesses to become storytellers, it might be mother who begins by telling how she met father, giving her view of the joys and struggles of the marriage. She is always asked how the illness has affected her, a question that evokes images of her own shadowy fears about dying and stories of other moments of disconnection in her life, such as when parents or grandparents died. Her worries are for her husband's comfort and for the relief of his suffering; she may not voice some of the fears she has concerning future unknowns, leaving those to be spoken of after he has died. Yet many times in a family meeting I have heard a wife expressing fears about loneliness in the future, after her husband has gone. She says that she left home to marry when she was a teenager; she has never been alone and is scared at the prospect, although the children are around and she has other relatives and friends. Giving voice to what they both have been thinking is usually very helpful. Her husband has also been worrying how it will be for her after he dies, and to name the worry without having to come up with any plan of action is a relief for all. To hear that there will be emptiness and that life will be much changed but that she will somehow keep going is a reassurance for him. Now, he can give a sigh of relief and let go when he needs to let go, because she will be taken care of and will also take care of herself.

Many times a daughter will become a primary caretaker of aging parents, and when it is her time to speak in the family meeting and she is asked how dad's illness has been for her, she will perhaps unleash a torrent of feelings that have not been heard before. Married and the mother of two teenage children, she has a full-time job and comes here to her parents' home every day after work to prepare dinner and generally help out. She says that she always tries to be cheerful for dad, even though her heart is breaking, and she worries constantly about the stresses and strains on mom, who is in frail health herself. She does not mind the extra work but is constantly tired and often returns home to her family drained of energy, especially when dad has been having an unusually hard time. She is unable to talk to her husband about all this because he becomes too upset. His father died last year, also as a result of cancer; it was a nightmare for the family, and they never talked about it, nor will he speak to her about his dad in more than monosyllables. Her husband would like to visit dad because they get along very well and she knows they love one another, even though nothing like that has ever been spoken out loud, but it is too upsetting for him to see dad this way and so he stays home. Her two teenage children are also upset but talk very little and are staying away from their grandparents. So she is trying to maintain two households yet feels that everything is falling apart, and the only place that she can cry is occasionally with a friend at work, or alone in her own bathroom.

Perhaps in the middle of her story I might ask her to move and come over and sit next to dad. When she has finished I might invite her to ask dad if he would mind if she cried with him, and could he hold her when she needed comforting. While it may be a new experience, he says that it would be more than fine with him; it becomes an opportunity for him to give solace instead of being on the receiving end.

Variations on this theme are so common. Being able to speak about such pain to the whole family without it falling apart is often an opening for much deeper connections. The daughter's husband and two children need to visit, and they all need to gather in another family meeting, which can be so easily arranged. It is important that a father-in-law speak directly to his daughter's husband saying—if this is what he feels—that he admires him as a husband and father and loves him as a son, and has always been happy that he became part of the family and would like to give him a blessing. He might add that he also offers this blessing in the name of his son-in-law's own father, who would like to have given it himself.

If the relationship is more strained, he can still say something like: "I know it has not been easy for you and my daughter, and that you have had many struggles. I know how difficult it was for you last year when your father died. It was an awful ordeal for you and all the family, and I also know that it was not easy between you and your dad, just as there was great distance and often much heartache between me and my dad. You and I have not been as close as we might have been and I am sorry about that, but I am really glad you came to see me, and I would like to bless you."

We men are so much in need of being able to accept love as well as give it, especially from and to one another.

Some family "secrets" may emerge in the family meeting, a very common example of which is alcoholism. Mother might recall that the 20 years of her husband's drinking was awful for both herself and the children, and there was a repetitive sequence of drunkenness, abuse, financial problems, and absence, but she often adds that when he was sober he was wonderful. This may be the first time his alcoholism has been openly discussed and heard within the family. When it comes time for the children to say how dad's alcoholism affected them, feelings of embarrassment, shame, anger, fear, and a sense of never having known dad and constantly worrying for mom are commonly voiced. The object of such truth-telling is not to be judge and jury for father, nor to inflame his guilt—that is usually there in overabundance already. It is to acknowledge and speak of a piece of family history that had actually happened but had been banished into the underworld, there to ferment but almost always to reappear in subsequent generations if not aired and let go. The fact that the family can speak of all this, feel feelings, listen to one another and not dash out of the room is a source of wonder to them all. The story is out; it no longer needs to be hidden and there is now less of a barrier in dealing with the facts and fantasies of father's advanced illness. In addition, this airing may be the opportunity for other family members to take responsibility for their own alcoholism or other difficulties—there have been many instances of the family meeting being the catalyst for change in individuals within the family.

Some family secrets are harder to let go of than others but this letting go is no less liberating and life-changing. There was a family meeting around the bedside of a middle-aged woman who was dying of breast cancer. Her husband was by her side and had been extremely attentive and almost over-solicitous during her few days in the hospice Inn; her daughter sat at the end of the bed with her husband and their infant daughter. There was a stiffness and superficiality at the beginning of the meeting that was impenetrable. Mother lay with her eyes closed, saying she had no worries nor did she have much to say about or to her husband and daughter. Father held his wife's hand, rhapsodizing about her and their marriage and how heartbreaking her illness had been for him. The daughter was initially quiet and said few things about her mother, but suddenly stood up and delivered one of the most unexpected and heart-rending stories I have heard. She said that she had been immersed in an incestuous relationship with her father for ten years and talked of the pain, shame, and nightmares of her childhood, from which she was only now emerging with the help of both a therapist and a loving husband. Her father made several interjections of denial but her mother listened with eyes open, and it was to her mother she was talking. This dialogue continued for several days before she died; bit by bit the daughter forgave her mother's lifelong closed eyes as they struggled with their new intimacy. Father remained denial-coated and disconnected.

Even when relationships have been rich and deep and family secrets nonexistent, it is extremely difficult for children to voice their fears and their worries and speak of the dark, soulful nightmare unearthed when they realize that even dad can die. He is no longer in front of them running interference against death. That this man will no longer be available with a word of advice or support or simply as their loving witness is painful and unfathomable. But with encouragement the children can speak and weep and hug and thank. It is not enough for them to say that dad knows how they feel, that they have no need to say the words. He probably does know, but we never tire of hearing words of love, especially at this stage of the journey. Saying words of love and thanks allows us to let go with the knowledge that everything that needs saying has been said.

The family meeting is often an opportunity for family members to mourn other losses. For example, a daughter-in-law may grieve the death of her own father as she speaks about her father-in-law, saying that her father also died of cancer and that it was a long nightmare with nothing of any importance said by anyone, and that she wished that her family had been given the opportunity to sit down together like this and listen to one another. I would then usually ask her what she would say to him if he were in the room with us now. Almost invariably she would speak words that she had never been able to say before, and all of us witnesses would be so moved. I used to think that it was inappropriate to tell a story of this nature, one that is not directly related to the one who is dying, but I have found over the years that such a story is in fact proper and healing for all, and may be the prelude to a daughter-in-law being able to thank her father-in-law in a deeper way for being a wonderful father to her as well as grandfather to her children. Occurrences like this, which are not at all uncommon, have often made me wonder who the family meeting is *really* for! Often the dying person has let go of most of his burdens, and it is the rest of us who need this opportunity to speak.

Feelings are the connective tissue that binds us together, and the failure to express them ensures that there will be unfinished business within the family at the time of death, with some concomitant sense of disconnectedness and loneliness. It also makes it extremely likely that future deaths in the family will be handled with the same vow of silence. Skeletons in the family closet, such as suicide, alcoholism, or any hidden disaster about which the family has never shared soul-to-soul feelings and imaginings, are the source of generational pain. Even if the dying person himself will not let go of his silence, the family may be encouraged to talk and connect, thus breaking the chains that bind them to the past and isolate them from each other.

Reframing Family Stories

Reframing stories of awful pain and neglect unglues them from
the wall of the soul, allowing them to be relinquished. For the
betrayed or abused wife, it might be helpful to imagine a different
way of recalling her married life and of saying good-bye to her
husband. Knowing something of their story, I might suggest she
consider the following version in talking to him, keeping what is
useful and discarding the rest:

> *You know, Jim, we were so young when we married and were both
> trying to escape from difficult families. It was never easy for us. We
> had learned nothing helpful about living together from our parents
> and were so inexperienced in almost everything but sex. Yet there
> were some good times, and the children were a blessing. Later,
> there were many years of terrible pain for me when you were abusive,
> had affairs, and drank too much, and for my own self-esteem I
> should have left. I didn't, and here we are, and since your cancer
> was diagnosed we have been closer, even if it was forced on us. I have
> felt so sad and helpless about your fears and your pain, and feel
> apprehensive for you and for me now that your time is short. Thank
> you for being the father of our children. I wish you well on your
> journey and would like to give you a blessing and also receive one
> from you if you feel able.*

Heroic? Impossible? Untrue? Heroic, yes, for this is a difficult if
simple act of doing what needs to be done, and that is the essence
of heroism. The heroic is not a death-defying or death-denying act
but a simple affirmation of life and recognition of the soul or life
force of the other. Impossible? No. I have seen it done many times
with a generosity that is breathtaking. All judgment and
recrimination are left behind because healing and letting go will
not happen otherwise. Untrue? This is a truthful version in the
present moment, one that is no less true than any other version of
their story and infinitely more helpful.

For the neglected son or daughter, there might be another
script:

> *Dad, it is so painful for me to see you this way, and I don't know
> what to say. We never seem to have spent much time together, and I
> feel that I hardly even know you. Years ago, when you were drinking
> and away from home a great deal, it was awful for me. I would fear
> your coming home drunk and enraged, and I was in agony about*

the fights you and mom would have, but I missed you when you were gone and had so many dreams about how it could have been different. I know your childhood wasn't easy and that you were beaten by your dad, and I hated grandpa. You and I missed out on one another. You never got to know me nor I you, and that is really sad. And now you are not going to be with us much longer, and that feels very scary. I just want to put my arms around you and give you a blessing, and I need your blessing if you will give it.

One of the main benefits of such an encounter is that the awful cycle of pain and unfinished business, which is usually repeated generation after generation, is broken by the child who will speak to his or her father in this way. When they do get together despite their misgivings, they are often amazed at what they hear from one another, each having imagined that he or she is the only one to feel fear and loneliness and all manner of terrors for the future.

CHILDREN AND THE FAMILY MEETING

Children belong in the family meeting, and they need to be included in every phase of dying rather than protected from the pain of having to say good-bye.

Bertha was one of those enchanting grandmothers, a delightful companion for her grandchildren. An artist, Bertha had initiated her six-year-old granddaughter Mary into the magic of drawing and painting; her room next to the kitchen was festooned with many colorful images. As she became more and more disabled by advanced heart disease, Bertha seldom left her room, and Mary spent hours each day in her presence. The four-year-old grandson, John, was a little more distant and uneasy, especially toward the end, but when she was in bed he used to race into Bertha's room several times each day blowing kisses on the run. John's ritual reminded me of the custom many children have of holding their breath when passing a cemetery—a suspended animation in the company of death!

Bertha's daughter, Nora, was her warm and loving caregiver. On the day she died, Bertha arose and had a cup of tea with Nora in the kitchen and then went back to bed. An hour or so later when Nora looked in, Bertha was dead. Nora called Kathy, the hospice nurse, and when she arrived, Nora and her husband Bill were talking about calling the funeral home and having Bertha's body removed before the children returned from day camp. With Kathy's encouragement they decided to wait, and Bill went to the camp to fetch the children. Mary came directly into the room and stared at her grandmother's body. After a few moments, Mary proclaimed that her grandmother looked like Snow White, and then ran off to her room to get her book in order to show Kathy the picture. They agreed that she was very white, but unlike Snow White grandma would not wake up again, even with a kiss. "In any case," Mary said, "grandma doesn't need her body any more because she is not going swimming." That was that. A little while later Mary remarked to Kathy and Nora that grandma looked like her turtle who had died, and they agreed, because she did. John, who had been playing with a balloon in the kitchen, bounced it into Bertha's room. The balloon landed on her bed. "Hit it, grandma!" John cried, and when after a few seconds there was no response, he said, "She's dead!" And with that John took his balloon and went off to play.

Bertha was to be cremated, and Nora was uncertain how to tell Mary, so she and Kathy were fumbling for words when Mary came to their rescue: "Oh, you mean she is going to be melted! Good. Then, we can put her ashes down by the tree where we used to draw and paint." Children are in touch with their natural wisdom; it is often the terrors of adults that make death so frightening.

Though it seems to run quite contrary to the natural order of things, adult children often die before their parents, and sometimes even before their grandparents. When this happens, there is a natural wish to try and protect the older generations from the experience of consciously letting go and grieving for their child or grandchild.

Ann, a woman in her fifties who had been diagnosed with advanced cancer, told me about the death of her mother a few months earlier. Her mother had been in fragile health for a number of years but was still living on her own when she contracted pneumonia and died in a matter of days. Ann, who had been diagnosed about a year before her mother's death, had agonized for some time over whether or not to tell her mother. Her sister was strongly opposed, saying that the news would kill her, and so for three or four months Ann went along with the pretense that all was well. Eventually she decided that she needed to speak to her mother, and so she arranged to stay with her for the weekend. That weekend turned out to be the most intimate few days of their lives. There were many tears and much holding and giving comfort to one another; neither would have had it any other way.

When it is a younger child who is dying, there is often great reluctance to admit the fact on the part of both parents and medical and nursing staff. This denial is frequently reinforced by the continuation of futile tests and procedures right up to the end, so that there is less time to pause and absorb the pain of grief.

Quite early in the life of the hospice I was asked to see 17-year-old Marie who was in the intensive care unit, where she had been admitted on account of a serious infection attendant to far-advanced leukemia. I was told that Marie seemed very depressed. In assessing the situation, what I found instead was that everyone who had anything to do with her was depressed; now, for the first time in her three years of laboring with leukemia, Marie herself was obviously frightened, but throughout her long illness it was she who had been bolstering everyone else.

Marie was the oldest of six siblings, and her local family included her loving and supportive parents together with her maternal grandmother. In addition, she had spent so much time in hospital during the previous three years that her physician and several nurses had also become family. All were grieving, especially now that Marie was no longer able to hold them together with her radiant optimism.

When I first saw her, weak as she was—and she died three weeks later—Marie's sweet charm and fragility almost overwhelmed me. I had an urgent desire to snatch her out of that place and tell her that everything would be all right; after all, how could one so young be in such a dire condition with nothing to be done? But the reality of Marie's impending death was right there, and I realized how difficult it must be for both family and treatment team to let her go. Marie said that the recent chemotherapy had been more than usually unbearable because of the side effects, and that she wanted no more. She spoke of how difficult it was to tell both her family and her physician, and how hard it seemed for them to simply listen without trying to persuade her to do something else.

Perhaps it was the second time I visited that I asked if she would draw a picture of herself and what she imagined was happening to her. Marie drew a monochromatic, chaotic, and breathtakingly sad picture that was unrecognizable as a person. Even Marie was surprised by the portrayal which indicated that, beneath her self-composed exterior, she knew that her body was breaking apart.

The family meeting was poignant and painful but liberating for all, with her parents and siblings giving Marie permission to let go and thanking her for all that she had been in their lives. One of the nurses came to the meeting, but the physician and the other nurses stayed away, despite my urgings. Marie and her family were able to ask that she be transferred out of intensive care into the hospice Inn, where they stayed with her until she died.

Another experience involved the dying of a very young child. I had arranged to meet the five-year-old Fionna and her parents at their home. I arrived there one morning to find the mother, Ilana, cradling the comatose Fionna with one arm while with the other she held her three-month-old baby which she was breast-feeding. Her surgical-resident husband, Brian, was hovering close by. It was a touching scene of great beauty. Ilana told me that Fionna had a brain tumor which had been diagnosed nearly a year earlier. All treatment had been ineffective, and Fionna had become increasingly unresponsive during the past couple of weeks to the extent that she was now no longer rousable. Ilana described the heartbreaks of the past year, but also said that Fionna had taught her to be patient, accepting, and more loving, and that despite the awfulness of the situation, their time together was a precious gift that Ilana would not have traded even if given the chance. Brian was a great comfort during the ordeal despite the fact that he was unable to get much time off from the residency program because he was not, in the university's words, the "primary" caregiver! Fionna died at home a few days after my visit. Ilana and Brian both spoke of how heartbreaking it was to watch helplessly, especially in the early days of the illness when there was so much medical intervention and Fionna was so bewildered, but they also said that they would do it all over again. While they would have wanted Fionna to have lived a healthy life, they both felt so blessed by her brief presence with them and realized that she had taught them so much about suffering, holding on, and acceptance.

DEMENTIA AND COMA

I have guided many family meetings when the dying person was unintelligible or unresponsive, sometimes in coma. Coma is no barrier to having the family meet together with their loved one in order to talk and witness. While most of those afflicted by dementia as a result of Alzheimer's disease, major strokes, or injury seem to be unable to comprehend or communicate in ways that are familiar to us, we cannot be sure that they are not aware.

Stan was in his mid-seventies and had been admitted to a general hospital from a nursing home after developing pneumonia. He had been treated with intravenous antibiotics for several days but failed to rebound as he had on two other occasions in the past six months. He had started to become confused about ten years earlier, a year or two after retirement, but his wife of 40 years had taken wonderful care of him until her death five years ago. His only daughter, Frances, had looked after him for more than a year, but his increasing confusion and unsafe behavior led to her finding a nursing home that would take good care of him. Frances' husband had died when their three children were quite small, and Frances had raised them on her own, aided by her parents. Stan had been both father and grandfather to the three children, and they were all distraught when he had to enter the nursing home. Because there was no medical directive, the family had no specific instructions from Stan as to how he would want to be cared for if he lost the capacity to make his own decisions, so the burden of decision-making fell on Frances. On the previous two occasions of pneumonia, she had permitted hospital admission and treatment because that seemed to be expected by the nursing home physician, but on this occasion she decided that further treatment would have no effect on the quality of her father's life, and so she asked that treatment be stopped and that Stan be moved to the hospice Inn.

We had a family meeting that included Frances, her three sons, their wives, and two infant great-grandchildren. Stan seemed unresponsive, but I am not at all sure that he did not hear and sense what was going on. This gathering was an opportunity for these loving people to mourn what they never had mourned. Frances talked about the life and death of her loving husband, who had died of a heart attack when he was 32. She talked about how supportive his parents had been, and how she was devastated by their deaths in the past five years. She talked of her mother and father in their prime, and how much fun they were, and how mother's death had been another drastic blow to them all. And she talked of dad, and how she was the apple of his eye and he of hers, and how the decline in his awareness was another slow death for her. Frances' sons were equally passionate in their mourning of all the losses in their lives, recognizing the blessings they had received, particularly from their mother and their grandfather.

They all blessed Stan, with water, tears, and loving words. Did he hear? A natural but quite irrelevant question. He was blessed, and his presence allowed grieving that was long overdue. He was a silent witness to their grief—grief for him and for all the others who had blessed their lives. After that gathering I had no doubt whatsoever that the presence of the silent witness always offers the opportunity for soulful connection, and it is of no importance whether or not everyone present understands what is happening.

If there are members of the family who are afflicted by dementia, I still recommend that they be included in the family meeting, unless they happen to be extremely agitated. This is also true for those who are deemed to be developmentally disabled. They need to be included both for their own benefit and for that of the person dying. One of the major worries for a dying mother, for instance, is what will happen to her retarded child after she dies. She needs him there to give him a blessing and hand him over to the care of others; she also needs his blessing, and I have witnessed this happening on a number of occasions.

Some families exacerbate the agitation of the confused person by putting pressure on him to understand or respond in some way; others believe that their relative would become upset and so they try to protect him by excluding him from such meetings. This was the case with the Fahys.

It was Good Friday, and I had arranged to meet the Fahy family in the afternoon. I had been told by one of the daughters that their mother, Annie, was barely conscious and had said little or nothing for some days. Jack, their father, was very confused as a result of Alzheimer's disease, and they had decided that it would be less upsetting if he were out of the house at church instead of being present when the family gathered. I requested that he stay home, but the daughters were not to be persuaded. However, either by accident or design I arrived earlier than expected, and Jack had not yet left, although he had his coat on and was ready to leave in the company of his sister. I convinced the family to let him come upstairs to see Annie, and he sat by her bed holding her hand. The daughters were tearfully amazed that he spoke clearly and coherently to Annie, with complete understanding in that moment that she was dying. They said that he had not spoken in consecutive sentences for several months, and they had no idea that he understood what was happening to Annie.

Jill Regan was admitted to the hospice Inn already in coma, and we expected her to die at any moment. Jill's three daughters, now living in different parts of the country, had been estranged from one another for some time; her husband had left the marriage early in the lives of the children and she had raised them on her own. Jill had been strict and abusive, both physically and emotionally—her daughters had little good to say about their childhood, nor did they have good memories of their relationships with one another. They had all left home as soon as they could, had not attended one another's weddings, and were only in touch at holiday times.

It took the women a couple of days to reach the Inn once they heard of Jill's illness, but they all arrived and stayed with Jill until she died nearly four weeks following her admission. The time Jill gave them together was immensely healing to all of them, and the daughters were even able to soften their feelings toward their mother, whose own childhood had been one of constant giving while at the same time receiving little that was loving from anyone.

Many times I have seen someone in coma whose continuing presence has allowed healing among those in the family who were willing to avail themselves of the opportunity—thus it was with Jill and her daughers, who would otherwise have parted from one another without any resolution of their differences. Other families have attended a comatose family member with great discomfort, saying only that they wished he would soon be out of his misery. Those who think in this way are quite oblivious to the fact that it is their own discomfort and not that of the dying person that they are experiencing.

Family meetings are also of great importance when one of the family is resident in a nursing home, as is often the case if he has dementia or Alzheimer's disease. There is obviously no need to wait until the family member is dying or has reasonably clear thinking in order to gather together in the nursing home. The time for the meeting is always now.

SUDDEN DEATH

Sudden death is a great shock and tragedy for most families, and they are often in even greater need of a family meeting than those who have had more warning of death. I have had family meetings in emergency rooms and other places within the hospital, and I have also met on more than one occasion with the family at home on the day following an unexpected death. In these instances the meeting has proceeded along lines fairly similar to those which would have been followed had the now-deceased person been present. Someone in the family tells the story about what happened to father, and each recounts how the news was for them. I ask what they imagine would have been his worries for them, and they tell stories of their relationship with him together with any real or imagined unfinished business. I often ask how they imagine he would have responded to what they said had he been with us, evoking his presence to help them say good-bye and give him a blessing.

Most families do not say good-bye to the one who dies suddenly; because the soul, together with the feelings that are a part of it, is timeless, there may never be resolution without a good-bye. As there is no time in this dimension, time does not heal this ache, which stems from words unsaid and blessings ungiven, so there needs to be a ritual like the family meeting to make resolution possible. Individual therapy is a less effective method of letting go than a ritual involving the whole family as witnesses and storytellers.

REFLECTIONS ON AIDS

AIDS is a particularly devastating personal and social scourge of our times. For families affected by AIDS, the family meeting is an urgent part of healing relationships. Those whose AIDS has resulted from intravenous drug use may have children who are infected, and may have exhausted all family connections so that few if any family members are willing to assemble. In the gay community, friends and lovers are often very attentive and supportive, but their numbers may have been decimated by earlier AIDS deaths. In addition, a partner may view the death of his lover as a fearful prelude to or rehearsal for his own death in the not-so-distant future.

It may be difficult to ask biological family to gather because of unresolved or unspoken differences and disappointments related to lifestyle, but I have witnessed many miracles of healing when blame and other judgments are discarded. I remember a young man, Paul, who had been living in New York City. His lover contracted AIDS, and Paul cared for him until he died. Paul had always kept in touch with his sister, Mary, but had not seen his parents for several years because of the bitter rage of his ex-Marine father over his lifestyle. When Paul's AIDS became active and debilitating a few months after the death of his lover, Mary negotiated for his return home, and Paul agreed to the arrangement with much fear and trembling. He was home for four months before he died, during which time he spent two weeks in an acute care hospital. Following that hospital stay, Paul decided that he wanted no further active treatment.

I met the family at home just after the hospital stay, and while there had been no active warfare between Paul and his father during his first weeks home, peace had not been declared. The family meeting was exactly what they needed. In addition to mother and father, Mary and her husband were present, and it was as if these loving people had gathered to witness this reconciliation and embrace between father and son, one that was so very moving for all of us. It also felt to me as if Paul's father represented the judgmental and uncaring world that was finally opening its arms in love and receiving all of its wounded sons, welcoming them home.

BLESSINGS

It took several years of working in the hospice before I really understood blessings and became comfortable enough to initiate them. I had been brought up in the Catholic Church and had been immersed in Latin, beautiful music, gold vestments, incense, and intricate rituals, all of which inspired great awe and wonder. And there were blessings for every occasion—blessings at mass and through the sacraments, blessings with relics of the saints, blessings before and after meals. All were associated for me with the practice of this religion and seemed to be really effective only if performed by priests. In fact, at that time it was believed that *only* priests could bless the dying and perform this final sacrament that might be crucial to their eternal life. It was almost as if the attainment of heaven depended on the priest not being detained somewhere else.

In hospice work it also seemed as though blessings belonged to the realm of chaplains. But at the hospice Inn we were fortunate to have as chaplain, Sister Jean, whose whole life was a blessing to those who knew her. It was she who encouraged me and others on the staff to give our own blessings. Eventually, after much foot dragging and fear that I would be thought of as a fool or one who was intruding into matters that did not concern him, I introduced blessings at the end of each family meeting. Most often I use water, although one man asked to be blessed with his life-long friend, whiskey. Or a blessing ceremony can take place in which each family member lights a candle and speaks words of love and dedication.

I begin this final stage of the family meeting by asking the dying person if I might give him a blessing. I have never been refused in my request. Each blessing is unique, based on what I feel as a result of being present, listening to all the stories, witnessing the whole family, and being moved in a variety of ways. I might bless a father's ears that have listened so well, or his big heart, or his fertile mind. I might bless his feet that have carried him so far, and the afflicted area of his body that it may become more peaceful. Often I have asked his blessing in return, especially during times of pain and stress such as when I was leaving the hospice, which was a time of dying for me. The blessings I received were so refreshing. I know they were willingly and lovingly given, and were a chance for the dying person to give as well as receive.

Having initiated the blessing ceremony, I then invite others in the family to follow suit. I have witnessed many miracles of healing, forgiveness, and love in this ritual. For those who have had difficulty with words, this is their most touching statement. For those who had been able to speak, the blessing is like a seal on their love, an expiratory sigh that signifies that all possible has been said and done, and it is now time to let go.

Obviously some family meetings never really get started or become painfully bogged down. But in the great majority of gatherings the family members speak together and exchange blessings, and almost all is said and done in a very short time. The stories told are important, but the effect of the meeting goes far beyond the words said. It is as if the intention and willingness to be present and as open and truthful as possible about what lies within the soul makes it all happen, whether words are spoken or not. Families will so often remark that there was a greater sense of intimacy in those few moments than in decades of living together. This is true knowing: the simple, nonjudgmental witnessing of the light and dark of another soul. This is pure connectedness.

CHAPTER 8

Living and the Family

The most important discovery I made in almost two decades of work in a hospice was that family healing and intimacy of a quality that may never have been experienced before is often possible around the time of death. There is nothing like the real or imagined threat of death to focus attention on our values and the superficiality of our exaggerated disputes and differences. There is an urgency about this time; it is a now or never opportunity to speak from the heart.

The problem for most of us is that it has not been easy to say what we need to say in our family, and to say it without interruptions or judgments. We imagine that anything of a painful nature that we might say will cause feelings to be hurt irreparably. In this kind of scenario the family cocoon is not permeable; tears and feelings of all sorts are not allowed to mix with the family dynamics and catalyze healing, with the residue flowing out so that the family within is softened and nurtured. When the cocoon is impermeable and not even permitted to allow in the knowledge of the inevitability of death, it is difficult to say loving things and speak of grief for fear of breaking down. If that were to happen we imagine that chaos would ensue, since we have no experience that would lead us to think that this could be a time of breakthrough rather than breakdown. Consequently, even at this most poignant time, many will not take the opportunity to speak, to touch and be touched, for a variety of fear-based reasons.

From the outset of my work at the hospice we offered an atmosphere of caring for those who were dying. The hospice provided competent and loving staff who had the time and dedication to witness and guide the whole family; the awful pressures and stresses of the general hospital environment that are a part of the war on disease were left behind. But in the early days of our hospice work, family dynamics seemed to be more or less off limits unless we were invited in. And such an invitation would be forthcoming only from those families who appeared to have least need of us—those with permeable webs who were open to outsiders, welcoming them as witnesses and supporters in their ordeal.

Once in a while we would be invited in to the family when they were in some kind of uproar, with the idea that we would settle them back into their pre-explosive mode of living so that there would be the illusion of peace and quiet for the one who was dying. The majority of families, though, did not want to gather with hospice staff. They claimed that they did not need to meet because they had said all they needed to say to one another individually; sometimes there were long-standing feuds and furies among the members that caused them to refuse to come together.

After a few years, when we realized that there was great potential for healing as a result of these gatherings, we began to ask all families to meet. Once we were clear about the importance of the meetings, we had much less difficulty in persuading most families to gather. Arranging the meeting was the responsibility of the nurse who was assigned to the family. The nurse would usually say that the medical director likes to meet the whole family, and that was enough of an explanation for most. However, there was great resistance from some families. Often a daughter would act as spokesperson, responding to the nurse's request for a family meeting in some very guarded way such as this:

> ... *Yes, but what is he going to say? Is this going to be upsetting? Dad does not even know that he has cancer and certainly does not know that he is dying, and I do not want him to know. You want me to invite my brother? He hasn't been around for years, ever since he and dad had a big fight when they were both drinking. And in any case we don't get along. And grandma? She is much too old, and we have tried to protect her from the fact that her son is dying. And then you ask me to bring the kids! Ridiculous. There is no need for them to be exposed to all of this. It is upsetting to dad, and it is upsetting to them, and it would cause dad to start asking all sorts of questions, and I don't want that. No, I will not bring the children. Furthermore, is the doctor going to answer our questions, because all I have had so far is evasions and unanswered calls?*

This is a not uncommon type of response from a daughter who

has always tried to rescue and protect everyone in a family of great unhappiness and turmoil, and it is only a skillful and well-trusted nurse who can persuade a family like this to meet. In the early hospice days this kind of family would terrify me, and I was usually glad when they refused to come together. But as I became more clear about the intention of the gathering, understanding that I did not have to rescue them nor give guarantees about what would occur in the meeting, it became much easier for me, and I was then able to be much more effective, even with the most resistant families. There were always some families with whom I felt quite helpless as a guide; these families were a great test of my urge to rescue and so have the illusion of being effective. For all families, the intention was not to judge or attempt to explain an unhappy past but to get them to listen to one another's stories and allow themselves to let go of their resentments, disappointments, and betrayals. This may sound like an impossible task, yet around the time of death it usually becomes apparent, even to the most angry and wounded of sons or daughters, that now is the last chance to connect with their father and forgive him for the pain he has caused, thank him for giving them life, and both give and receive a blessing. The daughter may actually be thinking that she wants to give him a piece of her mind and rage at him for all his misdeeds, but as guide I would gently tell her that while this is very understandable, it is unskillful and would get them nowhere. There *are* no good answers, so dad would be quite unable to say why he abused her or drank too much. I would encourage her to tell herself that she *is* lovable and deserved much better, and that both she and her father lost out by having a relationship that brought pain rather than love and healing. I would remind her that the catharsis of explosive rage would last only a short while, that she needs to let go of the past in order to be free, and that this is the perfect time to do it. It is a miracle how many daughters do summon this courage, who *will* give thanks and bless. This is, of course, what the wounded soul-child within them has always wanted.

In the exercise in Chapter 5 when we imagined our own death, we invited the family to our home some days before we died. We had a taste of the impact of that gathering when we imagined speaking to all the family members in turn while the others witnessed. In this exercise we will actually speak out loud, before witnesses, to each one in the family.

Hospice staff who had themselves participated in a workshop, who had visualized their own family meeting and been amazed by the possibilities for their own healing, were the best advocates in encouraging the families of their patients to meet. Other hospice staff were more guarded and protective of both themselves and their patients, and they would sometimes scare off some family members from participating without necessarily being aware of what they were doing. But usually, with very few exceptions, at least some of the patient's family would agree to meet, and often as many as 30 people would gather.

For most people, the notion of family is restricted to close relatives, and they are the only ones invited to the family meeting. The idea of inviting "outsiders" to tell their stories and be as witnesses in this intimate and vulnerable gathering is almost unthinkable. Yet many have a much broader view of family and may wish to invite friends and colleagues to this gathering, most of whom would be eager to come and honored to have been asked. In this exercise, you have the opportunity to take this all-embracing view of family and imagine who you would ask to attend.

The exercise that follows is an opportunity for you to participate in a rehearsal for your own family meeting. It is similar to the experience of visualizing your dying when you gathered your family together in your room, only this time you are actually going to speak to each person one by one. In the workshop setting the group again breaks up into triads. Each configuration of the triad lasts 30 minutes; again there is a storyteller, a witness, and a guide. If you are working alone with this text you may very usefully rehearse the family meeting by requesting a friend to act as witness, and the roles could be reversed after half an hour if you wished. It becomes a little easier to imagine conducting a family meeting once you have practiced. The ultimate hope is that you will have a "real" family meeting, gathering your family and some friends together, long before you die, because the gift of this gathering is the guidance and insights it offers for everyday living.

VISUALIZATION: A FAMILY MEETING

I suggest that the storyteller reclines on the floor or in a bed propped up with pillows. Before starting in the role of storyteller, take a brief moment to think about who you will ask to the gathering; as before, you can invite anyone you like, dead or still living. Or you might simply let the gathering unfold on its own, seeing who arrives in your consciousness. The witness will stand in as the family members. As storyteller you will simply say "Now, you are my mother," and then begin to speak to the witness who in that moment is mother. When you have finished, you introduce the next person "Now, you are my six-year-old child, Mary." After approximately 20 minutes the guide tells you that you have a couple of minutes more before the meeting closes. As in the earlier sessions, a further five minutes are spent with each one of the triad describing the experience of each role.

Throughout the family meeting the witness does not respond but simply absorbs what is said. If there seems to be some hesitation, or gaps in the storyteller's delivery, the guide may give the occasional nudge, such as "Is there anything more you would like to say to your father?" But the guide's input is minimal; most of the time, as storyteller you will be your own guide.

When you have finished speaking to all the family, I suggest that five minutes or so be spent in the exchange of blessings. You will bless the witness as the manifestation of all the family, and then the witness will bless you, the storyteller, on behalf of the family. Most of us are unfamiliar or feel awkward about giving blessings, but it is very easy. Simply have a little water in a cup by your side, and be spontaneous. Perhaps you might touch with water the hands that have held all in the family with great tenderness, and the heart that has loved, and the mind that has been so busy. Just let it come to you, and realize the power of this act of acknowledging the soul or vital force of another.

In the workshop setting, we suggest a five- or ten-minute pause in silence between each storytelling. If you are doing this visualization at home using a friend as witness, it is important to have this pause before changing roles.

You may ask what can possibly be accomplished in this very brief time? Perhaps you have been in therapy for years and have spent many hours struggling over your relationship with your father, or a child, or your partner. What can you possibly say in just a few minutes about something that has taken so long to journey through and is still unfinished? The startling truth is that a few minutes is enough time if a few minutes is all we have. And if we live our lives in the present moment, as if this is the only time we have, then this moment is always enough for the miracle of healing to unfold.

Speaking to the Living

One of the difficulties most of us have in speaking to our relatives is that we frequently fail to complete our stories, or we may not even begin them in the first place. If as children we are continuously corrected, if the expression of our experiences and feelings is reframed by parents and older siblings time and time again, by adulthood there is often the sense that family members will never really understand. So we give up trying to communicate, seeking others to be our witnesses.

Often there is a formidable barrier between father and son that is never breached, generation after generation. Men may form an intimate connection through business interests, or outdoor activities like fishing and hunting, but although sports events may lead to the exchange of a kind of convivial warmth, communication about the eddies and turbulence of the soul seems to be beyond most of them. I have witnessed many a son rushing from the room when it is his moment to speak to his dying father, and many others who sit dumbstruck, choking back tears and gasping for breath. When a father is speaking of his son, it is usually to list his accomplishments and to say how proud he is of "my boy." There are reminiscences of reading to him as a child, teaching him to ride a bike, watching innumerable sports events in which he participated, graduation, marriage, children, fatherhood—all expressions of his passion and desire to connect and love. But it is often so difficult to speak directly of that love, and it is that absence of direct expression that seems to be at the core of loneliness in so many men.

Many years ago I saw a play—*Philadelphia Here I Come*, by Irishman Brian Friel—about a boy in Ireland who, while growing up, was always trying to attract his father's attention, but dad was always too busy, barricaded behind a newspaper. As the play continued I perceived the newspaper becoming thicker and thicker until it was like stone, and dad would not have been able to put it down even if he wished to. When the boy was a young man ready to strike out on his own, he went to his father and said: "Well dad, I'm off to Philadelphia." "Are you, son?" was dad's reply, now quite unable to shed his newspaper armor. "Well, good luck then." And that was that. This heartbreaking tragedy, so well expressed, is a universal expression of the father who is aching to put down his barriers and hug his son but is so disconnected from the experience of his heart that he does not know how to do so. And there sits a son who is desperate to be held and loved by his dad.

Many men will claim that they have no need of a family meeting because father and son both know how the other feels. The truth is, however, that most of us do not even know how we ourselves feel until we put these feelings into words, and so we *do* need to voice them, face to face. The well-being of our heart and soul depends on it. Perhaps our grandfather never spoke loving words to our father, repeating a pattern established many generations earlier. We need to break this dreadful cycle if we are not to hand it on.

There are fewer barriers to the expression of feelings between most mothers and daughters. They are more in touch with the soul, with all its darkness as well as its light. Since we are unable to see or x-ray the soul, it is difficult to define. Yet, soul is the vital force that magnifies us into something that is far beyond a thinking machine. Soul is essentially feminine, having to do with the vicissitudes of everyday life, with ever-changing feelings and with the delights and heartbreaks of relationships. Women are usually more in touch with this feminine essence, although there are many men in whom it is well expressed. Perhaps amongst other things it is the earthiness and regularity of menstruation that remind women of their role in the continuity and connectedness of the human species; the feminine is also in touch with the vitality of love that is the necessary fuel of the soul. Women know that their protective gossamer—the relationship they have with themselves—needs to be permeable if the blood and the tears are to flow out and they are to be renewed for another cycle. The masculine or spiritual is more otherworldly and detached, seeking purpose and meaning. We need both the feminine and the masculine if we are to be in healing relationships with ourselves and others.

So it is that many mothers and daughters are more in touch with their soulful feelings than most fathers and sons, and a daughter is often able to speak and weep and laugh and tell stories more easily than her brother. Some young children are more open and clear in the expression of their feelings than their elders, perhaps because they are in closer touch with soul and have not yet erected barriers to hide it. It is important that they have the opportunity to participate in the family meeting. Children are often partly or completely excluded from participation in the dying of a close relative, and they will frequently remember the exclusion. A child will remember that she was unable to say good-bye to her grandmother, and this will remain with her into adulthood, manifesting as a sense of something unsatisfactory and unfinished. Her parents' failure to allow participation in dying will probably be repeated by that child when she has her own children, unless she becomes fully conscious of the omission.

The family meeting visualization will make you aware of how difficult it will be to say good-bye to your own children—of any age, but especially very young ones because you will feel they still need you. Of course they want you to be around forever, but what they really *need* is to be loved. When you are dying it is a heartbreakingly loving act to speak to them directly, telling them that you will not be with them for very much longer, and that you do not want to die and leave them but that is the way it has to be. You can tell them that you are a part of them, and that part of you with all your love will always be with them, even though you may not see one another again. You can tell them that the blessing that you are about to give them will always be a part of your connection together. At this point you might give them a blessing in much the same manner that you and the witness exchanged blessings in the family meeting, in which you have just participated. Once again, it is not the actual words that are important because they may not be fully heard or understood. What is important is the fact that you express your love to your children and you do not leave them without saying good-bye.

Speaking to the Dead

In the exercise you may have spoken to a relative or a friend who died years ago, and this probably felt very real. If soul is the vital energy of our oneness, and we have had the experience of connectedness or oneness or relationship with another soul, then they and we are a part of a larger whole. We are one, and so we can talk to them whether they appear to be present or not.

Many people torment themselves for many years after the death of a parent, continuously berating themselves thinking: "If only I had been able to speak to my mom and tell her that I loved her. I wonder if she knew, because all she seemed to experience from me was trouble, and she will never know how much I have missed her." Most of those who missed this opportunity fail to realize that they can speak to her right now by asking a friend to sit in for her as witness, and then allow themselves to speak.

ON MEETING WITH OUR OWN FAMILY

Having imagined a meeting with your family when you are dying, what do you consider to be the barriers to having your own family meeting right now? How might that help you to live in a more vital and open way with one another? The idea of a family meeting to discuss feelings is, to most of us, almost unthinkable. We believe that the idea would be rejected by most of the family, or that dad would ask if we had gone mad or thought that someone was dying. And there would be the burning question of who would guide the gathering, or dare to be referee? If we were to give the idea even more thought, we would come to the conclusion that certain family members would not speak, and we would be in a cold sweat at the thought of some of the darker family secrets emerging into the light of day. Buried years or even generations ago, we might clearly imagine an awful scene upon their disinterment. No wonder the thought is daunting in the extreme and usually aborted as soon as it is conceived! Very little energy is given to the possibility of secrets being released and let go of, and of love being expressed and blessings given as never before!

The Talking Stick is an impeccable guide, and if we can still our fears and anxieties, all we need to do is make the occasion, which is always already there, maybe when the family is assembled at holiday time or a birthday, or at any other time. We would deeply enhance the family well-being if we had an annual family meeting, at which time the Talking Stick was passed. We should invite as much of the extended family as it is possible, because our ability to judge who should and who should not be present is flawed at best. In my experience, the one predicted to be silent frequently has much to say; it is often the daughter-in-law who is hardly considered to be part of the family who produces the story that moves and touches all. Her story may open up the family, allowing the members to say to one another what they could not have said without the courageous modeling of this "outsider" and catalyst for healing.

FAMILY MEETINGS AND FAMILY MEDICINE

Family meetings are tribal gatherings at which the pulse of the family is taken. The family practitioner is in the best possible position to encourage and suggest family meetings in the first place, since it is he or she who is most likely to be aware that healthy relationships within the family are essential for healing and relationship-centered care. The presence of this trusted guide would be a powerful initiation of these healing events. In the family medicine program at Albany Medical College where I currently work, we are encouraging more and more family meetings, and not simply at times when a member is dying. For those physicians who believe that the result will always be peace, harmony, and the exchange of blessings, disappointment is in store, but something is always learned.

I remember once being asked by two family-practice residents and the social worker to facilitate a family meeting in which the whole family was allegedly very willing to participate. This sounded like a wonderful opportunity for the caregivers as well as the family, so we arranged the meeting. The family consisted of an aged and ailing mother in her late seventies, five sons, one daughter, and four spouses. With the exception of the mother, all the family members were very large physically. More striking, though, was the tenor of disturbance and unrest I felt as soon as I joined the gathering. I have seldom, if ever, experienced so much violence in one room. There was no way that anything other than the dark side of the soul would be allowed to emerge from that vulnerable group, who had learned very early how to be fighting mad. And at that they were experts. We discovered that the only reason they had agreed to meet was to present mother with a united front in their determination that she should go to a nursing home, because none of them was willing or able to take her home. They wanted my stamp of approval for that decision, and nothing else. In spite of their obvious, omnipresent rage and fear of mother, a few family vignettes emerged in their less-guarded moments. Their father had died 20 years before and had been a role model for their alcoholism and violence. Mother was not far behind as a teacher. All of the children were alcoholics, and the four spouses present were obviously terrified of verbally exposing any of their own personal pain and discomfort, which was quite palpable. During the gathering, which probably lasted about 40 minutes, although it seemed like a timeless nightmare, three of the sons left the room at different times, either just after they had said something violent or heard something violent from another. One of the brothers explained his behavior quite bluntly, obviously speaking for them all when he said: "If I didn't leave, I would have to hit someone." One of those times, when I asked why nobody was able to take mom home, I thought that someone might be me. I only realized later what a very provocative question that was for this wounded family.

We ended on a note not much different, I imagine, from boxers after a fight. We shook hands all around and left the ring, with mom more or less resigned that she would go to a nursing home and the children happy that they had accomplished what they had ganged up to do in the face of their powerful mother.

For the family practice residents this was a breathtaking opportunity to witness the context from which their patient, who hitherto had seemed to them like a "mild little old lady," had emerged. But the meeting did not end there. When the residents, the social worker, and I were discussing the experience, one of the residents, inspired by all this family pain, began to talk about the death of his grandfather three years earlier. Grandfather had been his inspiration and advocate throughout his life, especially through his college and medical school years, and they readily expressed their love for one another. Cancer had been grandfather's lot in the last year or so of his life, and his death came rather rapidly in an intensive care unit as the result of complications of chemotherapy. His grandson, wrapped up as he was in exams, was unable to visit him before he died. I asked the resident whether, if his grandfather were here now in this room with us, there was something he would like to say to him. The words the resident spoke were a sensitive and moving mixture of love and thanksgiving, coupled with sadness that he had not been present in those last moments.

Another story of a family meeting that never seemed to go much beyond the stiff and the painful involved 17-year-old Diane, who had been seen in the outpatient clinic because of vague symptoms of weakness, and whose physical examination revealed little other than proteinuria and sadness. The only family event we were told about was the death of her mother some two years earlier. The attending physician thought that a family meeting might shed extra light and so invited Diane's father Robert, and Bob, her 20-year-old brother; the physician also invited a resident as another witness. Diane was monosyllabic, even when speaking of her mother (who had actually died *four* years before, when Diane was 13). When a tear emerged as she spoke of this, Diane's father dived in to the rescue, which I did not divert since Diane seemed unable to move any further. Robert said that his wife Ruth, to whom he had been married for 18 years, developed a headache one day and rapidly became unconscious, dying later in the day from a ruptured brain aneurysm. He said that she had been the light of his life, and that his only meaning in life now was to help the two children survive through college. He felt guilty that he had worked long hours, so that Ruth and he had not enjoyed enough time together. He had no interests outside of work, which he did not like very much, and gave no thought to any new relationship at this time, at least while the children were living at home.

Bob was enrolled in a local college. He lived at home, though he spent most of his time in his room. He would seldom speak to Diane, and like his father he displayed no feelings even when talking of his mother's death, which he described as "devastating." One month prior to our meeting Bob had been in a car crash in which his Jeep was demolished. I could not help but wonder how much that accident had to do with the care-less way in which he was living his life since his mother's death.

117

Apart from the couple of tears from Diane, this family was as distant from their feelings as the earlier described family was filled with rage, and I felt equally helpless.

In discussion after the meeting I expressed my feeling that mother had been the custodian of soul in that family; it was around her that living and loving feelings had swirled. With her death soul had seemed to disappear and the family members had all shut down with a paralysis of feelings, presenting a sense of apathy, the depth of which was heartbreaking to witness. Diane's tears and weakness seemed to have been the only opening offered by this devastated family in four years, and even there, Robert had rushed in to stem the trickle, probably fearful that it would become a flood. Yet we all had a sense that we might be able to help Diane express her grief, and that in doing so she might be able to become alive. Robert seemed like a heart attack waiting to occur, and Bob a time-bomb set to go off. While the family meeting itself did not appear to create any opening, without it we would never have known of the depth of hopelessness and helplessness among the individuals in this family, who had been fairly successful at hiding the impact of their loss from others and from themselves. Having the meeting allowed us to plan a strategy which involved each individual in the family, rather than waiting to respond at some later date to the crises of heart attacks and other explosions.

The family approach to well-being is much more complex than the relatively simple way in which we imagine caretaking someone's state of disease. We believe that a disease is a pathological entity that happens to an individual, something we can treat, eliminate, or quell. However, if we look at the whole family and see what is there before our eyes, we realize that in this "illness" something is happening to everyone. The disease concept does not capture this reality; on the contrary, it ensures that we will attempt to fix and patch but ignore most of what is really happening, just as Robert and his family were ignored in, around, and after the death of his wife. This neglect caused them to hold their breath after mother died, ensuring a living death for all of them. A family approach to a disaster of this kind would have encouraged them to mourn and to breathe.

Every family, especially those in which one of their number is dying, needs to meet together for the purpose of healing the family wounds and taking their leave of one another. As mentioned earlier, this will probably not occur unless caregivers—particularly, but not exclusively, physicians—stress the importance of this meeting, give encouragement, and join in. Physicians without this kind of experience may be anxious about being the guide to such gatherings, and they might be concerned that they will uncover such pain and trauma that they would create a situation that was worse after the gathering than before. However, if the intention of the meeting is clear, all will usually be well. The guide only needs to remember that the goal is to have each person tell his or her story and be heard, and that apportioning blame is pointless and unskillful. The guide is also there to help the family forgive transgressions and to say good-bye. When these guidelines are kept in mind, only an occasional nudge and a tincture of humor are necessary to keep the meeting on its true course.

QUESTIONS AND ANSWERS

If family meetings are to become a part of normal care during times of life-threatening illness, then the health care system will need to become familiar with the goals and intentions of the family meeting, and be prepared to answer questions of scared and skeptical family members. Among the questions commonly asked are the following:

Q. Should all *families be encouraged to have a family meeting when one of their members is dying?*

A. Without any doubt. For its vitality, the soul of the family requires the circulation and nurturing of love that is expressed in words as well as actions. Words *are* important, and this very human way of circulating our sense of connectedness and oneness is essential for heart and soul. In addition, the spirit of the family requires the expression of love to others for its health and well-being. The widespread belief in families that the others "know" how we feel without us having to say it may contain some truth, but most people still wish with all their hearts to hear it in words.

Q. Do all families agree to a family meeting when it is suggested?

In my experience less than 1 percent of families decline in cases where they are given sufficient encouragement. However, the majority of families have considerable fears and apprehensions initially, and would refuse without this support and guidance. Three situations come to mind, all involving sons of widowed mothers who were dying. Two of these men were physicians, and I have always imagined that their chosen specialties offered a clue to their attitudes. One was a dermatologist who had a large practice and little time for each patient. He probably imagined that he needed to go no more than skin deep into his relationships with his patients, and this was certainly the way in his relationship with his mother. However, he made it much more difficult for the rest of his family, particularly his children, to give thanks and say good-bye. The other physician was an angry anesthesiologist who insisted on controlling his mother's pain medication and everything else about her care, and was enraged by the suggestion that the family should gather together and speak. Then he would not be in control, and feelings would emerge. The third man was the oldest son of a rich and powerful family that had never dealt with the feuding and fighting left over from the death of father some ten years earlier. This man vetoed all thoughts of a family meeting. Instead, the family literally stood watch over mother, allowing very little expression intimacy or love.

Q. What do you say to family members who are reluctant to meet that may help them to change their minds?

A. I tell them that the intention of the meeting is simply to express love, give thanks, and end with some sort of blessing. There is no intention to judge. I make clear my recognition that the expression of rage and hurt along with angry questions as to why a parent did this or that is futile and unskillful. There are usually no answers to such questions, and any reply would be experienced as unsatisfactory. I encourage and coax a child to say that a parent's alcoholism or neglect or abuse was painful and created a barrier, but I also urge her to let it go and move on to the expression and reception of love and thanks. This sounds very simple, but it is not at all easy when there has been a lifetime of pain. I stress that this is a perfect opportunity to become free of this anguish, and it really can be done. For all families, I remind them that speaking about their fears and worries removes barriers between them, and that in connecting in this way, many of the concerns are lessened.

Q. Should the patient be a part of the meeting when some in the family express serious reservations?

A. The prospect of being in the room and talking with a dying relative is terrifying for many people, and some families insist that they meet without the patient. In the early days of facilitating these meetings I gave in to these pressures and met with the family alone. On most of those occasions we joined the patient after a while, but not always. After some years I realized that the separation was the result of my own discomfort; I imagined that I would be frightened or incoherent meeting my parents in a similar situation. In recent years I have always met with the whole family, including the patient, because dying affects everyone, and it is even immaterial whether or not the patient is conscious or seems to understand.

Q. What are the ground rules of a family meeting?

A. Only one person speaks at a time, and must be allowed to do so without interruption until finished. The rest of the family act as witnesses. If there is no outside guide, the Talking Stick can be a very effective alternative. I remind the family of the intention of the meeting—to speak in order to become connected, not to judge and to blame. Quite often in a family meeting I will suggest that members change places, at least for a while. For example, a father may be having great difficulty speaking to his son, and if the son is sitting some distance away I will suggest that he change places with the person sitting next to his father.

The meeting continues until everyone has had a chance to speak. Even with very large groups, this does not take as long as may be imagined, since the essentials of what people wish to say at this time can usually be said with a handful of words.

Q. If anger and sadness are expressed, do people leave the meeting feeling very hurt?

A. That is possible, and some will leave the meeting holding on to the hurts and resentments that they brought in. However, at this particular time, when a family member is dying, it is easier to let go than at any other time in life, and most will usually do that. Does the letting go last? Always, if it has been a true letting go, even when the abuse incurred earlier in life has been enormous.

Q. But doesn't it take years of therapy to change attitudes and behavior and to forgive self and others?

A. Years of therapy may or may not work, but in a family meeting a miracle of freedom can occur in a moment. I have witnessed this happen innumerable times. Sometimes it may appear that there has been little or no movement toward healing or a change of attitude among the family members, but I have often heard—even some years later—about the profound effect of the meeting on various individuals. As a result I have learned, with difficulty, not to judge a family meeting as good or bad, even though I feel more at ease when it seems to go smoothly.

Q. What happens when a family member cries uncontrollably or when another storms from the room?

A. Tears are far more common than stormy eruptions. I often encourage the person who is crying to come and sit next to the dying relative, who can give consolation. But there is no necessity to stem the tears. Tears are the healing solution for the family, and there is no need for them to be surreptitiously wiped away or shed alone. The tears of one person may encourage tears in another whose feelings have been dammed up for an age. On the rare occasion that a family member leaves the room, after a short while I will encourage someone to go and urge her to return. This is often the prelude for the one who leaves to speak her soul and spirit in the presence of the family, and I will offer her this opportunity, perhaps suggesting that she sit next to me.

Q. Does the guide sometimes get attacked in the meeting?

A. In the early days of facilitating family meetings this did happen from time to time, and it was very uncomfortable for me, sometimes causing me to doubt the wisdom of having family meetings for every family. However, in those days I was acting as a psychiatrist, analyzing and judging what was said, giving the occasional interpretation, and trying to keep my distance. When after a few years I discovered that all I needed to be was a guide to storytellers and a witness to the stories, and that it was imperative that I *not* keep my distance, the incidences of personal bombardment were exceedingly rare. When I became clear that my role was to encourage and nudge family members to go deeper into the soul of their feelings and to facilitate family circulation of the loving kind, and that analyzing and judging had no place, then all was well.

Q. What about those family members who will not attend the meeting?

A. I used to have the delusion that the family meeting could only be successful if all the members were present, and I used to put pressure on the patient's nurse to see that everyone turned up. This was a ridiculous imposition on my part, and in retrospect I regret any pressures I brought to bear on both the nurses and the families. Often, not all family members were present, but with more experience I came to realize that simply having these meetings changes the family and the way in which we deliver care, because we are present at and witnesses to a sacred event. Even if only three people out of six are present, the meeting still takes place. Just as violent and abusive happenings in the world cause pain and damage to the *anima mundi* or collective soul of the world, so also these sacred and loving occasions have an effect much more widespread than we can ever imagine. What often happens is that the absentees hear reports or have some intuitive feelings about what went on in the meeting, and some of them will request another gathering.

Q. What is the essence of what needs to be said at a family meeting?

A. Ideally a family meeting will include a brief acknowledgment of how family members may have missed out on really knowing one another, apologies for hurts they have inflicted, expressions of their love and connectedness (as long as it is really felt in that moment), and the touch of blessings given and received. At this particular time it is so easy to see that love is all there is.

Q. I left my family years ago because it was so painful. Why meet and rekindle the pain?

A. Saying that we can do without the family is like saying that a tree can do without roots or that limbs can thrive without the body. It is also like a large group of young people who were reported in a newspaper recently as saying that they had no need of history since it was not part of their everyday job. We *are* connected to our families and our history, like it or not. If there has been some sort of malignant sclerosis of our connecting linkage this is the time to revitalize the circulation. Otherwise we will hand on this family malignancy to subsequent generations.

Q. But what if my efforts are met with further rejection?

A. That may happen, but if it does, it is quite different from past rejections. This time, within the family meeting, you determine to let go of the rage and the hurt and to offer love and blessings. If they are not received that is sad, but you will have done what you needed to do. Consequently you will be free of the awful burden of handing on family secrets and family rage to younger generations—quite literally clearing the air for the family so that its members can breathe and eventually expire in peace. The morphic field within the family will have been cleansed so that the curse is no longer a part of it and will not be handed on.

Q. Why do we wait until the last minute to speak our minds to one another?

A. The family meeting is not one in which to speak the mind. The mind tends to chatter too much and invent stories, most of which are far from the truth. This meeting is a chance to speak from the heart or from the soul, something that may never have happened before in the forum of the family or anywhere else. We leave it so late, or more likely never experience it at all, because relationship-centeredness—storytelling, witnessing, and guiding—are not a part of our everyday life. So it is only very late in life, in most instances, that we wake up to the fact that we need to express love and to receive it at all times if soul and spirit are to be vital. Otherwise we simply exist on commercial life support.

Q. Should children be present at family meetings?

A. Yes. A family meeting is so important, even for small children, when a parent is dying, and it is equally important for grandchildren. Children are part of the dying, so they need to be folded in to important events or rituals that take place along the way. Often people will say that the child is too young to grasp what is happening and would be too disruptive to the proceedings. Yet I have been repeatedly amazed at the wisdom of very young children. When given permission and encouragement, they are often able to speak more clearly and directly about their feelings than the adults present, and, having spoken and cried, move on. In any event, with our own very limited comprehension of the mysteries surrounding death—and much of life—it is presumptuous for us to say that children do not understand. I believe that children should not be forced to stay in the meeting and need to be free to come and go, and if a very small child is disruptive, an adult or a rotation of adults may need to leave with the child for a while. Children are offered the opportunity to say something (and other family members usually have the urge to push them to speak), but I believe that they should never be coerced. While a child may not remember the meeting in words, it becomes an important part of the family mythology. She will be able to ask one of the adults to tell her the story of what happened when grandmother or dad died, and this story, like any good tale of the soul, will be told over and over again.

Q. *Remind me again about the role of witness in the family meeting.*

A. The witness is fully present and attentive and is like an open vessel that can contain anything that is poured into it. The witness uses the sense of hearing in particular, because hearing offers easy access to the soul of the witness if judgment is suspended. The witness *does* nothing since the experience of witnessing is simply the experience of *being.* Many of us were taught something about active listening, which promoted attentiveness but also encouraged the mind to be active in analyzing and occasionally interpreting what was said. Witnessing is passive listening with full consciousness and attentiveness. The mind is as still as possible so that the vessel is open and receptive.

Q. *What are some of the characteristics desirable in the guide?*

A. The intention of the guide is simply that he or she will lovingly attempt to facilitate connectedness within the family. It is a spiritual practice in that it is principally this offering of love by the guide that creates a cocoon that feels safe for both storyteller and witnesses. There is no script. There is no series of questions to be posed. The model for the role is the god Hermes, the friend of man and familiar traveler in the underworld, whose task it is to nudge and encourage the storyteller to go deeper into the tale.

Q. Is it necessary to have a guide from outside the family?

A. If there is an outsider who has experience and is skilled, this is most desirable. There are still insufficient guides from among the ranks of professionals because they receive no training. Many physicians say that they have conducted family meetings, but they usually only discuss technical matters, and in attempting to remain in control they stifle the expression of feelings in the suffering family. I remember a television program in which a physician met with the family of a patient—the father of the family—who had been in the intensive care unit for four months. The father had never been fully conscious, and the treatment had obviously been futile for many weeks. The physician stated a few facts and suggested to the family that now was the time to remove the respirator, although he said that the decision was completely theirs. There was no real guidance, no emotional presence, and no storytelling. The family seemed so painfully on their own, and the family would always have a residue of guilt and of things unsaid and undone. In two other vignettes from the same program, two families that obviously held great love and compassion within struggled to speak. All was *not* said and done in these instances, and in one of the families there was considerable unexpressed pain because the family tried to shield and rescue one another rather than witness. I believe that because there was no external guide available, several rounds of the Talking Stick would have woven miracles of healing for both of these families.

Q. Do you have any suggestions for the storyteller?

A. Apart from the occasional minimal nudge from the guide, the storyteller should continue the story until it is finished, and the witnesses neither interrupt nor ask any questions. Occasionally the storyteller will seem to ramble on and on in one part of the story, and it is the job of the guide to gently move her along. She may be dwelling at length on a particular segment of the story to delay moving into deeper realms of feelings, or it may be a way of protecting others from having to speak. The difficulty for most guides is to know when and how to move a story along with love and tact. When the Talking Stick is the only "guide" for the family, it is curious how it seems to induce the storyteller to become her own guide, moving the story along. It is surprisingly rare for the holder of the stick to talk for too long. It is as if the Talking Stick has a momentum of its own, or perhaps the holder realizes that if she fails to tell an important piece of the story, she can tell it on the next round.

Q. Should family meetings be part of the care of any life-threatening illness?

A. While we have little or no certainty about what lies ahead—and many people burdened with a life-threatening illness *do* recover—a diagnosis of this kind is at the very least a wake-up call. It is a confrontation with our denial of death. It is a reminder that it is time to look at our priorities in life, do what needs to be done, and say what needs to be said. The family meeting has an important place in this discovery and should be a part of every relationship-centered diagnostic work-up. Technocentric medicine has an established routine of tests and procedures in and around the diagnosis of any life-threatening illnesses. Just as it would be negligent if certain tests were omitted, it is also negligence for any brand of medicine that imagines itself to be relationship-centered if a family meeting is not strongly urged. This meeting should certainly take place within a month of diagnosis. It will transform the care of life-threatening illness.

CHAPTER 9

⚜

Suffering and Dying

When family members are asked what is their greatest worry for the one who is dying, they usually reply that they hope there will be no suffering. When asked to elaborate on the concept of suffering, it almost invariably comes down to not wanting to see their loved one in pain.

Pain and suffering are often thought of as synonymous, and yet they are not necessarily related. The pain of childbirth, for example, is intense, but in a wanted pregnancy it is not necessarily accompanied by suffering. Suffering has to do with attachment; when we refuse or resist or in some way are discouraged from letting go, we suffer. Suffering is also related to denial of death which is less easy to maintain during the loss of control that may accompany a life-threatening illness. Suffering is the name for the anxiety and intense discomfort that emerge due to the terror of death when it can no longer be easily denied.

Perhaps pregnancy and delivery are rehearsals for death in that they enable us to discover that if we really do surrender and relinquish control, we will cease to suffer. This is as true for dying as it is for birth. In the process of delivery, pain arises as the child propels itself toward the world outside the womb, and then the pain departs. If we are not attached to the pain but instead regard it as a necessary part of the desired outcome of welcoming the child, we will not suffer. If we will not let go and are frightened by what is happening, suffering will be added to the pain, which will then intensify and be accompanied by anxiety.

Cancer pain or the pain of angina or a heart attack is usually accompanied by considerable suffering, at least initially—before we revive denial. We read into the pain that we are not at all in control and imagine that we are about to die. We believe that the continuation or worsening of pain means that we are closer to death, and that when the pain diminishes or is absent, all must be well, or at least much better. It is the meaning that the mind ascribes to pain that is the cause of the anguish and suffering. The mind is a great architect of stories and fictions, trying to explain what is happening despite having very little knowledge at its disposal, so that often the stories it fabricates become the cause of suffering. We need to remember that the mind is not to be trusted too far or taken too seriously if attachment and suffering are to be kept to a minimum.

If it were possible for us to be detached, then we would not suffer. Detachment does not mean that we do not love or care, but only that we make no attempt to hold on, either to agony or to ecstasy; both need to be relinquished. If we did not believe that we had a *right* to good health, or that the children we have been privileged to bear are *ours*, or that all the things we have acquired are *ours*, then there would be no suffering. Yet it is our nature to be attached for fear of being swept away if we have nothing to hold on to. Furthermore, we usually determine our worth by the number of friends we have and the importance of our position, as well as the value of our goods and chattels. If we were able to acknowledge our value simply in terms of our being, then suffering would not be part of our lives because we would be free of attachments and expectations.

Suffering often arises when we attach dire meaning to pain and will not let it go. Sometimes suffering may be the only way in which we can legitimize the receiving of the care for which we crave. Sometimes it is seen as the only way in which we can legitimately get the attention of the family; mother who is well may feel herself to be a burden for her busy daughter, but mother who is sick and in pain feels less guilty about making demands on her daughter's time.

Apathy, from the Greek *apatheia* (*a-*, without and *pathos*, feeling), is the state in which we are unable to feel anything and the soul is numb. In a society or a family where it is unacceptable or too painful to express feelings or emotions—either for fear of rejection or because of the awful loneliness of once again not being heard or acknowledged—apathy reigns, and there is no vitality of soul. In these circumstances there is a real or apparent sense that nobody cares, which itself creates awful loneliness, and the perceived apathy in others becomes the source of apathy and non-caring in ourselves. A society in which children can be battered and killed—even when there are those who know about the abuse but fail to act—is one that is mired in apathy. A hospital where physical and psychological terrors and suffering are treated with medication of an ever-increasing strength and not with the witnessing and guidance that is sought is one that contributes to suffering by its apathetic indifference. This is the formula for a health-care system that prescribes apathy as an antidote for suffering. It is a system that has become swept up by technology, and in its industrialization has lost sight of the need for loving care which will vitalize the soul, ameliorate suffering, and provide a healthy environment for body, soul, and spirit.

When I think about suffering, Gloria often comes to mind. She was a woman in her early sixties who had been referred to me because she seemed unusually unhappy and angry. Gloria was also trying the patience of her oncologist with her constant stream of calls and complaints. When I first saw Gloria, she was weak and miserable as a result of both physical and emotional reactions to the chemotherapy that she was receiving for advanced colon cancer, but she was going about her everyday life most of the time. And she was angry! She told me how she, being an only child, had given up any ideas of marriage on account of her mother who had been sick for as long as she could remember, and who, according to Gloria, had used guilt and other cajolery in order to pressure her daughter to stay home and take care of her. Gloria's mother had been very demanding and was never satisfied; she had not expressed any appreciation for the care given to her, enjoying ill health and miserable moods unremittingly for years before dying of heart failure in her eighties, ten years before Gloria came to visit me. On her deathbed she had made Gloria promise that she would always look after her father until he died. Gloria's father had been as helpless and silent as her mother had been demanding and nasty, yet Gloria did her duty until his death three years before we met.

For those three years, Gloria had felt free and ready to enjoy the life she had suspended for so many years, even though she had experienced very little happiness and would most likely have been unable to recognize it were it to come her way. Then, six months prior to our first meeting, Gloria had been informed that she was afflicted with advanced cancer. With that awful news she immersed herself in what seemed like a paralytic fury, and in both words and behavior had angrily folded her arms across her chest, saying that if there was a just God who cared anything about her He would release her from this ordeal, and she was going to sit there until He did! And that is precisely what happened. Gloria spent the last several months of her life angry, with arms metaphorically crossed, moving from one physical crisis to another. She was pain-free but suffering intensely; the release she demanded only occurred with her death.

Gloria was bathed in rage and held on to it through all the vicissitudes of her experiences with cancer, unwilling or unable to let the rage go. She was a great teacher, reminding me about the anger I ignite within myself when confronted by my own helplessness. The Demeter in me wished to comfort her, but Gloria would not be comforted. The Hermes in me wished to guide her beyond anger and into and beyond the fear and terror of being out of control and dying, but she refused to make the trip. It is hard to remember that our love and skills as mother or guide may not be accepted at times, either by our own family members or those to whom we offer care, and that this makes us no less loving and skillful. Sometimes there are those like Gloria who we are unable to reach and who will continue suffering to the bitter end.

Alan Klein was also dedicated to suffering. He was a lawyer who had always been devoted—or attached—to his work, and kidney cancer had been his lot in the four years before he came to the hospice Inn. Even toward the end, Alan was difficult to like. His incessant, irritable demands were never softened by a word of thanks, and he angrily dismissed anyone who ventured close. He had no friends; only his ex-wife visited, and she only once. His ex-wife said that he had been financially successful as a lawyer, but as her husband and father to their daughter he was a disaster. They married while he was in law school, and for a while his personal lack of warmth was obscured by sex and excused by the trials of being a student. Their daughter was born soon after he graduated but he took little interest in her, dedicating himself to law. He never seemed happy, with himself or anyone else, and after ten years of a mixture of criticism and neglect salved only by financial security, his wife left him. He had maintained little contact with his daughter and had not attended her wedding, which had taken place a year before his illness. His daughter would not visit Alan now, even though he was dying.

We never learned much of Alan's story. He died rigid and alone, in much the same way in which he seemed to have lived his life. I imagined that he had cold and demanding parents whom he could neither satisfy nor let go of, carrying them with him to his grave. It seemed as though any show of love and affection would have been a distraction from Alan's rule of law and might cause him to lose control, so he had instead lived a life of soul-destroying suffering, spreading it around to all who came across his path, ensuring that nobody would be there for him at the end. If health of the spirit depends on giving love and care and letting go, then Alan was spiritually barren. If health of the body and soul depends on receiving regular care, Alan had never been vibrantly alive because he never gave care to himself nor allowed it in.

Another story of suffering gives me the shivers when I think about it because I see myself in the more unconscious periods of my life, and I also see many others who I know and care about. Geoff was a man in his late fifties who developed lung cancer and came to see me because he was extremely depressed. He told me that he was the vice-president of a small but very successful company, and his job required that he had to travel much of the time. In speaking of the pressures and tensions of the job and always having to be on the move, he said that when he was awake within the hustle and bustle of his life, he always seemed to find himself in an airport, either coming or going. With two sons in college and another in high school, his expenses were enormous so that he felt unable to slow down. I will always remember him saying: "This is all too hectic. I can't wait to retire." Of course he never did retire. He died a few months later.

Geoff suffered trying to hold on to a killing job until the end, feeling trapped by his social and family obligations as if they took precedence over self-care. He seemed to have given no thought to the possibility that children do not have to go to college or that lifestyles can be simplified. We hold on to jobs that seem to offer security but are often pressure-filled, conflict-laden, or deadly dull and soul-destroying; we hold on to marriages and relationships that have died and yet we will not relinquish the corpse. Instead, we suffer. I have seen many individuals and families in which death has been a relief and a release from a deadly bondage. For the survivors, at least, there still needs to be a letting go; when the relationship was one of unremitting suffering, this can paradoxically be very difficult, as the resulting guilt may often lead to protracted bereavement.

WHY SUFFER?

It is the most natural thing, in the face of suffering, to ask "Why me?" Bad things *do* happen to good people every day, and we imagine that there must be some explanation, because the mind reasons things out even when it has so little to go on. It is very difficult for us to acknowledge the seemingly random nature of events over which we have no control and for which we have no explanation. We so easily forget that we *do* have control of our responses to the bad things that will happen.

We ask how a loving God can allow all the suffering of the world and of the planet. If He brings suffering upon us as a test or a trial or stands back and watches as a spectator, He must be a tyrant, for only tyrants cause suffering or stand by and do nothing when those who they love—if they love anyone at all—are suffering. Our mythology is filled with stories of powerful tyrants who impose trials on their subjects: Venus giving impossible tasks to Psyche, tasks that must be successfully completed if she is to be reunited with her lover, Eros; fairy tales replete with stories of kings and giants who set absurd conditions that are unattainable except with the help of charms, animals, or spirits. These powerful people are sadistic; they enjoy their real or imagined power by watching the less empowered suffer. It is likely that these tales are simply projections of our own sadism. Perhaps on account of our terror of death we derive some passing relief from watching puny folk like ourselves immersed in terror. We derive some fleeting consolation that it is other people's names that appear in the obituary notices; similarly, earthquakes and disasters involving others provide another moment of relief that death has not yet come our way. The projection of our terrors and our innate sadism provides an illusion of control, but the cost is that we abandon our fellow beings, failing to lend them a hand by joining in their suffering. Life contains both death and suffering and they are woven together, and if we really are to acknowledge our connection to one another, like the cells in the body, then we must acknowledge our connectedness in life, death, and suffering.

SUFFERING IN SILENCE

When we are in physical or emotional pain and are frightened—when we imagine that our life is threatened and we grasp and hold on like a person who is drowning—we suffer. We then have a choice: we can speak or wail about the suffering, or we can suffer in silence. Society prefers the silence—our culture is most uncomfortable with suffering and would prefer to walk away and not see it, like all those who refused to see the human carnage during World War II. Vocal suffering disturbs the peace, raising the specter of death and helplessness at a time when society is expending great energy in banishing these realities from consciousness. The patient is expected to suffer in silence, grateful for all that is being done for him by the "good" doctors and others. It is the "bad" patient who complains or takes nothing for granted, asking difficult questions, assessing treatment protocols, and refusing pills that would help him not to shout. Suffering in silence requires apathy; it requires the suspension of feeling, which in turn leads to paralysis of soul. The soul that is awake to the fears and terrors of the threat to life and to the loss of all of the connections that we have ever known will scream and rage, asserting life. To be "good" and silent is unnatural—to be a "good" patient or a silent sufferer is bizarre. If we are not to suffer, we must reach out to God and our physician and anyone else who will listen and tell the story of our fears and worries, re-establishing our connectedness with life.

PHYSICAL ILLS AND THE SOUL

Many physical ailments—especially in the early stages, before they take on a pathological life of their own—are expressions of a soul that is desperate to be heard. It is the sense of not being heard—and hence holding on to the feelings of fear and desperation—that is the cause of suffering, and it is with the dying that this is most obvious. A significant component of pain arises from the fears and terrors associated with loss of control and the waning of life. If family and caregivers do little more than focus on the pain, juggle with narcotics, and ignore or deny cries from the soul, pain and suffering will continue. Sometimes it will be muted, resulting in apathy or depression. Patients need to be able to tell their story and we need to bear witness without rushing in too soon to *do* something.

Sleeplessness, a common discomfort, is usually treated with sleeping pills, although this is not what the child within the patient is crying out for. Insomnia is frequently the response of a frightened soul who is terrified of going to sleep for fear of never waking up. This scenario requires a witness who will listen, and a guide who will tell the patient that sleeplessness is a normal response. The guide might even add a few words, such as: "It is true that we may die in our sleep, although that does not happen to most of us. It is also true that your time here is short. But even so, it is safe to let go into sleep, and we will be here with you. If you die during sleep it will be a peaceful departure, and if you awaken we will be here to greet you." As usual, it is not the actual words that are important but rather the naming of the fear and the reminder of the loving connection and relationship, so that the person who is dying knows he is not alone on his journey.

Restlessness is a state that is frequently distressing. Much of it stems from the physical debility attendant on advanced illness, but there is often a component of struggle by the terrified child within that adds to the discomfort and exhaustion. In the language that surrounds cancer, for example, there is much that is belligerent. The word cancer itself inspires terror, and some will not even mention it. Then there is the almost automatic response that we have to "fight" this thing, and the warfare begins. The toxic weaponry of chemotherapy is augmented by the nuclear forces of radiotherapy and the surgeon's knife. In moments of remission we are triumphant in having "won the battle," and when treatment efforts are unsuccessful we are deemed to have "failed," or we may even imagine that we have "lost the war." Our intention, illustrated by our language, is to eradicate this monster at any cost, even if it kills us—and it often does. The child within us would have plenty to say about this attitude toward ourselves and toward this sacred shrine that is our body, if we would only listen. He would be appalled by the environmental desecration of our body as a result of the treatments, and he would be even more shocked by everyone's belligerent attitude, especially our own. He would say that he is terrified, and everyone is too busy fighting the war to listen. He would remind us that we have told him that to voice fears and worries is negative, and that we must have a positive attitude, but this brand of "positive attitude" may not be what he needs. He would say that if we have to use these forms of treatment, we must use them with love and caring, and not in the spirit of all-out warfare that will be the death of him.

GIVING VOICE

There are a number of ways in which we can give voice. We can tell the story wrapped in tears and rage and laced with resentment, if anyone will witness without interruption. If, in their attempt to rescue us or cut short the fearful story, the listeners interject that it is nobody's fault, or that we need to put ourselves in God's hands, or they use some other soporific to still our voice, we will most likely become silent and turn blue with depression and apathy. However, if we simply rage without end against the coming of the night, maintaining our fury and righteous indignation to the end, unwilling to modify the story, after a while most of the witnesses will walk away, ensuring the isolation we so greatly fear. If we demand retribution or the death penalty—for ourselves or for others—we are not letting go and moving on. We are not forgiving ourselves or others for real or imagined wrongs, and we can never move on to a place beyond suffering.

A definition of neurosis is that it is a state in which the individual repeats the same story over and over again without allowing it to change. Like Gloria, many sufferers hold on to the story of their suffering, remaining stuck in its mire, refusing or apparently unable to give it up.

Giving voice may take us beyond suffering with acceptance as a possibility—acceptance that death is at hand and need not be repulsed; that it is possible to let go, give thanks, and say good-bye. When the family moves beyond suffering, if the stories and the lessons are remembered, there may be great transformation as the family members are able to aid other sufferers by entering into their suffering with them.

One of the terrors of dying is that we will die alone—and lonely—and this is the way it is for most people, whether or not they have loving families. If we have not allowed the barriers to be broken through and not connected with others way beyond the mind, with all the darkness and light of our feelings and imagination, we will die alone even though we are surrounded by intimate strangers. It is no wonder that those who have some degree of consciousness about this terror, yet feel unwilling or unable to do anything about it, should wish to commit suicide or have a physician help them die.

PHYSICIAN-ASSISTED SUICIDE

The topic of physician-assisted suicide has generated much heat and passion. There has been much talk about the right to die, and to die with dignity. Death used to be quicker when there was little or no treatment. It is only relatively recently that we have become much more conscious of dying since we have more time to observe its course. Many people have life-threatening illnesses for which there is no cure, but their dying may be protracted over months or even years through treatment of various kinds. Also, because we are living longer, it is commonplace to see the elderly fading away in their dying years.

To use the metaphor of the rape of Persephone, in the myth she was in the garden one minute and whisked into the underworld the next. In the modern equivalent of this tale Hades does not have an easy time dragging her down from the garden into his realm—she fights and she draws a crowd, some of whom stand around and watch while others fight vigorously to keep her with them. We see Persephone being dragged under, with her head barely above the surface, asking or screaming to be put out of her misery, and we are up there witnessing this awful struggle. It is difficult for us to do nothing—other than say that we will accompany her on this journey and that we will *be* with her— especially if death terrifies the life out of us because we too have spent a lifetime keeping the underworld at bay.

The thought of suicide is perfectly understandable when control seems to have been lost and we feel that we are faced with the specter of abandonment by life and a horrible death. Most of those actively involved in the debate concerning physician-assisted suicide are as terrified of death as those who are dying, although they will say intellectually that they are accepting and unafraid and have seen death many times. But the issue has little to do with the act of dying; it is more to do with feeling disconnected and experiencing shattering loneliness, and suicide is a solution. Yet there is always something that can be done about this malignant loneliness if we recognize the issue and will act as guides and witnesses.

The debate on physician-assisted suicide takes place in the environment of denial of death, with little understanding of what can be accomplished for the well-being of everyone in the family during this time.

All physicians receive some training about birthing, and those who are going to be regularly involved with childbirth during their professional lives will focus their studies in obstetrics and take post-graduate refresher courses. While only a relative few clinically based physicians will ever be involved with birthing, all will be entangled sooner or later with dying and death, and yet there is no training. If there is no training, and physicians and other caregivers have not taken conscious heed of their own loneliness and disconnectedness, no wonder there is bluster and fear, with talk of hurrying up the unimaginable. Since dying involves body, soul, and spirit, the usual lectures or instruction manuals are inadequate since feelings are very much involved; the physician is personally drawn in to dying, imagining his own as he witnesses that of his patient. In order to be a truly competent guide, a physician's training needs to be very personal, helping him to imagine his own dying and the dying of those he loves. Only then will he be in a more comfortable position to help others, since he himself will be more at ease in the presence of death. Only then will he be able to become a loving witness and guide to those who speak of suicide.

What is feared by all of us is that there will be unremitting pain and suffering during dying, and that the time will be an agony for all. Better and more dignified, we think, that we get life over with as quickly and painlessly as possible. Intellectually this seems to make some sense. Nobody wants to experience or witness unremitting pain and suffering, but the fact is that adequate pain management is possible in almost all instances regardless of the disease. Some physicians are untutored or uncomfortable with pain control, and their reluctance or ignorance will cause great distress among those in their care. Patients and families need a physician who is comfortable with the care of body, soul, and spirit, and they should not hesitate to seek the services of another physician if they are not receiving the care and the pain control they need. Many families who tolerate inadequate and insensitive care by their physician are reluctant or unwilling to dismiss him, perhaps on account of a superstitious fear of offending one who seems to have the power over life and death. Yet while even the best of physicians has technical limitations, none has any excuse for not being well versed in pain management and in the emotional stresses that will occur towards the end of life.

Suffering is addressed when the person who is dying is allowed to tell his whole story, replete with fears and worries, to the family witnesses, and in turn be witness to their feelings and concerns. Letting go is then much easier, as has been suggested in the stories I have related, because the loneliness melts into the oneness of the family or of the surrogate family of caregivers. Among the many people for whom I have been witness during their dying, only two killed themselves, though many more talked about suicide and their wish to be helped to die as quickly as possible. It is my impression that when loving care is available for those afflicted by a life-threatening illness, and when they know that there are guides and witnesses who will accompany them on their journey, some of the fears and terrors abate, and there is less thought of suicide. Even when the best technical treatment is offered, if there is little or no loving care there is an awful sense of aloneness, and it is this that induces the urge for suicide.

While there will be instances when pain and suffering are impossible to relieve, it is never impossible to give loving care. The self-styled mercy-killer or suicide-facilitator is not necessarily a good guide or witness who has confronted his own denial of death and his own loneliness. In fact his apparent ability to control dying in others may have boosted his sense of control over his own life and death; the sadist is not above assuming the disguise of an angel of mercy. There is also no guarantee that he understands much about soul and spirit and the essential elements of care.

Feeling uncared for, either by self or others—that is, feeling intensely alone—is an understandable precursor of the quest for suicide at any stage of life. I have imagined that most of those who ask to die or be assisted in their suicide are asking not to be left alone, not to have to go alone along this strange and frightening journey in the underworld; they are asking for Hermes or Virgil and not hemlock. It is *real* care, with its opportunity to give as well as receive, that is the antidote to suicide, whether or not it is assisted by a physician.

CHAPTER 10

Living and Letting Go

At the end of life, when all is said and done, the family members who are attending their dying relative as both guides and witnesses will often encourage their loved one to let go. Holding on to one another for dear life (or for grim death) in boundless dependency is a way of life in many families, but this makes it painfully difficult to die.

When I was eight years old and growing up in England, I was sent away to boarding school. Many years later, paying close attention to the size and maturity of my own five children as they passed through their eighth year reinforced my long-held belief that this particularly British middle-class practice of sending children to boarding school at a ridiculously young age—whether the family could afford it or not—was an exceptionally cruel and unusual punishment for having been born into that culture. My lasting memories from those years are a series of tearful good-byes to my parents at railway stations, then leaning far out of the train to catch one last glimpse of them. School itself seemed to be one long ordeal of home sickness. Coming from a troubled family, my departure for school should have been a relief, but those of us from dysfunctional backgrounds hold on to the family with even greater tenacity, all the way from childhood to death. It is only possible to let go freely when we are not grasping and holding on, but we also need others to let us go.

Letting go would seem to be very simple, but it is not at all easy; in fact, it goes against everything we believe that we stand for. We are taught early on to hold hands for safety; later, to "hold our horses" or hold our tongue as we are urged to take and retain control of self. Through years of struggling to gain the next foothold in the material world, we hold on to judgments of others who appear to us insincere or downright contemptuous. And when the diagnosis of a life-threatening illness is affixed to us we "hold everything!" while we attempt to fend off the unimaginable. The image of the wreck of the Titanic creates powerful visions of holding on for dear life to the life-raft, or any flotsam and jetsam that we can grab. This is the natural response to fear of drowning.

The alternative is to surrender. The word surrender derives from the Old French *surrendre* or *sur-rendre*, "to deliver up" or "to hand over," and refers to the giving up of one's person or possessions. The question of personhood or ego seems to be central to both holding on and to surrender: if there were no personhood, there would be nothing to hold on to, and therefore nothing to let go. Personhood has to do with the cocoon that surrounds us, the protective fabrication that invests our inner life force or soul.

For most of us, surrendering this personhood that we have been at such pains to create is at odds with our upbringing, which stressed individuality, strength, and becoming our own person, armoring ourselves against the dangers of living. Yet many of us have experienced this loss of personhood in a concert, when the music dissolves our sense of boundary and we merge with the rest of the audience, or in any of the host of wonderful cathedrals throughout Europe or in temples in Asia, when personhood seems to dissolve and we become part of the magnificent whole. This surrender of our armor is a necessary part of lovemaking that is more than mechanical. And surrender is at the heart of relationship-centered caring.

This is all very simple, but it is not at all easy. Speaking of surrendering the self may conjure visions of cult members trusting their lives to messianic leaders who entice them up some mad yellow brick road. Betrayal and other atrocities are a part of the human experience, and may be visited upon us if we let down our self-defense. But there is no real alternative to letting go and surrendering—or at least making more permeable—our imaginary personhood unless we armor, police, guard, insure, and demand guarantees in a futile attempt to hold. There *is* no security in this life, no guarantee against betrayal, and certainly there is no way to avoid loss. Impermanence is our state, and to put so much energy into holding on to an imaginary sense of control is inordinately life consuming. Even when these security measures appear to work for a while, they operate at the expense of muting and containing our vital life force or soul; we may feel "safe" for a moment, but we also deaden our sense of wonder. Real love is then no longer possible, since it contains impermanence.

In the workshop exercises that I have described, there is often the sense as we work in the triads or when we come together in the large group that individual personality disappears, and to a greater or lesser extent we feel as one. Quite unwittingly we give up our person and become part of something much larger. This suggests that allowing the protective coat to become more permeable—because sometimes it appears to imprison the soul rather than protect it—is a relief and the prelude to a greater freedom of being than that allowed by an egoistic view of self.

We need to practice letting go for the sake of the soul. Though it is not easy, we must start now, for if we have had no practice it will be difficult to let go at the time of death, and letting go is the prelude to a peaceful death much as it is required for a fully engaged life. We need to watch as the clouds roll within and around us and the storms rage or the sun shines, and not become attached to any one of these manifestations—even the "good" weather, because it too needs to be let go. We need to watch with love the parade through our conscious awareness of ideas, lovers, children, accolades, losses, disasters, and ecstasies—and try not to hold on to any of them. The way in which most people were raised makes this very difficult. It is even subversive in some way, as our national economy depends on our holding on to all that we think we need, and much more. I also have difficulty letting go; the list of the things that I believe I "possess" is long and detailed, and I cherish and hold on to that list. But having been given the gift of being able to grow older in this lifetime has also given me the opportunity to develop a little wisdom so that the list is now much shorter than it once was. And I am still working on whittling it down. Wisdom is a gift that is beyond the rational mind; it helps us to sort out what we need from what we want. And wisdom also tells us that the list really contains only one item: love.

As part of my training program for caregivers (outlined in the Postscript to this book) there is a delightful exercise that is a study in letting go. Before coming to the workshop the participants are asked to choose something that has considerable meaning for them that they can bring to the workshop and then give away. The monetary value of this gift is of no importance, but it must have a story.

The group members are asked to stand up and move slowly around the room in silence with gift in hand. Some quiet music is played, and every 20 seconds or so a bell is rung, at which time the participants stop and exchange gifts, still without speaking, with the person nearest to them. This exchange takes place about ten times, and then the group is invited to sit in a circle. At this point, anyone who wishes may open and describe their gift, and this is followed by the giver telling the story behind the gift. She then opens her gift, and the process continues until all the gifts are opened and all the stories told.

The stories that emerge from this brief exchange are always amazing. Selection of the gift is itself an interesting process. We look around our house at all our story-laden trinkets and discard one after another as either unsuitable as a gift or something we do not want to relinquish because of some ascribed value. I remember a man who forgot to bring any gift with him and grabbed a candle stump on his way into the ceremony. It was not too surprising that he should have forgotten because in his life he was always very busy and in a rush. The man who received this gift was obviously a little taken aback by the nature of the gift, but said nothing other than to describe the candle; the giver was obviously embarrassed as he told the brief story of how his gift came to be. We moved on to other gifts.

Then two days later, toward the end of the workshop, the recipient of the candle told us that he had been quite preoccupied by his reactions to the gift ever since he received it. Initially he had made judgments about the giver, but then he became aware that it was one of the most precious gifts he had ever received. He realized that at Christmastime he would leave shopping until the last minute, and then dash into an expensive department store armed with a credit card and gather up an assortment of gifts that had little or no thought behind them and no story, other than that they were expensive or that they were a bargain. "No different at all from the gift I received," he said, and most of us gasped in recognition of ourselves.

At another workshop a young man gave away the first love note written to him by the woman who became his wife. The recipient was a woman who was amazed by its beauty and delighted to receive it, but aghast that he should have given it away. He said that he had no need of it because his wife was there every day, and he thought it a beautiful gift to pass on. Another participant gave away the wedding ring from her first marriage, which she had held on to together with a whole variety of residual feelings from the marriage. She experienced a great sense of relief when she decided to give it away.

In another workshop, a magnificent man named John gave away a beautiful pocket knife, and he told us the story of his best friend Will with whom it was associated. They met in college and were bound together by their passion for climbing and for the sea, and it was through a number of climbing adventures in Alaska and sailing together that their friendship was forged. John later gave me a written version of the story he told us all in the workshop, and I continue in his words as he described writing to his friend:

> *I wrote a simple note to Will, stimulated by my need for a reprieve from the New York cityscape. I had been thinking about cedar trees that we had felled in southeast Alaska many years before. We planned to return and craft the wood into a sailboat to sail around the world. The note read, "You are one of the most magnificent beings to walk the face of this earth. Perhaps it is time to build that boat?" I closed the letter with my phone number, hoping for a rapid response, and I sent the letter to Will's parents in Alaska, with the requisite "Please Forward" on the cover. I knew that Will was somewhere working in Nicaragua at the time, and I did not have an address. The call came just before dinner. The voice on the line sounded like that of a ghost, detached yet familiar. It was Will! The voice fought for composure. "John, got your letter today and opened it because we just learned that Will was killed four days ago in Nicaragua." It had sounded like Will but it was not, it was Gerry, his dad. The note I had sent four days before on the day of Will's death—the note so simply expressing my love for him and a desire for adventure—gave Gerry reason to call.*

John went on to speak of his meeting Gerry years before:

> *Gerry was an imposing character to behold. His presence was large, his full face of white fur, formidable. He could have been a character who just stepped out of a Hemingway novel. His cool blue-gray eyes shone brightly and looked through you. I instantly understood some of the power Will possessed; it was genetic.*

John flew to Alaska to attend Will's funeral and the scattering of his ashes on a mountain in the Chugach Range, speaking movingly both of his intense grief and of the deep connections he had made with Will's family and especially with Gerry:

We created a strong bond in those few days, sharing our thoughts about Will and our passion for the great outdoors. Gerry invited me to sail with him that following summer. He was moving his 32 ft sloop from Juneau across the Gulf of Alaska to Seward ... Gerry and I shared one important yet uncomfortable attribute with Will—the dilemma of having two great loves: the mountains and the sea.

We stowed a bottle of champagne to help celebrate the beginning of this first journey together. As we left Elfin Cove, huge swells pushed us into the gulf, and we were talking of how we wished Will was with us, how much he would have loved this moment, when the cork on the champagne bottle popped of its own accord, and most of its contents spilled out onto the deck. We looked at one another and shivers ran down our spines.

It was later on this journey that Gerry gave John the beautiful pocket knife that John had so admired when they were provisioning the boat, and it was that knife that John gave away.

The recipient of the knife was a woman who, like the rest of us, was overwhelmed by the story, and she said that she could not have received a more precious and appropriate gift. In her own life she felt powerlessly stuck in both a relationship and a job that were suffocating her, and felt that the knife would somehow empower her to cut her way out, figuratively if not literally!

Occasionally in the circling of gifts an individual will receive back a present she gave away, as if it was not ready to go elsewhere. On one occasion I gave away a poem which came back so that I had it later in the workshop to give to someone who really needed it. Another time my wife gave away her father's ring. When it came back to her she said that she felt so relieved! I read somewhere that in some Pacific islands there are those who believe that a gift may be held only for a year or less before it is handed on. What a marvelous practice in letting go—and one with which I have difficulty!

Each story is a gem, and I am always surprised at the serendipity that accompanies the ceremony, with everybody receiving exactly the gift they need. Horace Walpole coined the word serendipity in 1754 from the Persian word *serendip*, an old name for Ceylon or Sri Lanka. There is a story of the three princes of Serendip who were always making discoveries of things they were not in quest of. This same sense of coincidence is very much a part of the giveaway ceremony, a sense that if we will give away a present, the right person will receive it. In this ceremony I have witnessed a woman give away a favorite scarf, one that was invested with powerful stories, only to receive another story-laden scarf as her gift. A physician who brought her one-month-old baby to the workshop gave him away in this ceremony! Although not a permanent situation, and she was reasonably sure that he would be returned, the experience of letting him go was very powerful for this mother. She witnessed not only her own pain at parting from him, but heard from others as he was passed from hand to hand what a precious gift and a blessing he was.

Letting go is not simply something we should be aware of as a necessary part of dying; it should become a way of life. We have a wealth of things in and about us that are aching to be given away and swept into the flow of connectedness and relationships between us as they pass from hand to hand—kind words, a few laughs, a poem, a story. There are closets full of story-imbued gifts waiting to be passed on. We have nothing that we *really* need except the talent for passing on love.

If letting go is to become a way of life, we need to practice it. If it were to become part of medical practice, for instance, the giving and receiving that is part of medicine would take on a different hue. At present, physicians give of their skills and their time and receive high social status, occasional thanks, and a generous supply of money. As the thanks and the status wane, the urge for greater compensation increases. If the practice of medicine were to become relationship-centered and more of a flow of love, back and forth as in the gift-giving ceremony, we would realize once again that it is the exchange of these personal gifts that is the real source of reward, satisfaction, and healing.

Those of us who are involved in the giving of care—and sooner or later that means all of us—need to think about what we are going to give away to those for whom we care, in addition to our tried and true skills. This usually means that we will need to give more of ourselves, and that relationships will need to become the hub around which our lives revolve. If loving relationships and the giving of ourselves become central in our lives, I predict that, like the three princes of Serendip, we will have the surprise of receiving what we really need in return.

CHAPTER 11

Mourning: Bereavement and Grief

Mourning is the process of letting go and then grieving for someone or something that is important in our lives. We are unable to grieve fully until we have let go. Bereavement is the state of being in rage, enraged because something that the ego thinks is *ours*—something that we own—has been taken away. Gloria was enraged because her health was taken away, along with the opportunities for life that she believed she deserved. She was never able to let go of that rage and grieve for herself, which is the last stage of letting go.

The idea of ownership is fundamental both in our social structure and in the way we imagine our lives. "This is my life, and I am free to do what I want with it." This, like any other statement about ownership, is a statement from the ego; if there is an "I", then this life is *mine*. But what if there is no "I"? What if we are simply a part of something much larger, as anyone who is comfortable with solitude knows from experience? What if we are on a par with one of the cells of the body? I imagine that cells do not pay much attention to the idea of "I"; instead, they each go about the business of being the best cell possible, taking care of themselves and sharing food and liquid, as well as giving and receiving messages from adjacent cells. Without ego or the desire to be something else, they are simply present as impeccable cells, ultimately connected to others, but not attached. When the time comes to die, they do not hold on, and so are ready to let go and be swept away in the rivers of change. Cells that do try to become something else and break out of their bounds we call cancerous.

If we believe that a cell is simply a reflection of a larger whole, we can understand how like a cell the human body really is, and how the democracy of cells parallels the human community. If we could imagine ourselves as being like a cell and practiced thinking in that way, we could change our lives and attain the freedom we are always talking about but seldom find. The world economy as we know it would require re-visioning, but we would suffer less and not feel bereaved. Imagine that!

I heard the story of Sarah, a woman whose mother and 12-year-old daughter Anna were burned to death in a fire. This had happened some three years earlier, and in that time Sarah had been quite unable to let go of her daughter. She had been able to let go of her mother after a while, and had shed many tears, but with Anna it was different. Sarah had left Anna's room exactly as it was when she died, had been unable to listen to music associated with Anna, and every day felt a deep physical ache in her stomach and chest when she woke up and realized that Anna would not be there. Her therapist encouraged her to look intently at a photograph of Anna—something Sarah had initially been very reluctant to do for more than a quick glance—and speak to the picture, telling Anna how painful this death had been for her. The therapist stressed over and over again to Sarah that she must tell Anna that she will never see her again, and that she must let her go. This Sarah did in a relatively short time, albeit with great anguish and grief. Sarah had never grieved in that way—deep within she had held on to the wish that Anna would return, and so had experienced the soul-grief of her loss. It was only after speaking to Anna and letting her go that she was able to grieve and then move beyond grief to the remembrance of Anna's delightful essence: she could listen to Anna's music and pack away most of her things, but Anna's presence—her soul and spirit—remained.

Untold tales are the repository of so many feelings of bereavement. A story the likes of which I have heard many times was told by Arthur a couple of weeks before his death. Arthur and his wife June had been introduced to the hospice a week earlier—Arthur had been in the hospital, and June needed some help in order to take him home. They were in their early sixties; this was his second marriage and her first. There were no children by this marriage which they both described as being compatible and companionable. When I asked whether they would have liked to have had children, Arthur said that he didn't care; after an uneasy pause, June added that Arthur had two children by his first marriage. Arthur became very angry with June for this exposition. He raged on that he had not had anything to do with them for years, and if they did not want to see him when he was well, he was not going to invite them now.

When he caught his breath, Arthur told the familiar story of a teenage marriage precipitated by pregnancy and four impossible and irresponsible years which ended with his wife leaving with another man. He continued to see the children for several years after the angry and miserable divorce, but he had not seen them since the older child was 12 and they had moved away.

I have heard many variations on the theme of this story, all having in common the feelings of guilt and anger which tick away like a malignant time bomb in the soul. Almost invariably there is a deep aching to connect or reconnect, but little or no understanding that the children are experiencing a reciprocal version of this malignancy which, if not defused by forgiveness and letting go, will be handed on down through the generations. Arthur was unwilling to try to find his children, and although his wife made some efforts, they never met together and Arthur never let go of his guilt. But I have seen many who have had meetings and been reconciliated with their children, and others who have been able to speak to them in absentia, both receiving and giving forgiveness and letting go the hurts that have eaten a hole in the inner fabric of the soul.

Some tales seem to lie in waiting, buried in the foundations and stunting growth as the roots rot in a bog of unshed tears. Such was the situation with Tim, a kindly man who had retired four years earlier. Restlessness in retirement led him to buy a small variety store to while away his time, and during a couple of quiet times in his store, Tim told me his tale. His wife had died six years before from heart disease, and her last two years had been miserable for both of them: several episodes of heart failure; much of her time spent in bed unable to do anything for herself; repeated hospital stays; oxygen assistance; fear; irritability; and finally death in an intensive care unit, with both of them frightened and disconnected. There had been no good-byes and no thanks spoken, only Tim's mute and helpless witnessing, observing his wife's discomfort, confusion, difficult breathing, and finally her death. Tim had left the intensive care unit for a few minutes to find something to eat, and his younger child was alone with her mother when she died. Tim and his daughter had never spoken of that experience.

As he looked back, Tim said that his wife was a good woman, and they had loved one another even if they had seldom expressed their love, but over the years there had been many arguments. All of them as far as he could recollect were about their mentally disabled son who lived with them most of the time but had been in and out of mental hospitals when his behavior became too bizarre or dangerous. Tim said that in fact they had done a good job with their son, advocating for him and making the situation as comfortable as possible, but he and his wife had talked very little about their feelings and had never given each other the support they both deserved. Instead, the helplessness and profound disappointments came out as rage toward one another.

He went on to say that he had seemed to manage quite well after his wife died. About a year following her death, Tim had a brief relationship which was a disaster and ended in a few weeks with him becoming profoundly depressed. With the help of medication Tim was able to mobilize himself. He had always smoked heavily and at about this time developed a form of asthma, from which he was still suffering.

Tim had never told this story except in occasional fragments to different people. Both he and his wife felt bereaved early on by their son's condition, and never took or were given the chance to speak about it as a prelude to letting go of their disappointment and guilt. Instead, they buried themselves in activities on their son's behalf, neglecting both themselves and their daughter in the process. For both of them, this sense of bereavement led to broken hearts and the inability to grieve, and Tim was unable to give and receive love and care when his wife was dying. I lost touch with Tim and don't know whether he was able to speak to his son and daughter about their family story as he said he would. I wonder, also, whether he was able to give himself more loving kindness in recognition of his dedication to his family, since this might have brought some relief to both his choking asthma and his guilt.

The suffering and bereavement of those who have lost a loved one on account of murder may be especially long lasting. I have spoken to a group of parents of murdered children, for whom the issue of holding on to rage at the atrocity of murder is particularly poignant and understandable. Some of these parents have horror stories that they have been reciting to others in the group for years, unable or unwilling to let go of their self-ascribed roles as chroniclers and torch-bearers for their dead children. It is of little use to suggest that the only ones who continue to be in awful pain on account of their frightful stories are themselves; the murderers are not affected, nor are their dead children revived by their grief and rage, so they need to let go. Yet many will not hear this, believing that they would dishonor their dead children if they were to let go of their fury. Some families of murder victims will attend the execution of the murderer of their child or relative in the hope that the viewing will bring relief through an experience of retribution. There seems to be very little understanding that revenge does not work, that the nightmare will stop only when they let go, and that letting go does not mean that they love the victim any less. Letting go recognizes that what happened was awful and that they had no control, and that they must live with the experience as part of their life story, but as it relates to the present, not the past. The story needs to continue to be told, but the rage needs to be relinquished and transformed.

When a child dies, I have often seen rage destroy a marriage which may have been fragile in the first place and unable to withstand the barrage of blame and fury. Parents will occasionally deal with the death of a child by never discussing the experience so that the child becomes lost to the family story. A number of times during a family meeting I have heard of the death of a child in infancy about whom the siblings, now grown, were completely unaware. Even 30 or 40 years after the event the bereavement and the suffering can end with the telling of the story, making the child an important part of the history of the family which they can all recount and honor. This is preferable to either one or both parents holding on to the life and death of the child as an awful secret suffering and feeling unable to share their bereavement. After the telling of such a story I usually suggest that we light some candles in memory of the dead child or in some other way invite the child into the soul of the family through a ritual.

Some families will transform their bereavement into a spiritual awakening. The parents of a child who has died as a result of leukemia or a birth defect may become involved with other parents and children facing similar difficulties, or family members involved in the outrages of war or genocide may become involved in working for peace. It seems so much easier to bury awful feelings, but that only leads to malignancy of one form or another. We may scream for revenge, but that changes nothing. We might sue the person allegedly responsible, but that at best only helps the bank balance and not the soul, and it does not necessarily help us to let go. The rage and indignation surrounding bereavement attempt to assign and apportion responsibility, and God frequently ends up with a share of the blame. Accepting the responsibility of knowing that we are not totally in control, that life often feels unfair, that things often seem to occur at random and that we have very little idea about what is going on is not easy, but if we did, our sense of bereavement would be much less intense.

BEREAVEMENT VERSUS GRIEF

Bereavement is a cover-up for grief. It is easier to feel rage and blame than to experience the awful pain and sadness of soul that is grief. If bereavement is of the ego, grief is of the soul. The soul *does* become attached. The soul *is* involved in the earthy and earthly feelings and loves of everyday life and finds it hard to let go, ignoring the spirit, which urges detachment.

Feelings are rather like the clouds; we may rant and rave against them and often judge that they have been around for too long, but if we leave them alone without trying to push them away or hold on to them, they will leave. The experience of grief *will* rise into consciousness if we do not try to ignore it. If we will tell its story to loving witnesses and if we will cry a solution of tears into which we will stir our grief, it will usually move on, like the clouds. The soul-threatening aphorism that we "need to get on with our lives" is often used quite early on in times of grief, as if we should grieve for no more than five days before getting back into our often apathetic way of living—and wonder why we still feel awful. The truth of the matter is that there is no time in the realm of soul—the soul's frame is timeless. We realize this when we have an intimate soul-connection with a friend we have not spoken to for years. When we call up this friend after a long hiatus, the conversation continues as if it had never been broken—as if there was no time between us. In the same way, grief of soul does not take any particular time. It may appear to be fairly brief because we feel we said everything there was to say to our loved one before he died and did everything that needed to be done. Or it may appear to be around for longer, as with Sarah whose daughter Anna was burned to death. We need to be able to tell the story, not like a broken record but by mixing it with our memories and insights in the present moment. Usually in such retellings the story gradually changes, softening at the edges until the grief-encrusted memories become more like a warm blanket than a breath-stealing gag. The family needs to be open to these stories, and it is better that we tell our stories within the family, because there they can be transforming. There will, however, be times when we will need to reach outside the family to a therapist in order to be healed.

MOURNING FOR OURSELVES

Usually when we speak of bereavement or grief, we are referring to the loss of someone or something outside of ourselves, but when we are dying, we are losing both ourselves—at least as the ego imagines it—and our conscious life as we know it. Self-care requires that we acknowledge this and tend to our bereavement and grief, and also that we enlist the help of others. If we are to lessen suffering when we are dying, we need to let go of our rage and our fear, otherwise we will not be able to go gently; we will be holding our breath, unable to expire. We also need to grieve for ourselves, reaching inside to the weeping child within, taking him into our arms, breathing deeply, stroking, singing a lullaby. All those things we did as parents were simply training for what we need to do now.

And this is what Rita did. She had metastatic breast cancer and experienced considerable pain from both the site of a mastectomy, which had been performed two years earlier, and from a number of bony metastases. In addition, there was a very noticeable and unpleasant smell from a large open area on her chest wall.

An attractive lady in her early forties, Rita held her head averted from the side of her cancerous breast and said that she was neither able to look at it nor apply the needed dressings, a task that she left to her husband. Rita had four young children and was beside herself with rage, both at the injustice of what was happening to her and at her own breast, which revolted her. She was taking a large dose of morphine but although it deadened the pain somewhat, she felt little relief. It is interesting that we imagine the relief of pain through deadening or killing it. I have a feeling that when we imagine it that way we may do additional harm to ourselves, killing or deadening more than the pain, as happens with chemotherapy, which damages far more than the malignant cells. It would be less violent to imagine softening or cradling the pain, but then we might be afraid that we were being too soft on ourselves! But to return to the story of Rita—while clearly holding on to the rage and disgust with herself that was causing her great suffering, she was willing to try a session of relaxation and visualization in order to let it go.

Since she had four children, it was not difficult for Rita to imagine a situation in which one of them was physically hurt by falling off a bicycle. She was easily able to imagine the child running to her, bleeding and frightened, and, after being taken into her arms, becoming soothed and unafraid. It was a little more difficult for her to imagine doing the same to her wounded breast, taking it into her arms and giving it love and comfort, but after two sessions she was able to do just that—to look at her breast with tenderness, and to dress the damaged area. The need for large doses of morphine decreased fourfold. The cancer did not disappear, and she died some weeks later, but Rita softened her feelings toward her breast and her inner self, immersing them in her compassion. It was only then that she was able to weep for herself, and that seemed to release energy for the awful but necessary task of taking leave of her husband and children.

A similar story involved Dennis Rae, a man in his sixties suffering from widespread melanoma, the principal manifestation of which was a leg painfully swollen and enlarged to three times its normal size. His rage at this monstrous limb was impressive. He said that he was disgusted with it, wanted it cut off, and was both terrified and preoccupied both day and night by its awful appearance, expecting somehow that it would explode. Visualizing, holding, and touching were not part of his life experience, and he had never paid his body much attention at any time in life, always expecting it to perform well, especially since he had faithfully taken it to his doctor for an annual tune-up. However, through guided visualization, Dennis was able to embrace his wounded leg and give it care and comfort in his imagination, and he was energetic and humorous during the little ritual we created around his leg as we touched it and gave it a blessing.

Dennis grieved for himself and for his wounds, giving himself the humor and compassion that is so much needed by the soul. If this is not done, if we do not mourn for ourselves and give our soul loving care and consideration, we will be unable to mobilize our spirit and so give the care, compassion, and comfort our grieving friends and family need.

A reflection about my own mourning relates to the men's group of which I have been a member for 15 of its 25-year existence. There have been many examples of fragility amongst us of late—surgery for failing hearts, tremors, forgetfulness, and problems with sleep. All physical signs that we are aging, if we care to look. It just recently occurred to me—and if it seems to you that this thought has been packed away in layers of denial, you would be correct—that sooner rather than later, one of us is going to be the first to die, and it might be me or it might be another. I have come to love those men. I am able to look on them without judgment—most of the time—and without the competitive edge that keeps men apart from one another, and from themselves. I make little distinction between one member and another, so it is easy to ignore individual fragility and the fact that death is not far away. In our weekly gatherings I have come to feel much warmer and safer in their company, as well as more love for myself, so this recent reflection does not seem morbid or in any way repulsive to me. On the contrary, it makes me feel more loving and thankful—toward both them and myself—and before it is too late, I simply want to say this out loud.

NEBAJ: THE LIFE AND DEATH OF A HUMMINGBIRD

Nebaj was 12 years old when he died in a freak accident at the home of a friend. Nebaj died instantly. He was the only biological child of Shawn and Valerie, who live and are totally immersed in the life of a village in Mexico. What follows are some words about their life and grief in the form of a letter that Valerie wrote to her friends after Nebaj's death.

THE WISDOM OF DYING

May 1996

When Nebaj was about one hour old, I was lying with him on my chest when suddenly he lifted his head and looked me intently in the eyes for about ten seconds. He then turned his raised head to the right where Shawn was standing beside us and held his direct gaze for a prolonged moment. I wondered what was going to happen in that moment. I knew that he was checking us out but now I feel that we were affirming our understanding of our investment as a trio.

We all knew that we had a special arrangement with each other, and living that, day to day, was a great joy and is now a precious memory.

In our lowest moments, Shawn and I remind each other of the time Neby caught a hummingbird in his bare hands about six months ago. When he shouted to me excitedly, I rushed over, disbelieving, and was astounded to see the shiny emerald-gold creature in his palms. He said he had seen it and wanted to play a little prank and so he had crept up on it and grabbed it carefully. He promptly let it fly off. *So* many times I was amazed by his actions and his words and I get a sense that everyone who knew him was fascinated by him. Even us!

The last day of his life was a full moon and we had planned to go for a night hike—all the plans, all the expectations, they're so hard to give up. The promise of who he was becoming ... and then the realization that he had now become, and it was us who were becoming and he was our teacher.

That last day, he announced that he was going to light a candle and watch it burn all the way down. He set it up on the stone floor and played around it all the while. When it became a puddle of wax and was about to extinguish he got very excited and said he wanted to see something ... soon after that he went down the block to play at a friend's and he was gone.

The past three and a half months have been very hard. They have encompassed an indescribable depth of emotions that are so much bigger than us and so all-consuming—there is joy as well as sorrow. For a time I felt I would die of a broken heart, but now I know I will just live with it.

We stay home a lot, work in the garden early and late. Friends have been very important, they have been wonderful.

We feel like we have been catapulted into the future ... we had plans to make some life changes when Neby was grown up and on his own. We had talked about opening an environmental education center for the Oaxaca area, and now we notice that it seems to be sprouting all around us ... so, we'll see when we're ready to start thinking about that.

Right now, we're working on getting used to his absence, working on that hard concept called acceptance ... it's a long road. Those who were close to Neby know how he was excited about life ...there was never a dull moment when he was around. It is that excitement that we hope to be able to retrieve someday.

Nebaj was our pride and joy—now he is our guiding angel.

Shawn and Valerie sent a copy of this letter to my son-in-law, Robert. They were friends and business associates—Robert bought Mexican rugs from Shawn, who oversaw their design and production in the village. I knew about the tragedy of Nebaj's death, having been present when Robert was called with the news, and was witness to the initial grief of Robert and my daughter, Sandra. They originally had planned to vacation at the ocean with Valerie, Shawn, and Nebaj two weeks after the time Nebaj died, and to take their one-year-old son, Dylan. After talking on the phone with Valerie and Shawn, they all decided to continue with the plan, so Robert and his little family became part of the intimate family mourning for a short while. They returned home so moved by their tragic vacation, their stories, tears, and silence all washed by the sea. Valerie and Shawn told them how the whole village had joined together in a vernacular ritual of mourning that lasted for a week; it was as if the village had cradled them both in its arms. It takes a whole village to mourn a hummingbird such as Nebaj.

Soon after reading the letter and hearing the stories from Robert and Sandra, I wrote to Shawn and Valerie, and Valerie replied:

October 21, 1996

Dear Mike,

It has been almost nine months since my world was turned upside down. I think of the nine months when I contemplated who my child would be ... I must admit that his being far exceeded any expectations I could have had. The enormity of his physical presence is transformed into his immense absence—now I need to find myself again amid all the huge and conflicting emotions ... and missing him.

157

You have seen a lot of grieving—I think that would be very, very hard work. Grief is like a fog that cuts you off from everything else. I'm in no rush to get through this stage of the process. It is a very special time and a time for *feeling*. I know something important is happening.

Please be in touch!

Valerie

Grief is like a fog—there is no rush to get through. It is a very special time for *feeling*—something important is happening ...

I feel so honored and blessed to have heard about the beautiful Nebaj and his amazing parents. They have been so generous in sharing their love and their grief: only good can come of it. Theirs is a spiritual gift that unites us all.

CHAPTER 12

Living with Loss

Loss is death, the ending of something. One of the effects of loss and the upsetting of stability in our lives is that it triggers our usually dormant and well-denied terror of death. Such a loss leads to bewilderment and rage, the intensity of which is related to how dependent we were on the person or situation for our feelings of identity and stability. For example, the physician or executive who is dependent on work for feelings of self-worth and well-being might feel emotionally undermined when the job comes to an end on account of retirement, poor health, or any other reason. Similarly, the woman who is largely dependent on her husband for care and soulfulness in her own life may collapse and die—physically or emotionally—upon the event of his death, since she depended on him for her basic vitality.

A common response to loss of stability is a frenzied attempt to restore the status quo. If disease is the problem, cure it. If we lose something, find it or replace it. If we lose a friend, forget her. If we lose the stability of childhood—and especially if we never experienced it in the first place—we may continue to search for it and attempt to reclaim it through the course of a whole lifetime. When we understand that the world is in a constant state of change, and that instability and our inability to hold on to anything is normal, the feelings that accompany loss become more acceptable. When loss is understood as normal, grief will occur, but the rage response of bereavement—which emerges only when our ego believes that something has been taken away that *belongs* to us—will not overwhelm us. Grief and heartbreak will occur with every important loss, but the grief will pass away like the clouds if only we will have patience and compassion for ourselves.

When loss is consciously apprehended and pondered over without any great hurry to push it into the past and heal the wound prematurely, the heart will mend. Conversely, when loss is denied or feelings negated, or there is a vigorous attempt to busy ourselves in work or other distractions, the heart may not be allowed to break. Then there is the danger of heart attacks or other inner explosions of grief.

In dying and death training for caregivers, one of the exercises that takes place early on in the program is related to loss. A careful look at an important loss highlights what we need with regard to care for ourselves at such a time.

EXERCISE ON THE EXPERIENCE OF LOSS

I would like you to list to yourself the more important relationship losses in your life. Loss of relationship can occur not only through death, but also through betrayal, misunderstanding, addiction, or simply growing apart. Take just a few moments, and then select one of these losses to work with—perhaps one where there is still unfinished business, or one that is still painful when you pause to think about it. If loss through death is specifically what you wish to work with but nobody close to you has yet died, you might imagine the future death of a parent, for example. Work with that, imagining that your parent is dying and this is your last visit together.

Work in groups of three where one is the storyteller, another the witness, and the last is the guide. First the storyteller spends ten minutes telling the other two people the story of his loss. The guide will keep an eye on the time and suggest to the storyteller that she wrap up her tale at the close of the ten-minute period.

At the end of that time the same storyteller will spend another ten minutes speaking to the witness as if he were the embodiment of the person lost. The storyteller will now have the opportunity of speaking directly to the person she has lost. The witness will not respond.

The guide will once again keep time, and when this segment is completed, each of the three in the group will spend a couple of minutes describing how the experience was for them. The storyteller will say a few words about how the experience of tellingthis particular story was for her, as well as how it was to speak directly to the loss. She will also say a word about how she experienced both the witness and the guide. The witness and the guide will then each give a brief report of their experience.

This segment of the exercise should take approximately 30 minutes. After taking a moment to pause in silence, change roles. Continue with the exercise until each person has had a chance to play the three roles.

The groups of three then reassemble into the larger group, where there is an opportunity for the experience to be shared.

Notes on the Exercise

For the Storyteller

The storyteller may have some initial difficulty in selecting a loss to work with. I usually suggest that it is best not to think too much, so that the mind can get out of the way and allow the loss to emerge on its own. The telling of the story is usually not too difficult; talking to the one who died or went away, on the other hand, is often an extraordinary experience. Some feel quite uncomfortable at first, thinking of this part of the exercise as play-acting and not real. They might say, "After all, how can I possibly imagine that the young man to whom I am talking is my mother? And in any event, is this not just an exercise of the imagination?" But we usually find that the young man who is acting as witness and the mother who died quickly begin to seem as one, and speaking to him is as if speaking to her. If this is of the imagination, it is at least as real as anything else. It is only the rational mind that thinks of the imagination as unreal, and the rational mind knows but a small fraction of what there is to know. The imagination is a manifestation of the soul, and when the storyteller is talking to the witness, she is talking soul to soul with her mother; she is really there, and it feels like it in the exercise. The wonder of this is that she can say things to her that she was never able to say to her when she was alive, and that she has always regretted not saying.

I had much to say to my mother, but had neither the courage nor the wisdom to say it while she was alive. She died in England,

and since I was never told that she was dying, I was not present during her last days. Even if I had been, I doubt that I would have said what I eventually said to her many years later in this exercise. She was a warm and witty woman who was considerably younger than my father from whom she received little loving attention—a not uncommon trait of Irish men of his time. So she lavished her attention on me, and her physical expressions were little short of incestuous. As a shy and insecure little boy, I found such attention impossible to handle. Later, in my adolescence, she began to drink heavily, and her alcoholism was also more than I could cope with. After some years I literally flew off to America. After years of pain from never having faced her loss and mourned her death, what I told her in one of these exercises was more or less as follows:

> Mom, I never was able to talk with you. I would like to have told you that the way you expressed your love for me was very difficult for me to handle as a child. I felt overwhelmed by both your needs and my own, and only knew that I had to try to keep my distance for survival. Then there was your drinking, which was very scary for me. I picked you up off the floor a few times, and there were other occasions when I thought you were dead, but you had simply passed out. Mealtimes were so awful when you were drunk, with dad sitting and glaring at you in those awful silences. What a terrible waste of time! I never got to know you, nor you me, and that is very sad. But now what I really want to say to you is how sorry I feel that you died and I was not there. I want to thank you for being my mother. I would not be here but for you. You gave me so many things, the most important of which seem to be life and a sense of humor. I want to give you my blessing, and I need you to bless me.

Quite simple. No particular questions about why my mother did this or that—she would not know, and even if she did know, it would not matter. No angry recriminations and finger-pointing. Just an exchange of love and thanksgiving, for it is that which frees us from all the strangleholds of the past. All we need to do, when all is said and done, is to give love and to receive it. It happened for me in this exercise, just as it happens for many others.

Once we were doing this exercise in a workshop for medical students, most of whom had not yet experienced the death of someone close to them. Some had grandparents who had died but they had not been very close; their parents, siblings, and friends were all still alive. Almost all of the women in the group decided to imagine the death of their father. The exercise was an amazing experience for all of them. One or two said afterward that they had hesitated initially for fear that thinking of their father's death would somehow bring it about, or that to go through with this imagining was in some way disloyal, but they all went ahead. Telling the story of their father was not difficult; in fact, for most it was a delight. But speaking to dad for the last time brought tears and a plethora of feelings that they had barely imagined. Yet, for each of them there was a great sense of relief. They became conscious that the unimaginable idea of their father's death could in fact be imagined and would actually happen sometime in the not-too-far-distant future. They also realized that they had things to say that had not been said, and that now was the time to speak. It is difficult enough to speak when dad is well loved, but it is even more difficult if he is neglectful or abusive. Somewhere deep within the soul there is the wish for reconciliation and for loving, and the approach of death announces that there is little time left for healing. But it is just as important that we take our leave of neglectful parents as well as loving ones.

The storyteller speaks first about how it was to tell the story and then to speak directly to the person she lost. She will then say a word about the way she experienced the silent, non-doing witness. The storyteller always feels his presence very strongly, and is much comforted by it. While this passive way of listening is not too true to life—we usually tend to nod, move, judge, analyze—experiencing the role in this way reminds us about *doing* less and *being* more.

The storyteller may have a number of different responses to the guide, but most often finds her to be supportive and encouraging, even though the guide may say very little. Occasionally in these exercises, but not as often as in everyday living, the guide may be a little overwhelming—pushing too much, trying to be too helpful, or sometimes going off at a tangent. Often it is the guide's personal agenda or unfinished business in life that motivates her to play the role in this way.

For the Witness
The experience of actively hearing the story is almost always difficult for the witness. It is hard to be still—there is always the urge to intervene or interpret or judge. I personally find the witness role to be the most difficult, yet this role has so much to

teach us. As many novice meditators find out, it is much easier to become wrapped up in the endless chatterings of the mind than to be still and yet alert and awake in the present moment. But it is this witnessing that allows us to experience real connectedness to another. Perhaps that is scary for many of us because we have been conditioned to hold on to our identity at all costs. Open witnessing causes us to lose that identity. All distance disappears and we become as one.

For the Guide

This is another difficult role, since most of us have been brought up to be rescuers. The guide is not a rescuer. The guide is a friend, but is not attached. This does not mean that she is not involved or concerned—only that she is able to let go and is not invested in the outcome. The guide does her best to be with the storyteller, encouraging her to go deeper into the story, but if that does not happen she is not offended, nor does she castigate herself for being a failure. In this moment she is Hermes, the traveler god who is familiar with the sights and sounds of the underworld, who is there to guide the frightened pilgrim on the unfamiliar journey through the territory of loss, pointing out the sights along the way and thus making them more conscious and manageable. Her task is not to rescue but to accompany, and through her encouragement and being, inspire the storyteller to complete her tale.

When the small groups of three have completed their tasks, they reassemble and speak about what happened in the triads. Always there is a wealth of stories that enrich everyone present, but over the years I have noticed something of great importance. In the triads an intimate experience unfolds that is felt to be unique and of an intensity that could have happened only in that particular situation with those particular people. Yet later in the large group it is discovered that all the other groups had a similarly rich experience. In our everyday pursuits we share a few "vital" statistics with others—a few ego-markers—and imagine how different and unique we are. However, when we scratch beneath the surface and expose what is *really* vital, we discover that we are all the same and simply a part of a larger whole. This is the fascination in our being alike.

This oneness or connectedness is what always happens when storyteller, witness, and guide gather together, whether it be in the family, in the workplace, or in a workshop. Such gatherings are all too rare for our well-being.

HOPE

At some point in every workshop, and often in the discussion in the large group following this storytelling experience of loss, the issue of hope arises. People ask whether we are letting go of hope when we talk directly to friend, family, or patient about their dying. It reminds me of the story of the elephant in the living room that everyone tries to ignore by stepping around it, and no amount of chaos or smell persuades them to do otherwise. This is frequently the case with family alcoholism; variations of the story I recounted of the deadly mealtimes in my adolescence with my mother's "elephantine" alcoholism are commonplace. It is often the same with dying. It becomes this giant presence in the household that nobody talks about, which makes comfortable living quite impossible. Life is thus suspended, and everyone holds their breath. We can actually live a very vibrant life in the face of death, but we cannot live with bated breath. When we hold the breath for too long, we suffocate.

There is a fear that if we speak of death to someone who is dying it will be like beating our loved one over the head with that reality, and we do not want to do that. When we have had no practice, any words are likely to come out awkwardly or even explosively. We imagine that we have to bombard the person with a statement such as, "Do you know that you are dying?" Words spoken like this—standing alone, wrapped in fear, uttered by a robotic fact-fountain rather than a person who is also willing to be witness and guide—are devoid of hope. But there are other much more loving approaches, ways that are full of hope because they break the dreadful silence and the terrifying aloneness, that can bring the dying person back into relationship within the family.

We might say:

Dad, we have tried everything we know in dealing with this cancer. I have been amazed at your patience and courage, because it has not been easy. We have always been looking ahead to CAT-scan results or new treatment protocols, but these things do not seem to be very useful any more. I have worried about you day and night, but we have never really talked, and I am really concerned how all this is for you. What do you worry about? Are you scared at times? I am.

In speaking this way we have identified the elephant in the living room. Now we can talk about it, and that is extremely helpful because now we are no longer alone. Hope has to do with connectedness—with the knowledge that we can talk and love together. Most people think of hope in connection with the removal of illness and the dream that we can once again get on with our regular, death-denying lives. This kind of hope is inspired by the denial of death and the terror of impermanence.

The denial of death on the part of many physicians leads them to say things to inspire hope. This was experienced by a medical student who participated in a recent workshop of mine. Her father had been diagnosed with invasive prostate cancer a few months earlier, and the surgeon had told the family standing outside the operating theater that he had "got it all." Over and over again I have heard patients with far-advanced cancer say that, after surgery, their surgeon had given them a clean bill of health or said in respect to the cancer that he had got it all. Sometimes the oncologist has persuaded them to undergo vigorous chemotherapy—even though it would be unlikely to do more than extend life for another few weeks—by regaling them with statistics that are both indigestible and irrelevant to quality of life. It seems as though some physicians feel that it is a caring act to lie in the service of "hope," even when they have not paused to ponder on the meaning of the word. The alternative to lying need not be to assault the patient with the brutal facts, but to move a little closer through truthful and lovingly direct communication.

This storytelling exercise gives us a firsthand experience of loss and with it the realization that we all have losses unmourned. We need to take seriously our own losses and our need to grieve. Heart attacks will follow for those of us whose hearts will not break. Ulcers will tear us apart inside from losses that we are unwilling or unable to digest. Malignancies will emerge from buried relationships that end or die with the ambivalence unforgiven and unreleased. The skin will weep from our failure to weep, and itch from chronic relational irritation. Examples abound, and while the association with loss cannot always be

proven or the loss itself is hidden or "forgotten," we *know.*
Treatment of the physical condition is necessary, but listening to
the soul with a witness and a guide is also needed to uncover the
rage and sadness that is a prelude to healing and letting go.

Impeccable self-care is an essential part of the practice of
wisdom. Greater consciousness of our own losses leads to greater
awareness of the losses of others and of the association between
the pain of the soul and physical malaise. We need to attain this
level of self-knowing, and we need to teach and guide others with
a clear understanding that such relationship-centered care is the
essence of healing.

CHAPTER 13

Rituals and Dying

Stories are the threads that weave us together in an endless patchwork quilt that covers us all. The vitality of our being depends on the telling of stories and myths, and rituals are their manifestation. Rituals are the celebration of the soul and of our connectedness with one another, and if we fail to keep them alive or create new ones, life will feel empty of meaning.

The word *myth* has been ascribed meanings in our time that suggest that myths are insubstantial and untrue. The modern rational-functionalist may have a patronizing view of them, speaking of myths as primitive, unbelievable, and rather amusing. Yet universally, myths are regarded as a source of cultural wisdom, a way of communicating archetypal energies. They are seen as spontaneous productions of the imagination to inspire awe, creativity, and comfort, like those of Sharazad and Persephone and countless others.

If myths are stories that arise from deep inside the senses and from within the vast dark matter of the soul, rituals are the eternal river that runs through these storied tapestries, sustaining their vitality. The word ritual is Middle English, deriving from the Latin *ritus*, meaning to flow or stream. A rite is the river itself. At the end of a journey, a French person might say "J'arrive," which literally means "I have come down the river, and here I am." The rite of passage signifies a flow from one state in life or story to another, and the ritual accompanying it is an age-old ceremony that celebrates the journey. Since the river is constantly flowing, the ritual can never be exactly the same, but a bored celebrant or a bevy of somnolent witnesses may make one ritual seem like another. In that case the river is frozen or stagnant and there is no life and the soul is not vitalized.

Rituals may often appear to be somber and serious, but the

parades of Mardi Gras, for instance, are joyous and perhaps bawdy, poking fun at our eccentricities as the floats stream along celebrating the flow of life and the changes of the seasons. Humor can lighten even the most fearful terrors of the dark, and we can even say as we parade or float down the river that death is fatal but not serious. "Going with the flow" is to let go and enter into the stream, which contains a limitless mythology of the unknown and is so much larger than ourselves.

Many religious rituals involve water. First there is baptism, through which we are cleansed of any real or imagined fault by the waters of the river. Confession has a similar function—an ablution of absolution, a letting go of our sins which we cast into the river so that they may be swept away. Then there is the rite of passage around death, when sins are let go and forgiven and the body is gently washed as the soul and spirit pass on.

In a world that has become ever more rational and functional and governed by profit and the bottom line, we are desperately short of rituals. Rituals honor and celebrate the soul and the spirit, and this industrial-mechanical age is nothing but anathema to soul and spirit. Rituals are not of the mind; they are of myth and dark matter and the river, and so make little sense. This causes them to become easy targets of the rationalist thinker and the budget-cutter, who may believe them to be a waste of time and money. They may even dam or divert the river, drying up the soul and spirit of a community and all who live therein.

Publicly, our rituals are few. In the US for example, the presidential inauguration is a celebration of the national soul and spirit, but it only occurs every four years and is largely ignored by the people and often chilled by both weather and politics. It took a presidential assassination to create a magnificent ritual that expressed the bewildered state of feelings and imagination; all who witnessed the rites surrounding the death of John Kennedy became part of the mourning of this atrocity to our collective soul. Most other national events in the US are commercially sponsored spectacles, and our most commonly and powerfully felt rituals center around sporting events. These may fall far short of what is essential for soul and spirit because sacred rituals, like any other form of loving and flowing intercourse celebrating our connectedness, are neither intended to be interrupted for commercials nor designed primarily with ego and profit in mind.

Countries that still sustain a monarchy provide many rituals for their people. While the monarchy makes little sense any more, it provides an almost visible link with the past; it offers a collective look at the origins of all who live in the realm, and this river to the past helps to keep the roots of all in the kingdom moist and alive. In the same way, traditional religions continue to provide and encourage rituals for their flocks. Prayer, the sacraments, singing, chanting, and a variety of other rites are the expressions of many established religions, providing opportunities for adherents to drift in the enchantment of the river.

Rituals transform. They remove something that seems overwhelmingly personal, as with the death of Nebaj for Shawn and Valerie, and cradle it in the arms of a larger gathering—as with the rituals created by the Mexican villagers—so that the loss is seen for what it is: a loss for everyone, and one that is a little more easily borne by the parents for it being shared by all. Ritual weaves relationships that may not at first glance seem very intimate into a colorful cloth that warms and shelters, making personal loss easier to bear. It is a mark of our aloneness that there are now very few community rituals for grieving; the funeral home wake involves a long line of individuals who do not become a group that can collectively grieve and support those who are touched by the loss.

Rituals transform an event into something larger and timeless by joining the participants with all others who have performed that ritual throughout the ages. The ritual of the Catholic mass, for instance, is the same everywhere and has been performed in the same manner for 2,000 years, drawing all who witness the event into something eternal, with a past, a present, and a future. It is less easy to maintain the lonely and isolating distance of the rage in bereavement when we are immersed in a ritual and bathed in the tears and grief of many, allowing our own tears and sorrow to emerge in the safety of the ritual's embrace.

What follows are some thoughts about rituals that may already have some place in our lives but with a little more conscious attention might take us further down the river, and provide more of the care craved by our soul and spirit.

FOOD

When lovingly prepared, food can be the focal point of rituals of great power. Once it was that families sat down to meals together; this was the time for communion and interaction. Some of it was not very nourishing—squabbles, fragmented stories, very little witnessing, and judgments galore—but at least the forum was present and there was a gathering. Now, in many families, fast-food reigns, and its advent has done much to destroy meal times as occasions for the consumption of food for both body and soul. Even in France, where eating and drinking are regarded as an art form, the amount of time that the family spends together at the dining table has been cut in half in recent years.

Many religious rituals involve offerings, usually of bread and wine. One of the most powerful rituals involving food and wine that I have ever attended happened early in the life of the hospice when I met Alice. Then in her mid-thirties, Alice was a patient in the general hospital who was overwhelmed by many complications resulting from far-advanced breast cancer. While Alice was extremely wasted and obviously had only a short time to live, I was quite unable to engage her in more than superficial conversation, with Alice saying that all was well and that she had no worries or concerns. She had two daughters, aged 14 and 16, and I met them initially without their mother. At first they were sullen and silent, but after a while they spoke of feeling so enraged and overwhelmed at what was happening that they were not able to visit their mother for more than a few minutes at a time without being beset by anger and terror and needing to flee from her room. They went on to tell me that their father had died of a heart attack when the older girl was three, but that their mother had been very loving and capable and was supported by a large Italian family. They also wondered and were fearful about what was going to happen to them after mother died, because nobody was talking about what was really going on. Having begun to open up, they were then able to rage and weep with their mother, giving her an opportunity to give them comfort as well as freeing her to talk and tell her story.

Alice, who had always been a warm, fun-loving person who relished cooking and giving parties, decided to host a going-away party in her hospital room. She commissioned one of her sisters—

the one who had agreed to become custodian of the two girls, much to their delight—to buy small gifts for her family, as well as food and drink for the party. The hospital authorities, who had never experienced anything quite like this, watched in awe. I have never participated in such a warm, loving, tear-stained communion. We were all moved way down the river, far beyond words, by the courageous gift of this young woman as she said good-bye to those she loved. Alice died three days later.

LIGHT

Rituals of light are illuminating for the spirit. Sunrises and sunsets offer opportunities to celebrate the very center of our soul—we gasp in awe at the sunrise and let go of the breath with an expiratory sigh on witnessing the sunset. An eclipse of the sun is a moment when we feel and can observe that we are in the presence of a power beyond imagining. At the instant of eclipse, even the earth seems to hold its breath in fear that there may not be another moment.

Candle-lighting can be a most moving ritual. I remember George, a medical student, sitting by his dying mother's bedside in the hospice Inn. They had an unusually intimate relationship— George was an only child and his father had left during George's infancy. Mother and son doted on one another, and there had been many warm and humorous stories earlier on in her stay at the Inn. Now she was barely conscious and close to death, and George, together with his mother's home-care nurse, was sitting by her side. This nurse had become a delicious blend of daughter and sister within this small family, and she too was grieving and had come to say good-bye. They had arranged a number of colored candles on the bedside table, and as I witnessed from the end of the bed, each lit a candle, describing as they did so some of the characteristics of mother that were inspired by that particular color. George had said that his mother's favorite color was yellow. Moments after he lit a yellow candle, she died.

Then there was a woman who had been moved to the Inn only an hour before she died. There had been no family meeting, and denial had been so formidable in this family that vigorous chemotherapy had never been discontinued. She had four children by her first marriage and a very caring second husband who was quite unable to console either himself or the children. When I arrived shortly after the death, there was chaos, with the husband, children, two sisters, and several other friends and relatives all in various states of disbelief. Three of the four children were too afraid to enter their mother's room.

I was unable to do anything useful with words, so I set up a large number of candles on the bedtable. With much fear and footdragging, all the friends and family entered the room, until it seemed as though every space was filled. The candle-lighting ritual was quite miraculous. One by one, each lit a candle accompanied by a few words, often from deep within the soul; it was hello and good-bye all in one. In the powerful silence after the last had spoken, we stood and watched the flickering candles and the dead face they lighted up, and after a while all those gathered left in peace. No words of consolation could have done more to comfort or move the family toward harmony and letting go than this simple ritual.

Prayer and Meditation

The word *prayer* often conjures up the question of whether or not one is a "believer"—which is understood as being a believer in God. The answer to this question supposedly determines whether or not we pray. But the question can be looked at so much more simply: it is the task of the spirit to give care, and it is also the task of the soul to ask for the care needed and give thanks. Prayer is simply the asking for care and the giving of thanks.

In the Buddhist world, one of the spiritual tasks of the monks is to beg for food. To beg means nothing more than to beseech or to ask. The monks ask or pray for what they need, offering an empty rice bowl, which is then filled. Then they give thanks. In their asking they have given a spiritual opportunity to another, allowing them to give what is needed. Very simple. Behind it all is the understanding that the monks are not asking for more than they need; they are not hoarding or selling, and there is no scam and no deception.

In the West, begging has taken on a meaning laden with judgment, and praying is something done in churches. Since many of us have far more than we need and are constantly in search of more of the same, there is usually a paranoid suspicion about those who beg. Does he really need it? Is that woman with the sad child a fraud? Are they all confidence tricksters simply trying to get more for nothing when they have plenty—are they just like me, begging and manipulating for more than I need? This lack of trust in self and others has brought begging or asking or praying into disrepute, except in relationship to God. We then go on to rationalize that we should work for what we want and always pay for it. Even a freely given act by a good Samaritan must be paid for, since we feel uneasy about accepting something for nothing. For good measure or bad, we add that we should be independent and not need one another. We should pay for all of the care we receive rather than pray or beg, and in every way possible obliterate the obvious fact of our interdependence and need of one another for our spiritual well-being.

If we are unable to ask, or feel that it is wrong or that somehow we are being too needy, then our spiritual health suffers, individually and collectively, and that is what we see and feel all around us. It is not the fact that religions are failing, or that we are not praying enough to God. The problem is that we are not praying or asking one another for what we need and have allowed our fear and judgments to stand in the way, and this creates intense loneliness and isolation.

Prayer does work. If we ask one another for care and love and give thanks for the being of one another, miracles can happen, because many of us are longing to be asked. I have often visited the dying in large apartment buildings and have thought that behind all those other closed doors there must be more than enough for the needs of the dying person, but the people who could give and be witness and nourish the soul and spirit of the one who is dying seldom come forth. There are probably many reasons why these fellow apartment-dwellers do not emerge, but I suspect the main one is the fear and anonymity of apartment living in these times of spiritual drought, with most people saying, "I mind my own business." But for the most part they are not asked because we are ashamed to beg and must maintain our nonexistent independence, even when we are dying.

Prayer works if we ask God and give thanks, but in prayer our spirit asks only for what it needs, which is probably not what the ego wants. The ego wants more—more life or more health or more strength—but what we actually need at the time, whether it be at the time of our dying or at any other, is usually way beyond our knowing. And there needs to be trust that we will get what we need—from God or the universe.

There is evidence that prayer heals physically, and it certainly heals spiritually. From all that has been said before, it is obvious that we need to pray because we are unable to be born or live or die alone. I have often heard people say that they are not religious, by which they usually mean that they do not attend any church. Some will add that they do not believe in God. The word religion derives from the Latin *re-ligio* or "the thing that binds." In fact, we are all interconnected or bound together, so we are all religious. And clearly there is a power or a knowing so much greater than ourselves, and one name for that power is God. I usually suggest to the non-believer that he not deprive his spirit of what it needs— that he pray or ask or beg for love and the spirit of connectedness from himself, his family, his neighbors, and the universe.

If our lives are to have meaning—if we are essentially here to give and receive love—then we need to pray or ask. We need to ask ourselves and each other. We need to ask ourselves to be more trusting and open to receive and to let go. We need to ask each other to be witnesses and give physical and soulful comfort to one another. We need to ask God—the Holy Spirit—to come into our souls and give us the love we need. And we need to give thanks.

Some of us who will not have had too much experience in praying will fall back on the only model we know: Santa Claus. We will have a list of things we want, with the childhood expectation that our God will follow instructions and fill our lives with those requests. If that is the substance of the prayer we have with God, we are likely to be disappointed. If we will trust, open up our arms, and let go—surrender—then we will get what we need, if not what we want.

Prayers to God may be formal. There are many prayers of great beauty that have been repeated over the ages, and in our saying them we become connected with all the souls who have ever said those words. There are rites and rituals in many religious traditions that are beautiful offerings set to words and music. They cause the spirit to soar, and if the mind is still, it is impossible not to experience the connectedness of all at such times.

Meditation is a form of prayer. If prayer is the act of asking or begging together with the grace to give thanks to an "outside"

God, then meditation is the act of holding still and doing nothing, allowing the God within to be manifested from within the dark matter of the soul. It is a passive act of asking and giving thanks by giving up both time and ego in order to be with God or in order to be a part of God. It is an exquisite practice that teaches letting go, detachment, and nonsuffering. It is a practice that is difficult for most of us because the mind is such a great distraction from the stillness necessary to experience God for more than a few glimpses. If we are willing to persevere, even through barren periods of fear and doubt, both meditation and prayer are readily available practices that will heal soul and spirit during dying or living.

MUSIC

The amazing thing about attending a concert is that all the differences between us disappear; we become one. The music seems to fill all the interstices between us and we all vibrate and are soothed or uplifted by the sounds we hear as we listen and experience as one. When the music ends there is a liminal pause—a brief silence between the sounds of musical ecstasy and the silence of coming down to earth—followed by a roar from the audience, a collective orgasm of relief and appreciation. I have noticed this particularly with a favorite of mine, Rachmaninoff's third piano concerto. This is a piece requiring the greatest virtuosity by the pianist, who dives and soars and stretches in a river of sound that ends in a crescendo that almost stops the heart. Even in recordings, the pause before the applause is included, because without this the work would be incomplete since in this moment the composer, the orchestra, and the witnesses so clearly become one.

Music is there for the celebration and caressing of all our various moods. There are lullabies for children and for dying. At one time in the hospice Inn we had a volunteer who played lullabies on the Irish harp that were a delight for all, even for those one or two who awoke to hear the harp playing and thought they had died and gone to heaven! There are songs that bring us back to our roots. For me, some of these are Irish songs sung by the mystical Noirin Ni Riain; I am also lulled and cradled by choirs and the liturgical music I heard in my youth. There are sounds for solitude and others for sadness or joy. In a letter to a friend,[1] Mahler said of his second symphony, *The Resurrection,* "The whole thing sounds as though it came to us from another world. And I think that there is *no one* who can resist it. One is battered to the ground and then raised on angel's wings to the highest heights." I certainly am unable to resist it, finding that it transports me on a journey into the dark matter of the soul that amazes me. From the most tender and sublime to the evocative and inspirational, music urges us to come to the river and immerse ourselves and be soothed, letting go of the stresses of our journey.

I have heard beautiful music in the hospice Inn over the years. I remember not only the celestial harp but also a magical flautist who also delighted in playing for whales, a mammal so obviously related to us. Then there was an exquisite professional choir that visited us a few times, and there were carolers at Christmastime, and Harvey, a warm-hearted honky-tonk piano player from a bygone age who regaled us every Friday at lunch. And I will always remember Don Paul, a delightfully colorful social worker who had once been a professional singer, singing lullabies and other pearls to families, creating this mystical oneness that is often so difficult to shape with words alone.

CREATING A RITUAL

We can create our own rituals to suit our particular needs and circumstances. In the hospice Inn the creative and soulful chaplain, Sister Jean, would invite families and staff to the Thursday morning prayer service where, with the imaginative use of color, sound, and song, she wove ceremonies that moved us all. She would lead a meditation on our hands, hands that have touched, held, created, punched, scratched, stroked, and performed an endless number of major or minor miracles; the meditation would then continue by looking at, touching, and appreciating the hands of those around us. Another time the ceremony might be a reflection on the magic of water, ending with giving each other a blessing. Or we might all create our own mandala, a circular creation filled with color and line depicting a mystical, soulful origination from the imagination.

---

1 *Selected Letters of Gustav Mahler,* ed. Knud Martner, Farrer, Straus and Giroux, New York, 1979.

In designing any ritual, the guiding spirit of the ritual in life or after death might be invoked by asking what it is that the person loved. If it was the family—and even when there is some doubt—then the family meeting is an obvious ritual, and this may also be the occasion to express the essentials of vows that have not been vocalized for many years. I have participated in several weddings close to the time of death of one of the celebrants, and there has been no ritual for them that could have been more perfect.

If food was always a joy in life, then there is nothing more appropriate than inviting family and friends to a communion around food, as Alice did. A going-away party may be difficult for most of us to imagine, especially when we think of the parties we have attended that were either too dull to repeat or too inappropriate for an occasion near death, but this is because many of those events were not designed to be celebrations of the soul; there may have been little trust, intimacy, or expression of love, because that was not the intention.

When the outdoors is a passion, a memorial service in the open air is perfect. I would like to imagine mine being somewhere close to water. I feel the draw of the Ganges or the Styx, but the river at the bottom of my garden would be just fine. I remember when Bob died, his loving companion and devoted caregiver, Julie, arranged his memorial service at a beautiful nature preserve that was so much an extension of both of them. I remember imagining how awful the ceremony would have been if it had been held in the dark confines of a funeral home. That ritual was so healing and so much more powerful for having invited nature to participate.

We do not need to wait until one we love has died to plant flowers or a tree; those are healing events for the living.

Whatever the ritual, we can devise it around the person whose life we are celebrating and make it personal by adding a dimension that expresses the love that radiates from soul. A candle ceremony could focus attention on a person's favorite colors as well as the music she loved and the flowers that enriched her life, and perhaps, like Nebaj, we would watch the candle burn to the very end.

At the time of death there needs to be a moment for candle-lighting, a blessing, and a few words of story or a prayer. If the death has taken place in an institution, I believe that it is of crucial importance that the staff be present at this ceremony of ending and thanksgiving. It could change their lives and the life of the institution.

The washing of the body has all but disappeared as a ritual; now it is simply a routine duty for nurses or funeral home staff. The Jewish and Muslim traditions still include ritual washing of the body, although it is not always performed by members of the family, and may exclude those not of the same gender as the deceased. I believe that the family should always be invited and encouraged to participate in this ritual washing. It can be a final loving act for those deeply connected to the one who died. This ritual washing has very little to do with cleaning and nothing whatever to do with hygiene. There is every reason for children to be involved, if they have loved the person, so as not to reinforce in them the collective fear and untouchability of death. Once again, this ceremonial washing could be accompanied by music, candles, prayer, stories, food, laughter, and tears. The ritual is for the soul and the spirit of both the dead and the living, and it is an expression of love—nothing more, and nothing less.

The stilled and oppressive air of a funeral home is no place for a celebration. The word wake has a number of meanings in the English language. The meaning usually associated with death has to do with keeping watch or guard over a body. If the object of the wake ritual is to watch or guard, we no longer do the job very well, except in the case of heads of state. We hand over the body to the funeral home, where it is held in the same manner that banks hold jewels and other valuables. A three-hour session in a funeral home may be a viewing, but it certainly is not a watch. I believe we need wakes as part of letting go and giving thanks, and we need more than a few hours in a reception line in order to keep watch before we let go.

If we need to use funeral homes because they are convenient and well organized in the face of the inconvenience and chaos of death, then we might think of hosting an all-night wake. We might ask about food and drink and candles and water for blessing. It is interesting that in New York state, food and drink are illegal in funeral homes, a ruling apparently initiated by the restaurant business who felt that funeral homes were taking trade that belonged to them! However, if there is enough demand, laws will change, and those that further inhibit our endangered practice of rituals need to change. Perhaps in the funeral home we could pass the Talking Stick—certainly we need to tell stories. If a chaplain is to be present, we would expect that he or she would know something of the soul and spirit of the one who has died and, through words, weave the family into the ceremony. Sister Jean from the hospice Inn and a few others I have met make this a most sacred occasion for the celebration of soul and spirit, but all too often I have heard clergy who appear to be soul-dead, droning from religious texts that have been sucked dry of any relevance, energy, and consolation.

We say that we are going to the funeral home to pay our respects, and we need to do exactly that for both ourselves and the family. The word respect derives from the Latin *re-specere*, to look back. A viewing probably does not offer much of an opportunity to look back, but a wake could be designed so that all would have that opportunity, in the same way that all have the opportunity to speak with respect in a family meeting.

Funerals are usually orchestrated by the various religious traditions, and it is a major problem of most churches that the benches are arranged in such a way that little human interaction is ensured. Some would say that this offers fewer distractions during our conversations with God, but distance from one another is not usually what we need in times of death. Many of those who attend a funeral service do not go out to the cemetery afterwards. For those who do, there is a short service by the graveside, but nowadays the coffin is not usually buried in the sight of all, and this seems to be another example of stripping away rituals that aid the soul in letting go. This practice, although carried out in the name of convenience, is yet another sign of denial of death.

Cremation is becoming more acceptable, yet for some it seems so final and too abrupt, and others feel the need to keep the body intact for its resurrection even though we become dust in no time at all. I have heard many stories of creative ceremonies around the disposal of the ashes: a folk singer whose passion was baseball having his ashes spread on Wrigley Field, Timothy Leary propelled by rocket into orbit around our planet, Bertha's ashes being spread around the tree where she taught Mary to paint, and those of John's friend Will being spread on a mountain in Alaska. All these ceremonies return our dust to the space or the earth we loved.

CHAPTER 14

Rituals and Living

The rituals that are so clearly an important expression of soulfulness in and around death are a vivid reminder for many of us that there is an absence of ritual in our lives. If we are to practice soulful living as well as soulful dying, and bring consciousness and honor to the soul, we must incorporate rituals that celebrate this way of being into our daily lives.

Rituals are expressions of the soul. They are neither rational nor functional, nor are they measurable in economic terms, so the logical mind may dismiss them as unproductive or a waste of time. However, without them we have no moments when we simply assemble and celebrate our oneness and connectedness.

Rituals are woven tapestries of celebration, with the warp made up of the elements of nature and the woof composed of the senses. Simple or exotic, rituals can involve the fire of candles, the cleansing and baptism of water, the breath of the Holy Spirit, the earthiness of ashes, and the spaciousness of meditation, mantras, and prayer. In addition, there are rituals involving the sounds of words and music, and the magical visual pageants celebrating both the seasons and the saints.

Healing is that which occurs as a result of loving relationships—with ourselves, with others, and with "all that is" or God. It is not necessarily related to cure or the elimination of disease, although this might also occur, but it mainly refers to the state of our loving connectedness. We can be without disease but in urgent need of healing because of being disconnected from ourselves and others; conversely, we can be dying and yet, at the same time, healed.

Dreaming is thought by some to be little more than electrical or chemical discharges during sleep that have little or no significance. Others believe that dreams offer a pathway into a realm of consciousness that is not normally available during waking hours. This realm might be akin to the dark matter of the cosmos, which is unknown and yet makes up the vast majority of the universe. This realm of the soul may be equally immense; dreams might offer glimpses into this unknown. Clearly this unknown may well contain inner powers for cure and for healing, and dreams may show the way.

RITUALS AND HEALING

An elaborate ritual enacted at Epidaurus in Greece more than 2,000 years ago, incorporated both healing and dreams. In the face of the impersonality and disconnectedness of modern-day technological medicine, there is a greater interest in healing and dreams and a longing for ritual. The scene at Epidaurus will be described here since it has much to teach us in our present day.

Apollo, the sun god, patron of music and poetry, was next in power to his father, Zeus. He was also patron of medicine and the physician of the gods, healing them when they were wounded and even wounding them in order to heal—reminding us of today's physician-induced illnesses and misfortunes. The caduceus of Apollo—which is also the symbol of modern allopathic medicine—consists of a staff around which is entwined a single snake. Like much in Greek mythology, the identity of the snake is not too clear. It is most likely that it represents the giant female serpent Delphyne, who was slain by Apollo. Again we can see a parallel in modern medicine, which has killed off the caregiving feminine spirit yet has the temerity to display as its emblem this lifeless female form draped around a staff. The caduceus of Hermes, with its two intertwined snakes representing knowledge and wisdom is often mistaken for the emblem of medicine, even though Hermes is not mythologically associated with medicine. This serendipitous selection of a more kindly totem seems like a yearning for the guidance and wisdom of Hermes by a medical system that is coldly Apollonian. It may also be a sign that we have a vague awareness of the healing power of storytelling, since it is Hermes who is interested in our stories, not the more rational Apollo. It is the hermetic quality of care that understands the importance of storytelling in healing.

Asclepius, son of the god Apollo, was born of the mortal

Coronis, who was also killed by Apollo, although Asclepius was recscued from his mother's womb at the last minute. Apollo gave Asclepius to the wise and kindly centaur, Chiron, to raise. It was Chiron who conveyed to Asclepius the warmth and loving kindness that is so essential for healers—characteristics sadly lacking in his father, Apollo. The divine physician Asclepius, offspring of mortal woman and the god of fire and light, had a great following among mortals. A Christ-like figure, he would not only heal mortals by restoring the warmth lost in their sickness, but also bring some back to life, reanimating their souls and restoring their vitality. Asclepius had many daughters, two of whom were assistants to their father: Hygieia, whose name means "health," and her sister Panacea, whose name means "all-healing." There were many centers of healing built in honor of Asclepius, the most important being at Epidaurus. The objective of the many thousands of pilgrims who traveled to Epidaurus more than 2,000 years ago was to have a healing dream while they slept in the temple.

On arrival at Epidaurus pilgrims were met by a priest or priestess whose duty it was to be their guide throughout their stay and prepare them for their dream by means of a series of purifications for body and soul. The purification consisted of a special diet, healing baths, athletics of all kinds, theater performances both comic and tragic, and the offering of a sacrifice. In a few days, when the priest felt the pilgrims were well prepared both in body and in soul, he took them up to the temple. There they would lie down to sleep, perhaps on the skin of an animal they had sacrificed, and the priest would offer a prayer invoking the healing of Asclepius during the night. The following morning the priest would be there to assist in interpreting their dreams. Some of the dreamers were healed of their malady, some simply felt better in both body and soul; others had a dream that offered guidance for their lives. Those few who experienced neither healing nor dreams were encouraged by the priests to remain in Epidaurus and return later to this sacred place until they, too, received their healing dream.

The experience of Epidaurus—and the experience of any pilgrimage, even one to a physician's office—offers a number of lessons about our search for healing.

The Quest

We set out in search of healing because we feel dis-ease of body or soul. Powerful places like Epidaurus, and physicians of renown in our present time, attract us like magnets, and we have faith and trust that the dis-ease will be relieved. We now have much less faith and trust in ourselves and our own healing powers, in part because of the impressive credentials and advertising of healing places and persons, and also because of our fears and sense of personal impotence and vulnerability. So we usually set out for somewhere, but when we arrive, the skillful healer will not only prescribe remedies but will also guide us to search for healing from within.

Fellow Pilgrims

There is something about being part of a group or crowd on a healing quest that is itself healing. I imagine those tired and frightened pilgrims setting off for Epidaurus telling their stories to one another, and in the telling and witnessing feeling so much more at ease and less alone. When I was a family physician in London I had two sessions daily, each of two or three hours duration, during which patients would come to my office. There were no appointments, so there might be 20 or more people gathered in the waiting room, and the stories flowed. Looking back I sense that what went on in the waiting room was often at least as important as what went on in my office, but in later years the convenience of appointments did away with this opportunity for healing. Any sacred quest undertaken with others offers the opportunity for connectedness, and it is this connectedness with others for which the soul yearns; this is healing. The journey is as important as the destination, because on the way we may meet both ourselves and others, and healing may have occurred long before we reach "Epidaurus."

The Preparation

Becoming prepared to receive healing is an essential part of the experience, at Epidaurus or anywhere else. Ritual cleansing prepares the body by washing it of the abrasive grime of everyday life. A feast is the opportunity for communion with others while providing loving nourishment for the body. Watching tragedy reminds us of the dark side of our human spirit and of death, as well as the fact that there are others so much worse off than ourselves. Comedy tickles the imagination, bathing us in the healing potential of laughter. Sacrifice acknowledges a power greater than ourselves, a power that we need if we are to be healed. Priests and priestesses embody our need for guides, with the masculine power for the spirit and the feminine nurture for the soul. Both are required, and while we can aspire to become our own guide, to have others in times of dis-ease and distress is a precious gift.

The Dream

Does the healing and the guidance offered by the dream result from the grace and favor of Asclepius, or does it originate and emerge from ourselves? Perhaps Asclepius is simply a part of ourselves, so that all of us have this healing power within if only we will prepare ourselves for it to appear. The fascination of the Greek gods is that they simply represent different facets of ourselves, facets that are occasionally obvious but are more usually hidden in the dark matter of the soul.

THE WORKSHOP RITUAL

Because the pilgrimage at Epidaurus is an archetypal ritual of healing, in the Dying and Death workshops we enact an event inspired by Asclepius, offering the group a rare experience.

The ritual begins in the evening and lasts until breakfast the following morning. Two hours prior to the start we meet as a group, and the participants decide which specific part of the ritual they will take responsibility for. Beyond the title of each event, no detailed instructions or directions are given, the form of each event being the result of the creativity and imagination of the small group of participants. The time allotted for each group to prepare for the ceremony is short, but the imaginative creations are always amazing.

The Sacred Walk

The ritual begins the way it would have done in Epidaurus long ago, with a walk that symbolizes the journey of the pilgrims to the site of healing. The pace and direction of the walk, which lasts about an hour, is in the care of the small organizing group. The walk becomes a study in awareness and attention to the present.

In Vipassana meditation there are two forms of practice that help focus on the present: a sitting meditation in which attention is focused on the breath, and a walking meditation in which attention is given to every movement and step in slow walking. Usually when we are walking we are thinking about something else—worries and concerns of yesterday or tomorrow. We often miss out on what is beneath our feet and before our eyes in the present moment. This lack of awareness denies us the opportunity of allowing the space we are in to absorb all our cares and refreshen our inner beings. Nature will always help us to let go when we are attentive and have the desire. The walk ends at the place where the remainder of the ritual will take place, and the initiation begins.

The Initiation

This event is a ceremony of welcome as it might have taken place for the pilgrims at Epidaurus. Each initiation is unique, but most involve a ritual of cleansing or purification with water, coupled with some combination of poetry, dance, chants, and candle lighting. An initiation announces that something special is about to begin. In everyday life, when nothing very much is seen as sacred or special (except, perhaps, marriage and death), there are few rites of passage and thus few special beginnings. The initiation in this Epidaurian ritual sets the tone for what follows.

The Feast

The regular evening meal is transformed into a feast with a blessing, decorations, speeches, toasts, and anything else which can transform this particular meal into something special. Mealtimes in families, and both at school and in the workplace, have become shorter and shorter, and there are usually very few occasions of sacredness in communion with a group. Most often nowadays, a meal is the occasion to swallow a few calories, and the opportunity for nurturing and healing is missed.

The Entertainment

While the entertainment in Epidaurus included both tragedy and comedy, in the several years that I have witnessed this ritual no group has ever performed a tragedy. Perhaps because we live tragedy every day and it is the subject matter for much of the rest of the workshop, we are loath to imagine more. Or perhaps we simply prefer to laugh, and in a workshop on dying and death we are particularly appreciative of the healing power of comedy. The creative accomplishments of the entertainment group in such a short time never ceases to amaze me, reminding me of the wealth of imagination at our disposal if only we will call it forth.

The Healing Dream

When I was first facilitating these workshops, this Epidaural ceremony was not conceived as a ritual but derived from my speculating about the experience of coma. I was curious how it would be if two participants were to lie down overnight, imagining themselves to be in coma, with the rest of us attending to them in any way we saw fit. In these early workshops, two participants would volunteer to be "in coma." They would lie down on a mattress early in the evening, and the rest of the group would attend and witness throughout the night, until breakfast the following morning. Some people would simply sit close by the pair "in coma" and meditate. Others would sing or chant, and still others would read or massage or turn the "comatose" bodies. Afterwards, those who were "in coma" said they experienced a feeling of great safety from being constantly attended by loving people. Details of the words spoken, the music, and the touchings were not remembered in any specificity other than as delicate strands of a web of love and security. This safety allowed many of those "in coma" to sink into deep dreams, which they later described to the group.

The coma experience was not unlike the ancient ceremony at Epidaurus. The power of that experience for the whole group led me eventually to use it as a model for the Epidaurian ritual which we use now for experiencing the power of ritual and healing dreams in the workshop. We invite two workshop participants to be the dreamers for the group, and the rest of the participants take shifts in witnessing and watching over the dreamers during the night. Any of the other participants may have a special dream during the night, and they often do, but it is usual for one or both of the dreamers to have a dream that is significant and even healing for most members of the group.

The Dreamers

A brief explanation of the ritual is given early on the day that it begins, and the group members are requested to consider if they would like to be one of the two dreamers. At lunchtime the volunteers announce themselves, and there are usually more than two. If that is the case, the volunteers are requested to meet together after lunch and decide among themselves which two will be the dreamers.

The Dreamers' Ritual

After the entertainment is over, there is a brief ceremony where the group gives its blessing to the dreamers as they take to their beds for the night. They bring a mattress and bedclothes to the main room of the workshop, and arrange their space in any way they wish. The remaining group members sign up for a two-hour period of watch, and there are always at least two witnesses present. The dreamers are asked if they have any requests of the witnesses concerning what they would prefer not to experience in regard to touching, massage, music, or anything else. Then there is an invocation after the manner of the priests and priestesses in Epidaurus who, on leaving the pilgrim-dreamers for the night, would invoke the healing god to bring sleep and with it the healing dream. After this the night watch begins; it ends with a short ceremony of awakening in the morning before breakfast.

The Process

When we reassemble after breakfast we usually start with the witnesses sharing their experiences, but at any time we make room for the dreamers to tell their stories, for their healing dreams seem to be ours, and we need to allow plenty of time for them when they are ready to tell their tales. We usually begin by recalling feelings inspired by the initiation, the sacred walk, the feast and the entertainment. At some point, those who intended to be dreamers will talk about the process of selection of the two dreamers. The witnesses tell of their experience of witnessing the dreamers; for some this experience has inspired tales of watching at the bedside of dying relatives and feeling profound helplessness and fear. In this ritual, witnessing—doing nothing other than participating with the dreamer—is in sharp contrast to these fear-filled tales. Others report being very aware of music and silence, watching the dreamer and wondering if she was asleep or awake and whether she would like a foot massage. Some noticed the timelessness of the moments of watch, and also told of their own dreams during the time they slept.

I was once in the role of dreamer in the early days, when we imagined the dreamer to be "in coma." The setting was in a small Buddhist monastery that sits on cliffs high above the Atlantic in southwest Ireland, one of the world's most beautiful places. Various people in the group reported how unsettling and frightening it was to have the guide or group facilitator "in coma." This was especially true of my wife who was a participant, and my daughter Paula who was a co-facilitator. My dreams were not particularly remarkable, but my "coma" companion had a dream of amazing clarity. It was shamanic in quality as he told the tale of moving from the place in which we were dreaming to an island close by, where he was a salmon; he then became a bird flying around the world. All this, he said, he did with a freedom borne of the safety of being part of this loving group. Perhaps we can only take off when we feel free and safe to go.

The following year at this same place in Ireland I was a witness. My watch was from 2 to 4 a.m., and I arrived in the room of the two dreamers with my daughter Paula. We replaced two witnesses, who stayed on for a while after we arrived; two others present in the room were quietly playing their guitars. A full moon reflected a silver triangle into the room, which was perched high above the cliffs looking down on the sea. The dreamers appeared to be asleep. Looking out at the sea sometime after I had settled in, two fishing boats came from the harbor, which was just out of sight to our left. They passed slowly, entering one after the other into the wedge of moonlight. It was one of the most magical moments of my life. I felt unified with the guitar players, with my daughter and the two dreamers, and with the moonlight and those fishing boats. I knew in those moments that the fishing boats were one with the dreamers, and the moonlight seemed so clearly to be the dreamtime that the dreamers were passing through.

In a recent workshop in Ireland I decided to act as an additional witness in the middle of the night, wondering, I suppose, whether something of the quiet magic of the previous year might recur. My only sibling had died in Vancouver two weeks earlier and I was still grieving, much supported by the whole group. After a while I decided to go into a corner and sleep, and I had a hazy dream of my brother. On waking I went over to watch one of the dreamers, Pieter, who is a good friend, someone who I think of as a brother. Gazing at him I appeared to see my biological brother, John, and wept uncontrollably. Later, when Pieter was describing his night, he said that he had the experience sometime during the night of actually *being* my brother, and a moment or so later he heard someone sobbing and knew it must be me.

The experiences of dreamers and witnesses alike are always of such power and mystery that none could ignore the impact of this ritual and the unifying nature of the experience, which is both healing and life-giving. We need time to allow the whole ritual to unfold, and we also need plenty of time for reflection after it has ended in order to appreciate and relish all that occurred.

RITUALS IN DAILY LIFE: EPIDAURUS AND BEYOND

The various elements of the Epidaurian ritual offer examples of activities that could be transformed into sustaining rituals for everyday life. For example, any walk could be transformed into a sacred walk simply by having that intention, and paying attention to everything that arose in the present moment during the walk. A meal is so easily transformed into a feast for body and soul. The spirit present in the initiation ceremony could be part of the welcoming of family or other guests into the household. Rituals only require the use of the imagination for them to happen.

The rituals that were referred to earlier as part of different exercises in the workshop, as well as a few others, are sketched here as examples of ways in which we can connect with the inner life of ourselves and others. These examples are simply intended to inspire and encourage you to devise your own rituals.

Water

The ritual of "taking the cure" at spas in Europe, mainly an adventure of the wealthy, was more popular in earlier years than it is today. The intention was to pamper body and soul with curative waters and with touch. The waters were drunk, douched with, and bathed in, and the body was massaged and oiled. Juices, good food, and sleep rounded out the prescription, and the result was to feel cured—well cared for by both self and others.

Water has amazing curative powers; for our well-being we need more of the moist relationship-centeredness of spas and less of the dry impersonality of hospitals. Water nourishes us through all our senses—with its enchanting sounds as it ripples down streams and crashes on the beach; with its gentle touch in a warm bath or a spa or the sea or when it is offered in a blessing; with the envigorating smell of the ocean or a mountain stream; with its cool taste; with its soothing and ever-changing forms which we watch with endless fascination.

The magic of the spas and the purification in the Epidaurian ritual are examples of the healing quality of water. The cleansing of the body at birth and at death is more in the spirit of Hygieia than of Pasteur—more for the soul than for the body, more like a baptism than a bath. Baptism is a ritual of the river that cleanses and purifies; likewise, the sacrament of penance or the telling of secrets allows us to cast our sins and our burdens into the river, where they are swept away. In this manner we are purged both of our unskillfulness and the loads with which we weigh ourselves down, and we are absolved.

Water is the life force of the river into which all our attachments, both painful and sublime, can be cast. Water is the element with which the newborn body and soul is wiped at birth, and it is the element for us to use in a loving ritual in the aftermath of death as we wash the body.

The water used in blessings given in a family meeting provides another cleansing. In expressing our love and forgiveness we are relieved of the weight of our ill-feeling, and are healed and lightened up as well as "enlightened." If we believe in this magical power of water that has been the essential element in so many rituals over the ages, we will use it in our everyday caregiving practice. Physicians and nurses will carry sacred water in their professional bags, and it will become a powerful tool in addition to their stethoscopes. If the bag is left behind, they will remember that tap water is also sacred.

I realize now that blessings are the most healing acts I have ever performed in medicine.

Fire

Asclepius the physician was fathered by the sun god Apollo, and the fire and warmth he inherited was central to his healing. We have lost sight of the need for warmth if we are to be healers. Therapeutic touch is a simple ritual in which the warmth and healing of Asclepius are transmitted from the guide to the sick storyteller. Massage is another such ritual—one that is mainly for the body when it consists simply of an athletic pounding of muscles, but one that is healing for both body and soul when it is performed with a warm and loving intention. Most people deprive themselves of this caring touch from others, often with vague discomfort about self-indulgence or visions of touching self or another that are colored with shame and sexual taboo. We need this touch from others for our healing.

Candlelight so easily becomes a focus for remembering: candles lit by all present at a death; candles lit at Thanksgiving, accompanied by stories of those not present, living or dead; candles lit in a cathedral accompanied by a prayer; candles lit at the end of a family meeting in thanksgiving, accompanied by a story about the meaning of the chosen color and how it relates to the one whose life is being honored; candles in the workplace to celebrate anniversaries of birth as well as the life and death of those to whom care had been given and who have recently died. Imagine if all board meetings started with the lighting of candles—there would be both light and profit.

Air

The breath is usually the focus of the ritual of meditation. Any work group could start with a short meditation. For some families, encouragement in this form of ritual gives them an opportunity to engage in a healing together. The breath is part of the ritual of confirmation, when the bishop breathes on to the one being confirmed as a manifestation of the Holy Ghost being breathed in to the occasion, fortifying the soul.

Solo or in chorus, songs of love and praise are released on the out-breath. Prayer is also uttered in the expiratory phase of breathing. Prayer is asking with the breath for what we need, and is a ritual available up until we breathe our last. Song and prayer are celebrations and thanksgiving for the love and joy of relationship with God, with other beings, with nature, or with all that is—or they may be expressions of pain and rage at the disappointments and betrayals that are also a part of the struggle to connect.

All this is preparation for healing and for being, for to become relationship-centered is to pause for breath; to ask and pray and sing; to light candles and bless with water; to take sacred walks and pause for comedy and tragedy; to feast with friends and family and to take our dreams seriously but lightly, with awe and amazement for the magic of what unfolds.

THE ANNUAL FAMILY GATHERING

The family meeting has proved to be such a powerful rite for healing that it is obvious we should not wait for the off-chance that we might be able to have such a meeting around the time of the death of one we love. Even the best of parents—those who prepare their children with love for living their lives—usually fail to prepare them for death. Sudden death is commonplace, and the chaos surrounding a final illness is such that we may not be able to create either the time or the opportunity for a family gathering.

We need practice. We need practice in saying hello, even to our parents and children, who we may have dreamed up so that we do not really know them. We need practice in letting go and saying good-bye, because the easy replacement of things nowadays suggests that we never have to let go, even to the bitter end. We need to practice storytelling and witnessing, because although they seem to be the essence of simplicity they are not easy, and we should not simply leave the role of guide to others, because they may not be there. We need to practice caring for the soul and for the spirit, because the ever-present need for the receiving and giving of love is not apparent to us in this age when it seems that bodily parts can be fixed and replaced quite easily without any necessity for becoming personally involved.

With all this in mind, I have devised an annual ceremony for the family, which I will describe here in some detail. It can be regarded as an antidote to denial of death, and thus a guide to living more fully in the present moment. It can take place at any time. A holiday or birthday may be chosen, but any other day can be designated as the Day of the Family. It is a ritual. It is a time that the family will spend together by the metaphoric river, casting off hurts and resentments, bathing one another in tears and laughter, and anointing one another with the loving blessings that emerge in the rite. If the family perform this ceremony a number of times over the years, or even once, they will know how to facilitate a family meeting when one of their members is dying, because the essentials of both gatherings are exactly the same.

When such a gathering is delayed so that it becomes a last rite without any previous practice, it is clear that many families are daunted by the prospect of such an intimate event. Those families who do gather regularly for a holiday or a summer barbecue will usually say that they want people to have a good time, and that food and drink is enough without getting into family feuds and secrets. They all gather, some dreading the occasion while others come because it *is* a ritual, and one of the few family traditions. Still others gather so as to meet together in a clique and gossip about the outsiders, and none expects that anything will be different from the way it has always been, year after year. The idea of each person being heard and witnessed but not judged by the others is either unimaginable or thought to be impossible without an outside guide to make it happen and a set of rules of order to control the anticipated uproar.

Yet it *is* possible for the family to meet and really listen to one another, even without the usual kind of outside leadership and with the simplest of rules. I can attest to the power of healing of soul and spirit through such a gathering, both from experience with my own family and from reports of others who have been encouraged to brave their fears and apprehensions and arrange a family gathering.

The following are some guidelines about how such a gathering might be structured, with the Talking Stick as guide. And what an amazing guide it is! What the Talking Stick does is bring out the guide in each of us, and it does this so well. All the family, including children, are invited, together with a few friends if wished. The ritual commences with the group sitting in a circle.

Part I: The Talking Stick
The convenor of the gathering will begin the Talking Stick ritual with a brief invocation, such as: "Will you listen with full attention to the sound of your heart speak?"

The stick is then passed from hand to hand in the circle, and only the holder at the time may speak. By virtue of the opening invocation, she is obligated to speak the truth from the heart, while all the others present listen without interruption, except for an interjection of "Ho" if they feel particularly moved. The anxiety accompanying the occasion usually ensures that the first round or two are awkward, but the passing of the stick seems to be like a spiral; with each round it goes deeper and creates more intimacy. When finished speaking, the stick-holder passes it on, or may pass it having said nothing. When the stick has made one full passage around the circle in silence, the ritual is complete. Someone may have the urge to ask for the stick in order to reply to something that has just been said, but this is not permitted until it is this person's turn to speak. The urgent need to respond or justify usually evaporates, and it becomes clear that listening and connecting with one another is often inhibited by the process of dueling dialogues, which are so often a painful part of family life. Usually the stick is only held for a couple of minutes, but there is no time limit; the number of rounds may be restricted to three or four, or they may continue without restriction until there is a complete round in silence, which may take several hours.

Part II: The Gift

After the rounds of the Talking Stick, there may be a brief pause before the ritual of gift-giving. All the participants are invited in advance to bring a possession of importance that they would like to give away, and they bring their gift to the gathering without knowing who will receive it. This ritual has been described in detail in Chapter 10, and it is suggested that this form be used.

The possibilities of this ritual gifting ceremony in the family are limited only by the imagination, ranging all the way from the giving of small trinkets to the handing over of all someone's goods and chattels! The choice of recipient is relinquished, but it is usually discovered that the right person receives the gift anyway.

Part III: The Memorial

For this part, the group sits in a circle, with at least as many unlit candles in the center as there are participants. Each person in the gathering has the opportunity of rising and lighting a candle in memory of a friend or family member who has died recently, or even in the remote past, or in honor of any intention they wish. As they light the candle, they say a few words about the intention. This memorial to the ancestors and to matters that are important to us is a reminder of our roots, connections, and disconnections. The tradition in some Eastern countries of having a family shrine or altar in the home is a vivid way of continuing this practice of honoring and remembering our ancestors on a daily basis

Part IV: The Ending

A single round of the Talking Stick brings the ritual to a close. It gives the participants the opportunity to say a few words about how they have experienced the whole gathering. In addition, those who have made a legal will are encouraged to give an outline of it to all present. The last will and testament is often a secret document read after the death of the will-maker, and it may be a post-mortem statement of unexpressed feelings and judgments with rewards and punishments meted out to the survivors. I have heard many times that the reading of the will has evoked great hurt and anger; transforming this into an ante-mortem testament leaves less room for unfinished business or allows it to be finished during the family gathering. This would also be an opportunity for participants to speak about their medical directive, a written document setting out their wishes and expectations in the event of irreversible incapacity to make medical care decisions, and naming a proxy who would see that these instructions are carried out. (An example of a medical directive can be found in the Appendix.) Finally, this round of the Talking Stick is an opportunity for the holder to offer a blessing to each of those present.

Reflections for the Skeptical

It might be feared that the annual family gathering will go on for too long! Perhaps, but usually it takes about the same length of time as a family barbecue, and is infinitely more healthy. There may be a worry that there will be the usual amount of mudslinging or expressions of rage and resentments, and that is certainly possible. If this happens, it would be nothing new. Usually, however, the guidance of the Talking Stick—or the hermetic spirit within each one of us—comes to our aid. This is coupled with the fact that there is no direct dialogue, so that responses to another person's utterances are delayed. This dissolves much of the usual reactive, unskillful, and violent dissemination of rage, and allows everyone to tap into the wish for intimacy and love that underlies family life. The family gathering really *is* worth the risk, and the health and vibrancy of soul and spirit of each of the participants and of the family as a whole depend on it.

When All is Said and Done

The wisdom of dying reveals to us that we have everything we need in and around us to live and die a life of meaning. The soul needs a constant infusion of love for its survival, and the spirit needs to give love, for that is what living and dying are all about. Dying strips away the masks, roles, and trappings—both beautiful and ugly—with which we have obscured our lives, leaving behind the basics of soul and spirit, which are related to the giving and receiving of love. We *are* terrified of death, but this terror will dissipate if we will only look at it, allow our shell to become permeable, and experience the timeless connectedness that is beyond ego. We will also discover that it is much easier than we thought to let go of disappointments, hurts, and hatreds and to forgive, thus becoming free.

At this time of unmasked vulnerability, we may tell stories and draw nourishment from our roots. We may be listened to and witnessed, perhaps for the first time in any consistent and fully attentive manner by our family, and we in turn may witness them; all this is exquisite care for soul and spirit and just what we need. In addition, we may allow ourselves to feel death at our right shoulder and become surprised that we no longer need to expend so much energy in its denial. As we continue to let go we suffer less, despite the fact that this is a time of great grief, as we mourn both for ourselves and our family and say good-bye.

Does this really happen? Is all this simply a longed-for ideal, or is death in fact an emotionally paralyzing event, with pain and suffering for all and cries for physician-assisted suicide? If we are prepared for dying by being clear about what we want for ourselves and for our families and friends, and we have our chosen caregivers to guide us, it is possible for us to die peacefully and consciously in the company of those we love. I have witnessed it so very often. If we are less well prepared when we are dying, but the skillful guidance that we have every right to expect is on hand, even up to the last moment we can give and receive love and witness what each person has to say, forgiving and being forgiven.

Most people will say when they are physically well that they are prepared for death and that they do not want to strive officiously to keep themselves alive when death is close and inevitable. They will even commit these wishes to writing in a medical directive so that their intentions are clear to all. In fact, in a survey in the UK only 10 percent of people who were well said that they would undergo a grueling course of chemotherapy that would at best add three months to their lives. However, 42 percent of cancer patients in that same study said that they would want the treatment. So up to the last minute, when we are clearly confronting death, many of us who had thought when we were well that we would be prepared to let go will change our minds and attempt to shore up our denial even in the face of death, and try to live a moment longer regardless of the quality of life.

Death really *is* inconceivable, and if we allow ourselves only occasional glimpses of it during times when we are physically fit, then our terror will be such that when death is close we will attempt to push it away. One solution is to imagine our death and the death of our loved ones long before they happen, and see to it that a family gathering occurs under the guidance of the Talking Stick when we are well. This makes death a more familiar companion and so much less terrifying, and also offers opportunities to practice ways in which we can give and receive the loving care we need.

However, most of us will continue to live in denial of our impermanence, putting off the care of soul and spirit until tomorrow, and so our lives will be governed by flight or fight. Flight will ensure that we keep busy and on the run, becoming dedicated to our careers and having little time for anything else, including ourselves and our families. Or we will be preoccupied with shopping or keeping up youthful appearances—anything to avoid the acknowledgment and acceptance of aging; anything to drown out the silence and the fearful void; anything that will give us a tangible and measurable sense of meaning, even if that is only a few numbers in a bank balance. The poet Dylan Thomas was an advocate of not dying gently, urging us to fight death every step of the way. Fight will engage us in futile heroics and immerse us in some cause or other to the exclusion of much that is of vital importance. And flight will impel us to keep moving, leaving little time for us to pause and simply be. Whether it is fright or fight that governs us, denial of death will ensure that we miss out on the present as we rush into the future. If we are to be awake to the present, then we need to accept death and allow it to be an ever-present and consciously apprehended companion at our right shoulder. When it is there and visible, when it is accepted as a natural part of our impermanence, we will not spend our lives trying to keep it at bay.

Witnessing dying or imagining our own death stirs up thoughts about the meaning of life. Ruminations by philosophers and others in their splendid isolation above and beyond the presence of death have led to volumes of words and uplifting stories about its meaning, but a few glimpses, as witness, of one who is dying in the family will help distill the essence of life down to the very simplest of ideas. Then we will see that life is simply about love—its presence and its absence. At that moment we will see clearly that our life task should be one of enflaming, moistening, and breathing love for the sake of the body, soul, and spirit of ourselves, each other, and our world. That is all there is.

It is vital that we honor our roots, for without them we could not be. We need to honor rather than judge and bemoan, to tell our stories rather than hide them in archives deep within the soul. These roots run deep. I once attended a past-lives workshop. Although I did not believe in reincarnation and past lives, I was curious about the subject and so took my skepticism with me to this weekend event. We were invited during this time to lie down with our eyes closed, with a partner by our side as guide, and imagine two countries—one that had the greatest attraction for us and another that most repelled us. Then we were asked to choose the one that inspired the most feeling and tell our story about it. I chose Ireland as an attractive force, but was totally resistant to the idea of telling a story. Those of us who were stuck were invited to invent anything at all, which I thought was quite ridiculous. How could a story I invented be anything to do with me in some bygone time!

But after a while, a story emerged. It opened with a scene from centuries ago of a young man standing with a donkey and cart in a field high above the Atlantic ocean, a place a few miles from where my father was born and where I had hiked around a few years earlier. In that scene, both man and donkey were totally immobile. The next scene was of the same man, although he was some years younger. He was stooping over the fireplace in a tiny white-washed cottage that had no furniture. Neither was there a fire in the fireplace. This man, too, seemed frozen in time. Going further back I saw a scene of boys, all darkly dressed, in a playground with their backs to me. None of them was moving. Then there was a scene of a young child sitting in the corner of a room curled up, listening to noises from the next room. After a while men emerged carrying the body of the boy's dead mother. As I was telling this story to my attentive witness I was overflowing with sobs and tears. The final scene was of a child just a few months old lying blissfully content in his mother's arms in her bed.

It was interesting to me that all the images up until the mother was taken out of her room were "still scenes"; scenes, perhaps, that somehow were happening to me still. Fixed and unmoving in my imagination, these images were stagnant, without any flow to move them forward and release them in time.

I have no idea where that story came from, knowing only that it was very moving. Having thought about it many times since that weekend, I have imagined that it emerged from the dark side of my soul as one of an almost endless array of memories that lie within my roots, stories of which I am not fully conscious. Rupert Sheldrake, a writer who explores the realm where science and spirit meet, would consider these stories part of my morphic field. This, he asserts, is a field somewhat akin to a magnetic field wherein are stored memories that lie beyond space and time. Furthermore, Sheldrake believes that the brain is more like a radio receiver than a computer storage facility. It receives signals from our morphic field and, if we are intuitive or broadminded, from the fields of others. So somewhere in my morphic field is the memory of a young man from long ago, perhaps a relative of mine and perhaps not, who lived a life of suffering because he was unable to let go of the mother who abandoned him at the time of her death. Without my knowing that story, I have always known the suffering of abandonment, and it has always affected my life. I also know that I had always been uncomfortable with and ashamed of my Irish roots, acclaiming myself to be English since I was born in

England, but I never felt that I belonged there either. What I remember is that after telling that story to a loving witness who also nudged me through my story as supporter and guide, I became Irish. Since then I have returned every year to facilitate workshops in a small and exquisite Buddhist monastery—the only one in Ireland—that happens to be just a mile or two from the spot where the man with the donkey stood! All this is another great reminder that we have very little idea about what is *really* going on; I know that I rediscovered my very earthy roots and found a marvelous and magical place in which to do my work.

The need to be more conscious of and subsequently nourished by roots is of the utmost importance for our soulful well-being, as is the need to tell stories. Our spirit requires that we offer our stories, with all their joys and sorrows, with all their blemishes and incompleteness, so that both we and others may hear and be nourished. Our spirit also requires that we be guides and caregivers. Our soul yearns for us to be witness to others and to ourselves, taking in their stories as well as our own, asking for the care we need as well as giving it to ourselves. The family meeting around the time of death and the annual family gathering are both sacred rituals that are expressions of these yearnings.

Our soul also pleads with us to slow down and give ourselves time to appreciate the flowers, gaze on the birds, put our feet to the earth and be nourished by our world, and in turn have our spirit sing its praises in loving acknowledgment of our connectedness with all things.

We are so negligent in giving ourselves care and in both asking it of others and expecting it from them as a human need. We have little awareness that we need care at every moment, and so neglect both body and soul much of the time. Many of us work in tense and overcrowded cities, stretching ourselves thin with long working hours during the week, and then, if we have the means, rushing along overcrowded highways into the country at weekends to relax. How nature is supposed to repair the wear and tear of this and other variations on the theme of stressful living is beyond imagining. If we were to take the need for receiving and giving care seriously and live consciously in the present, attentive to soul and spirit, we would have to change our way of thinking and behaving.

Ken, a physician friend of mine in his forties, is about to work part time. He says that he earns at present far more than he really needs, and has little time for himself and his family. He lives on 80 acres of farmland and wants to have more time to farm, tending to the land and being nourished by it. The ritual of spring plantings, for example, is a sacred event in which all his family is involved and during which he needs no outside distractions. He wants more time to teach, both in medicine and beyond. He wants more time to read because there is a wealth of nourishment in books, and he wants time for his music, for in that there is peace, and harmony with his fellow players. This kind of wisdom is in short supply. We hunger for it and need more models.

Just when I thought that I had finished this book, Barbara, a friend and colleague, returned home from looking after her mother in the last days of her life. She told the tale of those last six weeks, and it became clear to me that her story was the most appropriate conclusion that I could imagine, so here it is—an ending that is like a beginning.

Barbara's mother was in her eighties, living alone in Florida in a cozy condominium. For two years she had been in declining health on account of leukemia. When Barbara visited at Christmastime, she was startled to find that her mother was so frail. In addition, Barbara's mother was talking about her wish to die by taking an overdose of pills, if she could be sure that the dose would be lethal. Some of her mother's friends expressed their concern about the possibility of suicide and how helpless and fearful they felt when the subject arose. Because of concern about her mother's distress and the fact that she obviously had only a short time to live, Barbara decided to extend her stay until after mother died.

Barbara has worked with the dying and particularly with families struggling with Amyotrophic Lateral Sclerosis (Lou Gherig's disease), so she was very familiar with the experience of others. That was treasured preparation for her own journey. She is a creative, colorful person, known to her friends for the detailed and vivid dreams she could recall, which are a source of inspiration and wonder to both herself and all who listen. During the six weeks Barbara said that so far as she knew she did not dream; she was living a dream with absolutely no sense of time and a merging of experiences that blended the agony of mourning with the ecstatic moments of loving connectedness that she had with her mother, as well as with others who helped with her care.

The family consisted of herself, her mother, and a brother and sister, her father having died years before. There were three occasions during those last weeks when they sat together with the Talking Stick, and each ritual seemed to build on the last, weaving the family closer together so that there was literally nothing standing between them. After the first of these sessions mother told the children that she never realized how much they cared, and that she felt loved, comforted, and safe. From that point on there was no further talk of suicide, nor did she express any particular hurry to die. On the third occasion mother was in coma, which seemed to Barbara and her brother and sister to be of little importance at this time and certainly no reason to curtail the ritual. They had decided to focus this particular ceremony on the theme of journey. Each of the three children brought an object that represented this topic and told a story around it as both gift and blessing to mother. Barbara recalled how moved they all were by this rite. As she continued to speak to me of these weeks, it was obvious that each day, whether colorfully creative or darkly bowel-based, was filled with the sacred, and all was laced with tears and laughter.

Mother had made all the arrangements for her cremation. The family decided that the usual receptacles sold for the containment of ashes were impersonal and inappropriate in one way or another, so they decided to build a miniature sarcophagus. It would be made of wood with a hinged top and decorated on the sides with Egyptian symbols, because mother had a love of things Egyptian, and there would be family pictures embracing the lid. Barbara's husband George, a physician-carpenter, created the box before mother died, and the finishing touches were made both before and in the few days after her death.

The satin-lined sarcophagus was open during the funeral service, much to the bewilderment and surprise of clergy and friends, and the ashes were contained in a linen sack placed within the sarcophagus, which Barbara, in a whimsical moment, called the mummy bag. At the end of the ceremony there was an opportunity for any in the congregation to place notes or letters in the sarcophagus. This reminded me of the note I had placed in a crack in the West Wall in Jerusalem at about the same time that Barbara was looking after her mother.

They carried the sarcophagus into the churchyard, dug their

own hole, and buried it. Then they planted a tree on top, imagining that its roots would wrap around the box, embracing it, drawing the ashes back into the earth from whence they came.

That is what life is about, and therein is contained its meaning. Barbara went on her pilgrimage at Christmastime, and quite literally lived her dream of connecting with her roots. She gave and received love, told stories, witnessed and guided without being exactly sure who was doing what, and felt as one with the roots and trunk and branches of the family of which she is a part. She washed and held her mother, laughed and cried with her siblings, and when all was said and done, took a little of the tree, fashioned it into an ageless miniature sarcophagus, and buried mother's bodily remains in it under a tree, knowing that this would be the only way in which the loving memories would not be buried but would always be there as stories to sustain her.

May we all live and die this way.

A Curriculum for Living and Dying

The intention of this book has been to offer guidance through subject matters that prepare readers for accepting dying and death, and help them to absorb the wisdom that is readily available at this time in order to live lives in which loving relationships are fostered.

Professional caregivers may find it particicularly difficult to acknowledge their need for training in accompanying the dying and their families because many of them have experienced the deaths of a large number of patients and say that they have managed quite well. The majority of medical students have never taken the time to imagine the death of loved ones, nor is that in any way encouraged in medical schools or anywhere else. Yet once those students are released as graduate physicians, they will come across people like their parents hundreds of times—patients with the same name or age or occupation, with life-threatening illnesses, and near to death—and they will be unprepared.

Attendance at a family gathering can be very beneficial for professional caregivers. I firmly believe that it is imperative that professionals take time with their colleagues for their own mourning, and the shared experience of a family meeting may be the catalyst they need to take them into this personal terrain. The many personal stories told by hospice staff about their own losses and grieving speak of the importance of relationships between caregivers in creating a climate of healing. Many caregivers, feeling isolated and vulnerable, seem to believe that there is neither the time nor the interest on the part of their colleagues in hearing their story. A loving climate of caregiving depends on their giving this time to one another; they need it just as much as their patients do. Residents must have a place in which they can safely grieve and tell their story, and physicians who lose a patient need to have witnesses who will listen to the feelings attendant to that loss. A few moments to discuss the pathological state of the patient is not enough.

Relationship-centered care requires collaborative and supportive relationships between colleagues. This is not the situation at present except, perhaps, in hospices. Only a few moments are necessary; without that time, caregivers hurry on to their next patient overflowing with feelings—for their previous patient and for themselves—and are forced to shut off their grief and anxiety. Their inner soul is then shut off from the next patient, and while the mind may be able to function, they are unable to make a relationship-centered connection with the next person they treat, the connection that is essential to healing.

THE CURRICULUM

This detailed curriculum is offered in the hope that it will serve as a useful model for schools of medicine and nursing as well as for all other schools that teach about caregiving, that they may be inspired to develop their own experiential training program. But the curriculum is offered as a model for everyone since we all are involved in relationships in work and home, and the quality of these relationships will make the difference as to whether or not we live well and die well. While the program is ideally conducted in a group since witnessing the stories of others is a very important part of the learning, the reader at home can select any or all of the exercises and work through them over some weeks with a friend.

The curriculum is designed to cover a period of at least nine months, which is simply the minimum amount of time considered necessary for fully experiencing, understanding, and reinforcing loving relationships and for becoming more accepting of death—and life. After the nine-month program it is necessary to keep alive the soul and spirit of what has been discovered. With this in mind it is suggested that there be a *relationship-centered thread* that extends throughout medical, nursing, and teacher training, or any other college preparation. The training might begin in the first weeks of the college year and at the end of the nine months continue in the form of monthly meetings until the end of the final year. This would ensure that there is a relationship-centered supportive experience throughout the college years, and that the competitive atmosphere is counterbalanced by one that is collaborative and caring.

The ideal number of participants in each training group is between 18 and 24, although it is workable to have three more or less; if the number exceeds 27, the group tends to be too large for all to be heard. If the number of participants is not divisible by three (triads being the form for small-group exercises), one or two of the small groups can have four members each, with two members being witnesses in each rotation during the exercise.

The program comprises an introductory workshop, followed by seven day-long sessions at montly intervals; the seventh session is followed one month later by a closing residential workshop of one evening and two full days. The whole program thus requires 13 days for training, and includes five overnight stays.

The Introductory Workshop

The introductory workshop in the nine-month course lasts for four days. The workshop is residential so the time and space of four days together gives participants room to breathe and allows time to establish the relationship-centeredness of the group. The place is important—as is any place for care—and will add its own atmosphere to the workshop, as will excellent food and the spirit of those who manage the workshop setting.

Daily Meditation

At the beginning of each day before the morning session there is a meditation period lasting at least 20 minutes. Meditation practices are so powerful in increasing awareness of self and of all around as well as creating a readiness for healing. The facilitator may use her own guidelines for meditation; for others less familiar with meditation, a simple practice is Insight or Mindfulness Meditation (Vipassana). Information on this and other methods can be found in Joseph Goldstein's *The Experience of Insight* (Unity Press, 1972), and the works of other meditation teachers. Participants are invited by the facilitator to sit comfortably on a cushion or on a chair with back reasonably straight, hands resting on the lap, and eyes gently closed. The object of focus for mindfulness meditation is the breath. At the beginning of the first meditation the facilitator might say something along the following lines: "Be mindful either of the rise and fall of the abdomen as you breathe in and out, or the breath at the tip of the nostrils as it goes in and out. Choose either site of awareness and stay with it, simply observing the sensation of the breath going in and out. If a sensation in the body becomes predominant—such as pain in the back or restlessness—give it full attention without judging, avoiding, or expecting anything; simply watch or observe the pain or restlessness as gently and nonjudgmentally as you are able. After noticing the sensation, return to the breathing." The facilitator acts as guide to the process, and like the guide in other exercises, her role is minimal when it comes to interventions. Therefore she will speak only every few minutes, and then simply to offer brief instructions or a reminder to return to the breath. Another instruction might be: "Some people like to count the breaths up to ten and back as a method of maintaining concentration on the breathing. Try this if it might be helpful to you." And later on: "After a few breaths the mind will usually wander and become involved in some story or other. When you become aware of this drift, notice it without judgment or any other form of self-abuse, perhaps naming it ("mind wandering" or "thinking") and then gently return to the breathing."

The best preparation for guiding a meditation is attendance at an Insight Meditation or other retreat where there are experienced teachers. Learning from a book is helpful, but is no substitute.

While these initial four-day workshops may vary a little in both timetable and content, the following outline is typical.

Day 1

MORNING: After the meditation, each session throughout the duration of the workshop begins with a short piece of music, a poem, or a story. As the workshop matures, various participants take responsibility for these openings. Following this prelude there is a brief welcoming, and then an outline of any administrative issues that the participants need to know about.

After this introduction the Talking Stick makes three or four rounds. (Chapter 2 describes how the Talking Stick was used in a Native American ritual. Sitting in a circle, those gathered would pass the stick from hand to hand, the holder being the only one allowed to speak. When the stick had made a full round in silence, the gathering came to an end.) The usual introductions in workshops consist of name tags and brief biographical profiles; these are not necessarily a part of the Talking Stick ritual unless individual participants want to give a listing of personal details during their turn. The Talking Stick always provides stories, and it is from these stories that the group begins to know one another, not from a list of vital statistics.

Following the Talking Stick the group is led through the Personal Dying exercise, a meditation in which each person visualizes his or her own dying. The guided visualization follows the course of illness from diagnosis through physical decline and death, and includes imagining both wake and funeral. A script for this exercise appears in Chapter 5. After this visualization the group splits into triads with each person spending 20 minutes describing his or her experience. This is followed by an hour of reflection by the whole group.

AFTERNOON: After the music or poetry, the session begins with a few moments when the participants reflect on any thoughts or feelings left over from the morning session. The remainder of the afternoon is spent on the Loss exercise described in Chapter 12.

For all the exercises in the training program, participants work in groups of three so that they experience over and over again the three roles that are significant in relationship-centered care. To recap: the *storyteller* is the one who tells the story of her loss; if the loss is of a person, she will also speak to the *witness* as if that person were the embodiment of the one who was lost. The witness is always silent, but the *guide* offers the storyteller both supportive presence and the encouragement to go deeper into the story. Each member of the triad has an opportunity to play each role in all of the exercises.

EVENING: Free.

Day 2
MORNING: Participants are encouraged to share any dreams they may remember from the previous night. There is also the opportunity to share any new thoughts that have arisen in relationship to the first day.

The introductory period is followed by time for drawing. Paper and crayons are provided, and the participants are encouraged to draw their own family tree as a chart, or to depict it in any other way. Names are included, and the group members use pastel colors for those in the family for whom they feel (or felt, in the case of those who have died) warmth and affection without much of a sense of "unfinished business" between them. Those who are disliked or for whom there is considerable ambivalence of feelings are colored in dark shades, and those about whom little is known are accompanied by a question mark. Half an hour is allotted for these drawings, after which they are shared in the triads. The pictures of the family tree are taken to the afternoon session, in which the participants work in the same triads as in the morning.

AFTERNOON: The entire afternoon is devoted to the Family Meeting as described in Chapter 8. In this exercise the storyteller imagines that she is dying and has asked all of her family to assemble. Using the witness to represent the family, she speaks to each of them in turn. If the storyteller decides to begin by talking to her mother she says to the witness "Now you are my mother …" When finished, the storyteller pauses for a moment and then continues on with the next person "Now you are my sister …" In this enactment, even those who have died can be spoken to in this way, and the occasion becomes a very powerful opportunity to say what was never said during life. This exercise is usually the most difficult in the whole workshop as well as the most rewarding, as the possibilities for real communication and healing within the family become apparent.

EVENING: A ritual is created by the participants based on the ancient Greek ritual inspired by Asclepius (described in detail in Chapter 14). This ritual lasts throughout the night.

Day 3
MORNING: The morning is spent in processing all the events of the Asclepian ritual of the previous night. There are always powerful stories from all of the participants and occasionally this processing overflows into the early afternoon.

AFTERNOON: Free.

EVENING: The evening is devoted to circling with the Talking Stick. A time limit may be set (the participants are often quite tired after three emotion-packed days), or the circling may continue until the stick passes one complete round in silence, which can sometimes take several hours. Having been through intense exercises and a long ritual together up to this point, the participants are now able to speak with the Talking Stick at a deeper and more soulful level than they did at the beginning of the workshop.

Day 4
This final day includes the visualization on self-care (Chapter 6), a brief memorial ritual of candle lighting at which time the ancestors are remembered (as in the Annual Family Gathering: Chapter 10), and a ritual during which participants give away a gift they have brought with them (Chapter 14). The workshop ends in the late afternoon with one round of the Talking Stick, providing an opportunity for closure and saying good-bye.

The Seminars
Seven day-long seminars are held at monthly intervals to reinforce the learning in the introductory workshop. The seminars allow time for issues raised in the initial gathering to move to a deeper level, reinforcing the new learning and beginning a paradigm shift by making relationship-centered care the focus of caregiving and everyday life.

In the seminars particular attention is given to the role of guide, since caregivers will be acting as guides as well as witnesses both in their home and at work, and the skills necessary to becoming hermetic guides require practice. The role of guide is of the greatest importance in parenting, yet most of us have had very little modeling or instruction in the art. As parents, we may attempt to control and protect our children beyond reasonable bounds, impelled by our own inner sense of mortality and helplessness. The guide has a sense of the underworld and of death, and in knowing that each of us must pass through this terrain is in a better position to be a constant friend and mentor rather than simply a mixture of guard, fixer, judge, and jury.

Each of the seven seminars lasts at least eight hours and usually ends with the participants eating a meal together. The individuals bring the ingredients for the meal and it becomes an important ritual for the group.

The material presented for each seminar may be more than

can be used and is simply offered as an example of what has been valuable. The Talking Stick, which becomes a barometer for the connectedness within the group, will most likely take longer for each round as the participants become more eager to tell their stories and listen to those of others in this safe forum.

Seminar 1: Visualizing Dying
MORNING: After the meditation the Talking Stick is passed for one or two rounds. A visualization of personal dying (Chapter 12) similar to that of the original workshop follows the rounds of the Talking Stick. The experience of any exercise is quite different with repetition, and participants find they are able to notice details that were denied or avoided the first time they did the exercise. Practicing our dying makes it more familiar and less frightening; simpler, if not easier.

AFTERNOON: In the afternoon there are some brief exercises performed in triads. In these exercises there may be dialogue between the two principals, with the third person acting as silent witness.

For workshops composed only of medical students and physicians:

a) The physician tells the patient that she has but a handful of weeks to live.

b) The physician speaks to the patient at a time when pain has become a significant feature and she is clearly nearing the end of life.

For all participants:

a) The patient tells a family member her wishes in relationship to her wake and funeral.

b) The family member speaks with a loved one (the patient) after the physician's pronouncement of the fatal nature of this loved one's illness.

Each of these sketches lasts ten minutes; this is followed by five minutes for each in the triad to speak of his or her experience. The whole group reconvenes after completion of all the sketches for an hour of discussion. This is followed by one round of the Talking Stick to end the seminar.

At the end of this first seminar the students are instructed that they need to engage during the following five months in a project that they will report on in the sixth seminar. This project will be a practical experience in and around dying in a hospice, nursing home, intensive care unit or elsewhere. A few of the students may choose to investigate and participate in wake and funeral practices in their own or other cultures. The students design their projects with the guidance of the seminar leaders, and as a part of their project they will all make their own Talking Stick.

The students are also encouraged to think about how they will bring about a meeting within their own family sometime before the seventh seminar, at which time they will be asked to report back their experiences with this task. It is suggested that the students ask one of the other course participants to be with them at their family meeting as hermetic friend and guide or simply as a witness who in being present will provide loving support.

Seminar 2: Loss

MORNING: After the meditation and the opening round with the Talking Stick, the participants work in groups of three with a loss different from that aired in the introductory workshop. Similar guidelines to those in Chapter 12 are used.

AFTERNOON: Participants spend about 15 minutes writing a list of the significant losses they have experienced in life, plus those they anticipate are still to come. They are urged to notice if there are specific patterns to the manner in which they usually cope with loss. Some, for example, will discover that they spend little time with grief, having grown up in an environment where tears and sadness were not shared, and where they were told to be strong and get on with their lives without brooding on the loss. Participants then take 15 minutes each to discuss their list with the two other members of their triad. The second exercise of the afternoon involves the storyteller creating a ritual in which each of the more important losses is remembered.

Following this seminar it is expected that participants will give consideration as to how and where they can set up a family shrine at home, and how they will devise rituals to be celebrated at home on any special day of their choice. They will report back to the group on this at the beginning of the next seminar.

214

Seminar 3: The Family Meeting

MORNING: The opening meditation and round of the Talking Stick is followed by reports from the group members about their work during the previous month on the family shrine and rituals of remembrance. The remainder of the morning (at least two and a half hours) is spent on facilitating the family meeting (*see* Chapter 8). This repetition allows the storyteller to expand on her original encounter with her family during the initial workshop. At the end of this session the participants are encouraged to do further homework and research on their family tree, and are asked to bring their drawing to the final seminar.

AFTERNOON: Participants identify two members of the family with whom they have the most difficulty speaking. They then speak for ten minutes to each of those two people as if it were their last opportunity to do so. This is followed by discussion in the large group.

The triads then reassemble, with each storyteller spending 15 minutes in telling how she intends to arrange her own family meeting sometime before the final seminar. Participants are encouraged to consider requesting one of the other group members to act as guide (and provider of moral support) on this occasion.

The large group reassembles and after discussing this further work with the family, the seminar ends with a round of the Talking Stick.

Seminar 4: Rituals

Rituals are the art of celebrating and honoring the soul, and in their performance all who participate become connected and feel a part of a greater whole.

MORNING: The Talking Stick is passed for a round so that the group can check in with one another after the opening meditation. This is followed by a 40-minute session of Insight Meditation and then a 40-minute walking meditation, all in silence.

The walking meditation is, like the sitting meditation, an exercise in mindfulness. In the sitting meditation the breath is the object of mindfulness; in walking meditation, each movement of the foot is the subject of exquisite attention. So we notice the left foot rising slowly from the ground, moving forward, and being placed on the floor, feeling the pressure on the sole of the foot. Then the right foot is lifted and the next step witnessed. The walking is very slow, and as there is nowhere to go, there is no destination. If indoors, we need to find a place in which we can move back and forth for a few feet without bumping into others.

The object of meditation is to learn how to become more aware in the present moment. In everyday life we are usually thinking ahead or else preoccupied with what has already passed. In the morning on arising and stretching we are thinking about going to the bathroom. There we think about showering. In the shower we think about coffee. While drinking coffee we are reading the paper, and while saying good-bye to the family we are thinking about work. We are forever thinking ahead and seldom in the moment. The witness in us is fully attentive to what is happening, both with ourselves and with others, in the present moment. Most of the time we are not all there in the most literal sense of the words, and so are not witnessing anything.

The last hour of the morning is devoted to discussion in the large group about the various experiences in meditation.

AFTERNOON: Triads assemble and discuss three rituals they feel would be important additions to their lives and enhance their caregiving, both at home and in the workplace. For example, they could create a ritual in the office for the staff with whom they work, or one which takes place around the bedside when a patient dies, or one that would enliven a wake. Some of the group will focus on rituals for the home. Following discussion each participant, with the assistance of the two others in the triad, performs one of the rituals they have discussed. The group reconvenes as a whole for discussion before the final round of the Talking Stick.

Seminar 5: Self-care

As stressed in the initial workshop and subsequent seminars, it is important to take care of self by making time to get in touch with inner feelings and needs. This is practiced in each seminar at the start of the day with a short time for Insight Meditation but is particularly meaningful in this seminar on self-care.

MORNING: After the usual preliminaries the session starts with an exercise for meeting with the inner soul or the "child within" (Chapter 6). The group then breaks into triads to share their experiences. Discussion in the larger group follows.

AFTERNOON: Two sets of instructions for drawing are described, but there will probably not be time during this seminar to do them both (in which case the facilitator will select those felt to be most appropriate for the group). The first instructions ask the participants to draw a picture of themselves and add into the picture some details of where illness might develop if given the chance. In addition, the participants are asked to sketch in anything that may be of assistance to them in healing this disease. If a participant actually has some sort of illness, she draws it in. No further directions or clarification are given. After 20 minutes of drawing, the group breaks into triads, each participant experiencing once again the roles of storyteller, witness, and guide. Each storyteller takes 20 minutes to describe the drawing and anything it might have evoked. The guide may ask for clarification or invite greater depth, and the witness listens. In an hour the whole group reassembles for discussion of the exercise. This exercise always creates surprises: a picture, drawn fairly quickly and without much thought, often offers insights not ordinarily available as the storyteller/artist interprets the personal meaning of the colors used, explains why a particular site in the body was seen as being vulnerable, and describes the illness or disease chosen, and the assisting forces or lack of them.

The alternative instructions invite participants to draw a mandala, a circular design symbolic of a person's inner or outer universe. (The mandala is used in Hindu and Buddhist practices as an aid to meditation.) It is suggested that participants draw a colorful circular manifestation of their soul. As before, they gather in triads to describe and to guide and witness one another, and then everyone reconvenes. In the large group each participant says something about his or her drawing, with some commentary or observations by others.

AFTERNOON: The participants create a list of self-care behaviors that they will practice during the following month, reporting back at the next seminar. These lists will be shared in the triads in the customary way and discussed in the large group.

Seminar 6: Creative Project
This seminar is devoted to reports on the project outlined in the
first seminar and undertaken during the subsequent five months.
The participants report on their experiences in hospices, nursing
homes, or other situations, first in the triads and then in the large
group.

Seminar 7: Summary
The final seminar is flexible, designed to respond to ideas and
needs that have emerged during the previous six months. In this
seminar students report back about their own family meetings and
anything more they wish to add about the family tree. The
students design their own wake and funeral in this seminar, and
also write their own medical directive, based on an example which
I have drawn up (*see* Appendix).

The Closing Workshop
This 48-hour residential event begins in the evening and ends in
the afternoon of the third day, requiring two nights in residence.
It is an important opportunity to reconsider endings and
beginnings. On the first evening, after the time for meditation
and the opening music or poem, the Talking Stick is passed and
continues for several rounds.

Earlier themes in this training have been concerned with loss
and saying good-bye to friends and family members around
the time of death. This weekend provides the opportunity for the
trainees to say good-bye to one another. They have spent
considerable time together sharing stories, witnessing and
guiding, and now is the time to say good-bye. On the first morning
of the weekend the group split into triads, and each storyteller says
good-bye to the other two, spending ten minutes talking to each.
This powerful exercise may be repeated on the second morning if
no other issue has arisen that takes precedence.

Among other matters that may receive further attention are
self-care, relationships in the family, and the practicalities of
bringing more intimacy and connectedness into the workplace.

The trainees are strongly encouraged to continue meeting on
a monthly basis for at least two hours of passing the Talking Stick,
and if this is agreed a schedule is drawn up before the end of this
workshop.

SUMMARY

The total time spent by students on this training is 13 days, not including the time spent on their special project. The cost of training (including accommodation) is a very small percentage of the total cost of medical or any other education, and the complete program, including evaluation and all personnel costs, would amount to about $2,000 (£1,200) per trainee. The cost-benefit, however, is immeasurable. A responsible, balanced curriculum for students in medicine, nursing, or any other form of caregiving requires a training program of this kind; the potential benefits will affect caregiving practices as well as the well-being of both patients and caregivers. This training could become an important catalyst for a paradigm shift that would move caregiving in the direction of relationship-centeredness to balance the impersonal chill of the technocentric. The whole experience would allow greater comfort with and acceptance of dying. It would also give recognition to the fact that healing—that which occurs as a result of the giving and receiving of love—is a possibility for all, and is a vital and necessary art for living a life of quality.

Directive for the Care of Body and Soul

Instructions in the event of irreversible incapacity for
decision-making

I, ... appoint 1. ....

....

.... and 2. ....

....

....

to act on my behalf should I become unable to make decisions
due to injury, Alzheimer's disease, or any other illness. Either one
of my appointees may act alone, but it might be preferable for
them to act in consultation with one another, if circumstances
permit.

If my condition is such that it may be reasonably assumed that
I will recover consciousness and decision-making capacity, I wish
for whatever medical treatment is necessary and appropriate.

If treatment becomes futile in the opinion of my appointee(s)
after all reasonable efforts have failed, or if I become irreversibly
incapacitated and am not able to recognize or relate to those
significant in my life, *I wish all life-maintaining efforts to be
discontinued.*

I therefore request that:

- a Do Not Resuscitate order be implemented and respected.
- all intravenous or forced feeding of any kind by means of a feeding tube be discontinued or not started.
- no intravenous treatment, including I.V. antibiotics, be given.
- No surgical or other invasive interventions be undertaken.

I agree to comfort measures *only*, including:

- mouth care.
- pain medication as deemed necessary by my physician *and my appointee(s)* in *appropriate doses.*
- touching, massage, reading, and any other soulful connections that can be arranged.
- a family meeting in my presence of all relatives and friends who are able to attend, that they may tell stories, eat, drink, laugh, cry, give a blessing, and say good-bye.

Signed   Date   Address

....

....

Witness #1   Date   Address

....

....

Witness #2   Date   Address

....

....

The intention of this directive is to give clear instructions for life care. Whether or not it is legally binding in any particular location will need to be ascertained.

Further Reading

Adams, Richard, *The Unbroken Web*, New York: Crown, 1980

Bolen, Jean Shinoda, *Close to the Bone*, New York: Scribner, 1996

Borges, Jorge Luis, *Ficciones*, New York: Grove Press, 1989

Chopra, Deepak, *The Path to Love*, New York: Harmony Books, 1997

Eliot, T.S., *The Family Reunion*, Orlando: Harcourt Brace Jovanovich, 1939

Fox, Matthew, and Sheldrake, Rupert, *Natural Grace*, New York: Doubleday, 1996

Hillman, James, *The Soul's Code*, New York: Random House, 1966

Ionesco, Eugene, *Exit the King*, New York: Grove Press, 1963

Kerenyi, C., *The Gods of the Greeks*, London: Thames and Hudson, 1951

Levine, Stephen, *Who Dies?*, New York: Anchor Books, 1982

Moore, Thomas, *Care of the Soul*, New York: HarperCollins, 1992

_____ *The Re-Enchantment of Everyday Life*, New York: HarperCollins, 1996

Neruda, Pablo, *Selected Odes of Pablo Neruda*, University of California Press, 1990

Paz, Octavio, *Selected Poems of Octavio Paz*, New Directions, 1984

Remen, Rachel Naomi, *Kitchen Table Wisdom*, New York: Riverhead Books, 1996

Rinpoche, Sogyal, *The Tibetan Book of Living and Dying*, New York: HarperCollins, 1993

Soelle, Dorothee, *Suffering*, Philadelphia: Fortress Press, 1973

Index